abled. Plaintiffs primarily used the Rehabilitation Act of 1973 (29 U.S.C.A. § 701 et seq.), the earliest law of this type. But the Rehabilitation Act has a limited scope: it applies only to federally funded workplaces and institutions, and says nothing about those that do not receive government money.

With passage of the ADA in 1990, Congress gave broad protection to people with AIDS who work in the private sector. In general, the ADA is designed to increase access for disabled persons, and it also forbids discrimination in hiring or promotion in companies with fifteen or more employees. Specifically, employers may not discriminate if the person in question is otherwise qualified for the job. Moreover, they cannot use tests to screen out disabled persons, and they must provide reasonable accommodation for disabled workers. The ADA, which took effect in 1992, has quickly emerged as the primary means for bringing AIDS-related discrimination lawsuits.

AIDS and Health Care Closely related to work is the issue of health care. In some cases, the two overlap: health insurance, Social Security, and disability benefits for AIDS victims were often hard to obtain during the 1980s. Insurance was particularly difficult because employers feared rising costs and insurance companies did not want to pay claims. To avoid the costs of AIDS, insurance companies used two traditional industry techniques: they attempted to exclude AIDS coverage from general policies, and they placed caps (limits on benefits payments) on AIDS-related coverage.

In January 1995, the settlement in a lawsuit brought by a Philadelphia construction worker with AIDS illustrated that the ADA could be used to fight caps on coverage. In 1992, the joint union-management fund for the Laborers' District Council placed a $10,000 limit on AIDS benefits, in stark contrast to the $100,000 allowed for other catastrophic illnesses. At that time, the fund said the cap on AIDS benefits was designed to curb all health costs. In 1993, the EEOC ruled that it violated the ADA, and, backed by the AIDS Law Project of Philadelphia, the worker sued. Rather than fight an expensive lawsuit, the insurance fund settled.

AIDS and Education Issues in the field of education include the rights of HIV-positive students to attend class and of HIV-positive teachers to teach, the confidentiality of HIV records, and how best to teach young people about AIDS. A few areas have been settled in court: for instance, the right of students to attend classes was of greater concern in the early years of the epidemic, and no longer remains in dispute.

Certain students with AIDS may assert their right to public education under the Education for All Handicapped Children Act of 1975 (EAHCA), but the law is only relevant in cases involving special education programs. More commonly, students' rights are protected by the Rehabilitation Act.

Schools play a major role in the effort to educate the public on AIDS. Several states have mandated AIDS prevention instruction in their schools. But the subject is controversial: it evokes personal, political, and moral reactions to sexuality. During the 1980s, those who often criticized liberal approaches to sex education argued that AIDS materials should not be explicit, encourage sexuality, promote the use of contraceptives, or favorably portray gays and lesbians.

Civil Litigation TORT law has seen an explosion of AIDS-related suits. This area of law is used to discourage individuals from subjecting others to unreasonable risks, and to compensate those who have been injured by unreasonably risky behavior. The greatest number of AIDS-related LIABILITY lawsuits has involved the receipt of HIV-infected blood and blood products. A second group has concerned the sexual transmission of HIV. A third group involves AIDS-related psychic distress. In these cases, plaintiffs have successfully sued and recovered damages for their fear of having contracted HIV.

CROSS-REFERENCES
Disabled Persons; Discrimination; Food and Drug Administration; Gay and Lesbian Rights; Health Care; Patients' Rights; Physicians and Surgeons; Privacy.

ALLRED, GLORIA Gloria Allred, born July 3, 1941, in Philadelphia, is a flamboyant, widely recognized lawyer, feminist, activist, and radio talk show host. Though her critics dismiss her as a publicity monger and a dilettante, Allred has received praise from others who believe that she is a master at using the power of the news media to draw attention to the day-to-day struggles of ordinary people.

Born Gloria Rachel Bloom, Allred grew up in Philadelphia with her parents, Morris Bloom, a door-to-door salesman, and Stella Davidson Bloom, a homemaker. Her conventional middle-class childhood gave no hint of the outspoken activist to come. Allred graduated with honors from the University of Pennsylvania in 1963 with a bachelor's degree in English. She moved to New York to pursue a master's degree in teaching at New York University. Wh... interested in the CIVIL RIGHT... was beginning to gain mom... her master's degree in 19...

BIOGRAPHY

Gloria Allred

GLORIA ALLRED 1941–

Timeline graphic

1941: Born Philadelphia, Pa.

1963: Graduated from Univ. Pennsylvania, with honors

1965: Saw Martin Luther King active in civil rights movement.

1966: Received master's in teaching from NYU; moved to Los Angeles to teach in Watts.

1969: Watts riots in Los Angeles.

1973: U.S. Supreme Court upheld *Roe v. Wade*, legalizing abortion.

1974: Received J.D. from UCLA. Formed law partnership with Nathan Goldberg and Michael Maroko.

1980: Sued L.A. County to stop shackling of pregnant inmates during labor and delivery. *Larson v. Phillips*, 1980.

1985: Wrote "Prosecution of Prostitution" for *L.A. Times*, advocating legalization of prostitution.

1986: Sued El Segundo for sex discrimination. *L.A.*

1925   1950   1975   2000

Philadelphia to teach at a high school with a predominantly black enrollment.

Allred says her interest in the struggle for equal rights arose from personal experiences. While she was in college, she married, gave birth to a daughter, and divorced. Unable to collect CHILD SUPPORT from her former husband, she was forced to return to her parents' home. She also recalls being paid less than a man for what she considered equal work. The reason given was that the man had a family to support, but at the time, Allred was the single mother of an infant.

After moving to California, Allred taught in the turbulent Watts section of Los Angeles and became the first full-time female staff member in United Teachers of Los Angeles, the union representing Los Angeles teachers. The experience stirred her interest in CIVIL RIGHTS and collective bargaining and prompted her to go to law school. She received her law degree, with honors, from Loyola Marymount University, Los Angeles, Law School in 1974. Soon after, she entered a law firm partnership with her classmates Nathan Goldberg and Michael Maroko.

Allred is probably the most flamboyant and well known member of her firm. She has achieved notoriety and name recognition through staged press conferences and demonstrations publicizing and dramatizing the cause she is championing at the time. She also accepts controversial cases that naturally attract media attention. During her years in practice, she has successfully sued Los Angeles County to stop the practice of shackling and chaining pregnant inmates during labor and delivery; put a halt on the city of El Segundo's quizzing job applicants about their sexual histories (*Thorne v. City of El Segundo*, 802 F.2d 1131 [9th Cir. 1986]); represented a client who was turned down for a job as a police officer after a six-hour lie detector exam that included questions about her sex life; and sued a dry cleaning establishment for discrimination because it charged more to launder women's shirts than men's.

Allred relishes confrontation, and her showy tactics have earned her both praise and criticism.

"THERE ARE ENOUGH HIGH HURDLES TO CLIMB, AS ONE TRAVELS THROUGH LIFE, WITHOUT HAVING TO SCALE ARTIFICIAL BARRIERS CREATED BY LAW OR SILLY REGULATIONS."

Defending what many have called self-promoting publicity stunts, Allred says she tries to use the few moments she is in the spotlight to make her point as forcefully as possible. Her detractors say that she wastes her time and energy on trivial issues that do not advance any worthwhile cause and deflect attention away from serious issues. Yet, she points out, she is often stopped on the street by people who recognize her and want to thank her for taking on the small fights that no one else wants.

Some critics say she is all show and no substance. But Allred has many supporters as well. Among them is Justice Joan Dempsey Klein, of the California Court of Appeal, who credits Allred with moving women's issues forward. Klein also points out that Allred saves her dramatics for outside the courtroom and always observes proper decorum when before the bench. According to Klein, Allred is always well-prepared and, for that reason, is quite successful.

Dressed in her trademark reds and electric blues, her striking black hair set off by deep red lipstick, Allred is a potent combination of scholarship and theatrics. Her keen intelligence and shrewd understanding of the power of the media have made her a contemporary success story in the world of law and politics.

ARBITER [Latin, One who attends something to view it as a spectator or witness.] Any person who is given an absolute power to judge and rule on a matter in a dispute.

Annotations:

Cross-references at end of article

Timeline for subject of biography, including general historical events and life events

Biography of contributor to American law

Internal cross references

Quotation from subject of biography

Full cite for case

Definition enclosed in book logos with Latin translation provided

WEST'S ENCYCLOPEDIA *of* AMERICAN LAW

Volume 12

WEST GROUP

This encyclopedia is the result of efforts by numerous individuals and entities from the Twin Cities and around the United States. West Group wishes to thank all who made this publication, its quality and content, a priority in their lives.

In addition to the individuals who worked on *West's Encyclopedia of American Law*, West Group recognizes Harold W. Chase (1922–1982) for his contributions to *The Guide to American Law: Everyone's Legal Encyclopedia.*

COPYRIGHT ©1998 By
   WEST GROUP
   610 Opperman Drive
   P.O. Box 64526
   St. Paul, MN 55164-0526
All rights reserved
Printed in the United States of America
05 04 03 02 01 00 99 98   8 7 6 5 4 3 2 1 0
Library of Congress Cataloging in
   Publication Data
ISBN: 0-314-20165-3 (Hard)

West's encyclopedia of American law.
      p.   cm.
   Includes bibliographical references and
      indexes.
      ISBN 0-314-20165-3 (hard   :
      alk. paper)
      1. Law—United States—Encyclopedias.
      2. Law—United States—Popular works.
      I. West Publishing Company.
   KF154.W47   1997
   348.73′03—dc20
   [347.30803]   96-34350
                                        CIP

PRODUCTION CREDITS
Cover, interior design, and page layout:
   David J. Farr, ImageSmythe
Composition: Carlisle Communications
Proofreading: Wiest International
Photo research: Elsa Peterson Ltd.
Art research: Nanette E. Bertaut
Editorial research: Pat Lewis
Artwork: Patricia Isaacs, Parrot Graphics
Indexing: Schroeder Indexing Services

This publication is designed to provide information on the subjects covered. It is sold with the understanding that the publisher is not engaged in rendering legal or other professional advice. If legal advice or other professional assistance is required, the services of a competent professional person should be sought.

WEST'S COMMITMENT TO THE ENVIRONMENT

In 1906, West Publishing Company began recycling materials left over from the production of books. This began a tradition of efficient and responsible use of resources. Today, 100 percent of our legal bound volumes are printed on acid-free, recycled paper consisting of 50 percent new paper pulp and 50 percent paper that has undergone a de-inking process. We also use vegetable-based inks to print all of our books. West recycles nearly 27,700,000 pounds of scrap paper annually—the equivalent of 229,300 trees. Since the 1960s, West has devised ways to capture and recycle waste inks, solvents, oils, and vapors created in the printing process. We also recycle plastics of all kinds, wood, glass, corrugated cardboard, and batteries, and have eliminated the use of polystyrene book packaging. We at West are proud of the longevity and the scope of our commitment to the environment.

West pocket parts and advance sheets are printed on recyclable paper and can be collected and recycled with newspapers. Staples do not have to be removed. Bound volumes can be recycled after removing the cover.

Production, printing, and binding by West Group.

CONTENTS

DICTIONARY OF LEGAL TERMS

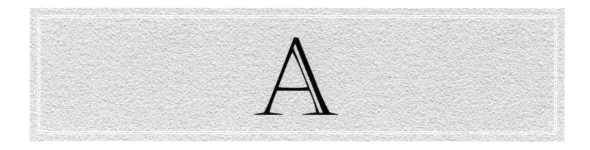

Abandonment The surrender, relinquishment, disclaimer, or cession of property or of rights. Voluntary relinquishment of all right, title, claim, and possession, with the intention of not reclaiming it.

The giving up of a thing absolutely, without reference to any particular person or purpose, as vacating property with the intention of not returning, so that it may be appropriated by the next comer or finder. The voluntary relinquishment of possession of a thing by the owner with intention of terminating ownership, but without vesting it in any other person. The relinquishing of all title, possession, or claim, or a virtual, intentional throwing away of property.

Term includes both the intention to abandon and the external act by which the intention is carried into effect. In determining whether one has abandoned property or rights, the intention is the first and paramount object of inquiry, for there can be no abandonment without the intention to abandon.

Abandonment differs from surrender in that surrender requires an agreement, and also from forfeiture, in that forfeiture may be against the intention of the party alleged to have forfeited.

Abatement A reduction, a decrease, or a diminution. The suspension or cessation, in whole or in part, of a continuing charge, such as rent.

Abatement of an action An entire overthrow or destruction of a suit so that it is quashed and ended.

Abdication   Renunciation of the privileges and prerogatives of an office. The act of a sovereign in renouncing and relinquishing his or her government or throne, so that either the throne is left entirely vacant, or is filled by a successor appointed or elected beforehand. Also, where a magistrate or person in office voluntarily renounces or gives it up before the time of service has expired. It differs from resignation, in that resignation is made by one who has received an office from another and restores it into that person's hands, as an inferior into the hands of a superior; abdication is the relinquishment of an office which has devolved by act of law. It is said to be a renunciation, quitting, and relinquishing, so as to have nothing further to do with a thing, or the doing of such actions as are inconsistent with the holding of it. Voluntary and permanent withdrawal from power by a public official or monarch.

Abet   To encourage or incite another to commit a crime. This word is usually applied to aiding in the commission of a crime. To abet another to commit a murder is to command, procure, counsel, encourage, induce, or assist. To facilitate the commission of a crime, promote its accomplishment, or help in advancing or bringing it about.

In relation to charge of aiding and abetting, term includes knowledge of the perpetrator's wrongful purpose, and encouragement, promotion or counsel of another in the commission of the criminal offense.

A French word, *abeter*—to bait or excite an animal.

Abettor   One who commands, advises, instigates, or encourages another to commit a crime. A person who, being present, incites another to commit a crime, and thus becomes a principal. To be an *abettor*, the accused must have instigated or advised the commission of a crime or been present for the purpose of assisting in its commission; he or she must share criminal intent with which the crime was committed.

Abeyance   A lapse in succession during which there is no person in whom title is vested. In the law of estates, the condition of a freehold when there is no person in whom it is vested. In such cases the freehold has been said to be *in nubibus* (in the clouds), *in pendenti* (in suspension); and *in gremio legis* (in the bosom of the law). Where there is a tenant of the freehold, the remainder or reversion in fee may exist for a time without any particular owner, in which case it is said to be in abeyance. A condition of being undetermined or in state of suspension or inactivity. In regard to sales to third parties of property acquired by county at tax sale, being held in *abeyance* means that certain rights or conditions are in expectancy.

Abiding conviction   A definite conviction of guilt derived from a thorough examination of the whole case. Used commonly to instruct juries on the frame of mind required for guilt proved beyond a reasonable doubt. A settled or fixed conviction.

Ab initio   [*Latin, From the beginning; from the first act; from the inception.*] An agreement is said to be "void *ab initio*" if it has at no time had any legal validity. A party may be said to be a trespasser, an estate said to be good, an agreement or deed said to be void, or a marriage or act said to be unlawful, *ab initio*. Contrasted in this sense with ex post facto, or with *postea*.

Abjuration A renunciation or abandonment by or upon oath. The renunciation under oath of one's citizenship or some other right or privilege.

Abode One's home; habitation; place of dwelling; or residence. Ordinarily means "domicile." Living place impermanent in character. The place where a person dwells. Residence of a legal voter. Fixed place of residence for the time being. For service of process, one's fixed place of residence for the time being; his or her "usual place of abode."

Abolition The destruction, annihilation, abrogation, or extinguishment of anything, but especially things of a permanent nature—such as institutions, usages, or customs, as in the abolition of slavery.

Abortion The spontaneous or artificially induced expulsion of an embryo or fetus. As used in legal context, usually refers to induced abortion.

Abrogation The destruction or annulling of a former law by an act of the legislative power, by constitutional authority, or by usage. It stands opposed to *rogation;* and is distinguished from derogation, which implies the taking away of only some part of a law; from subrogation, which denotes the substitution of a clause; from *dispensation,* which only sets it aside in a particular instance; and from *antiquation,* which is the refusing to pass a law.

Abscond To go in a clandestine manner out of the jurisdiction of the courts, or to lie concealed, in order to avoid their process. To hide, conceal, or absent oneself clandestinely, with the intent to avoid legal process. To postpone limitations. To flee from arresting or prosecuting officers of the state.

Absconding debtor One who absconds from creditors to avoid payment of debts. A debtor who has intentionally concealed himself or herself from creditors, or withdrawn from the reach of their suits, with intent to frustrate their just demands. Such act was formerly an *act of bankruptcy.*

Absentee One who has left, either temporarily or permanently, his or her domicile or usual place of residence or business. A person beyond the geographical borders of a state who has not authorized an agent to represent him or her in legal proceedings that may be commenced against him or her within the state.

Absentee voting Participation in an election by qualified voters who are permitted to mail in their ballots.

Absolute Complete; perfect; final; without any condition or incumbrance; as an absolute bond in distinction from a conditional bond. Unconditional; complete and perfect in itself; without relation to or dependence on other things or persons.

Free from conditions, limitations or qualifications, not dependent, or modified or affected by circumstances; that is, without any condition or restrictive provisions.

Absolute deed   A document used to transfer unrestricted title to property.

Abstention doctrine   The concept under which a federal court exercises its discretion and equitable powers and declines to decide a legal action over which it has jurisdiction pursuant to the Constitution and statutes where the state judiciary is capable of rendering a definitive ruling in the matter.

Abstract   To take or withdraw from; as, to abstract the funds of a bank. To remove or separate. To summarize or abridge.

Abstraction   Taking from someone with an intent to injure or defraud.

Abstract of title   A condensed history, taken from public records or documents, of the ownership of a piece of land.

Abuse   Everything that is contrary to good order established by usage. Departure from reasonable use; immoderate or improper use. Physical or mental maltreatment. Misuse. Deception.
     To wrong in speech, reproach coarsely, disparage, revile, and malign.

Abuse of discretion   A failure to take into proper consideration the facts and law relating to a particular matter; an arbitrary or unreasonable departure from precedents and settled judicial custom.

Abuse of power   Improper use of authority by someone who has that authority because he or she holds a public office.

Abuse of process   The use of legal process to accomplish an unlawful purpose; causing a summons, writ, warrant, mandate, or any other process to issue from a court in order to accomplish some purpose not intended by the law.

Abusive   Tending to deceive; practicing abuse; prone to ill-treat by coarse, insulting words or harmful acts. Using ill treatment; injurious, improper, hurtful, offensive, reproachful.

Abut   To reach; to touch. To touch at the end; be contiguous; join at a border or boundary; terminate on; end at; border on; reach or touch with an end. The term *abutting* implies a closer proximity than the term *adjacent*.

Academic freedom   The right to teach as one sees fit, but not necessarily the right to teach evil. The term encompasses much more than teaching-related speech rights of teachers.

Academic year   That period of time necessary to complete an actual course of study during a school year.

Accede   To consent or to agree, as to accede to another's point of view. To enter an office or to accept a position, as to accede to the presidency.

Acceleration   A hastening; a shortening of the time until some event takes place.

Acceleration clause   The provision in a credit agreement, such as a mortgage, note, bond, or deed of trust, that allows the lender to require immediate payment of all money due if certain conditions occur before the time that payment would otherwise be due.

Acceptance   The taking and receiving of anything in good part as if it were a tacit agreement to a preceding act, which might have been defeated or avoided if such acceptance had not been made. The act of a person to whom a thing is offered or tendered by another, whereby he or she receives the thing with the intention of retaining it, such intention being evidenced by a sufficient act.

The exercise of power conferred by an offer by performance of some act.

Access   Freedom of approach or communication; or the means, power, or opportunity of approaching, communicating, or passing to and from. Sometimes importing the occurrence of sexual intercourse; otherwise as importing opportunity of communication for that purpose as between husband and wife.

In real property law, the term *access* denotes the right vested in the owner of the land that adjoins a road or other highway to go and return from his own land to the highway without obstruction. Access to property does not necessarily carry with it possession.

For purposes of establishing element of access by defendant in copyright infringement action, *access* is ordinarily defined as opportunity to copy.

Accession   Coming into possession of a right or office; increase; augmentation; addition.

The right to all that one's own property produces, whether that property be movable or immovable; and the right to that which is united to it by accession, either naturally or artificially. The right to own things that become a part of something already owned.

A principle derived from the civil law, by which the owner of property becomes entitled to all that it produces, and to all that is added or united to it, either naturally or artificially (that is, by the labor or skill of another) even where such addition extends to a change of form or materials; and by which, on the other hand, the possessor of property becomes entitled to it, as against the original owner, where the addition made to it by skill and labor is of greater value than the property itself, or where the change effected in its form is so great as to render it impossible to restore it to its original shape.

Generally, *accession* signifies acquisition of title to personal property by bestowing labor on it that converts it into an entirely different thing or by incorporation of property into a union with other property.

The commencement or inauguration of a sovereign's reign.

Accessory   Aiding or contributing in a secondary way or assisting in or contributing to as a subordinate.

In criminal law, contributing to or aiding in the commission of a crime. One who, without being present at the commission of an offense, becomes guilty of such offense, not as a chief actor, but as a participant, as by command, advice, instigation, or concealment; either before or after the fact or commission.

One who aids, abets, commands, or counsels another in the commission of a crime.

Accident The word *accident* is derived from the Latin verb *accidere*, signifying "fall upon, befall, happen, chance." In its most commonly accepted meaning, or in its ordinary or popular sense, the word may be defined as meaning: some sudden and unexpected event taking place without expectation, upon the instant, rather than something that continues, progresses or develops; something happening by chance; something unforeseen, unexpected, unusual, extraordinary, or phenomenal, taking place not according to the usual course of things or events, out of the range of ordinary calculations; that which exists or occurs abnormally, or an uncommon occurrence. The word may be employed as denoting a calamity, casualty, catastrophe, disaster, an undesirable or unfortunate happening; any unexpected personal injury resulting from any unlooked for mishap or occurrence; any unpleasant or unfortunate occurrence that causes injury, loss, suffering, or death; some untoward occurrence aside from the usual course of events. An event that takes place without one's foresight or expectation; an undesigned, sudden, and unexpected event.

Accidental death benefit A provision of a life insurance policy stating that if the insured—the person whose life has been insured—dies in an accident, the beneficiary of the policy—the person to whom its proceeds are payable—will receive twice the face value of the policy.

Accidental killing A death caused by a lawful act done under the reasonable belief that no harm was likely to result.

Accidental vein An imprecise term that refers generally to a continuous body of a mineral or mineralized rock filling a seam other than the principal vein that led to the discovery of the mining claim or location.

Accidents of navigation Mishaps that are peculiar to travel by sea or to normal navigation; accidents caused at sea by the action of the elements, rather than by a failure to exercise good handling, working, or navigating of a ship. Such accidents could not have been avoided by the exercise of nautical skill or prudence.

Accommodation endorsement The act of a third person—the accommodation party—in writing his or her name on the back of a commercial paper without any consideration, but merely to benefit the person to whom the paper is payable or to enable the person who made the document—the maker—to obtain money or credit on it.

Accommodation paper A type of commercial paper (such as a bill or note promising that money will be paid to someone) that is signed by another person—the accommodation party—as a favor to the promisor—the accommodated party—so that credit may be extended to him or her on the basis of the paper.

Accommodation party One who signs a commercial paper for the purpose of lending his or her name and credit to another party to the document—the accommodated party—to help that party obtain a loan or an extension of credit.

Accompany To go along with; to go with or to attend as a companion or associate.

Accomplice One who knowingly, voluntarily, and with common intent unites with the principal offender in the commission of a crime. One who is in some way concerned or associated in commission of crime; partaker of guilt; one who aids or assists, or is an accessory. One who is guilty of complicity in crime charged, either by being present and aiding or abetting in it, or having advised and encouraged it, though absent from place when it was committed, though mere presence, acquiescence, or silence, in the absence of a duty to act, is not enough, no matter how reprehensible it may be, to constitute one an accomplice. One is liable as an accomplice to the crime of another if he or she gave assistance or encouragement or failed to perform a legal duty to prevent it with the intent thereby to promote or facilitate commission of the crime.

Accomplice witness A witness to a crime who, either as principal, accomplice, or accessory, was connected with the crime by unlawful act or omission on his or her part, transpiring either before, at time of, or after commission of the offense, and whether or not he or she was present and participated in the crime.

Accord An agreement that settles a dispute, generally requiring a compromise or satisfaction with something less than what was originally demanded.

Accord and satisfaction A method of discharging a claim whereby the parties agree to give and accept something in settlement of the claim and perform the agreement, the *accord* being the agreement and the *satisfaction* its execution or performance, and it is a new contract substituted for an old contract which is thereby discharged, or for an obligation or cause of action which is settled, and must have all of the elements of a valid contract.

Accouchement The act of giving birth to a child.

Account A written list of transactions, noting money owed and money paid; a detailed statement of mutual demands arising out of a contract or a fiduciary relationship.

Account, action on A civil lawsuit maintained under the common law to recover money owed on an account.

Accountant A person who has the requisite skill and experience in establishing and maintaining accurate financial records for an individual or a business. The duties of an accountant may include designing and controlling systems of records, auditing books, and preparing financial statements. An accountant may give tax advice and prepare tax returns.

Accounting A system of recording or settling accounts in financial transactions; the methods of determining income and expenses for tax and other financial purposes. Also, one of the remedies available to enforce a right or redress a wrong asserted in a lawsuit.

Account payable A debt owed by a business that arises in the normal course of its dealings, that has not been replaced by a note from another debtor, and that is not necessarily due or past due.

Account receivable   A debt owed by a business that arises in the normal course of dealings and is not supported by a negotiable instrument.

Account rendered   A statement of transactions made out by a creditor and presented to the debtor.

Account stated   An amount that accurately states money due to a creditor; a debt arising out of transactions between a debtor and creditor that has been reduced to a balance due for the items of account.

Accredit   To give official authorization or status. To recognize as having sufficient academic standards to qualify graduates for higher education or for professional practice. In international law: (1) To acknowledge; to receive as an envoy and give that person credit and rank accordingly. (2) To send with credentials as an envoy. This latter use is now the accepted one.

Accredited law school   A law school that has been approved by the state and the Association of American Law Schools (AALS), the American Bar Association (ABA), or both.

Accretion   The act of adding portions of soil to the soil already in possession of the owner by gradual deposition through the operation of natural causes.

   The growth of the value of a particular item given to a person as a specific bequest under the provisions of a will between the time the will was written and the time of death of the testator—the person who wrote the will.

Accrual basis   A method of accounting that reflects expenses incurred and income earned for income tax purposes for any one year.

Accrue   To increase; to augment; to come to by way of increase; to be added as an increase, profit, or damage. Acquired; falling due; made or executed; matured; occurred; received; vested; was created; was incurred.

   To attach itself to, as a subordinate or accessory claim or demand arises out of, and is joined to, its principal.

   The term is also used of independent or original demands, meaning to arise, to happen, to come into force or existence; to vest, as in the phrase, "The right of action did not *accrue* within six years." To become a present right or demand; to come to pass.

Accumulated earnings tax   A special tax imposed on corporations that accumulate (rather than distribute via dividends) their earnings beyond the reasonable needs of the business. The accumulated earnings tax is imposed on accumulated taxable income in addition to the corporate income tax.

Accumulation trust   An arrangement whereby property is transferred by its owner—the settlor—with the intention that it be administered by someone else—a trustee—for another person's benefit, with the direction that the trustee gather, rather than distribute, the income of the trust and any profits made from the sale of any of the property making up the trust until the time specified in the document that created the trust.

Accumulative judgment	A second or additional judgment against a person who has already been convicted and sentenced for another crime; the execution of the second judgment is postponed until the person's first sentence has been completed.
Accumulative sentence	A sentence—a court's formal pronouncement of the legal consequences of a person's conviction of a crime—additional to others, imposed on a defendant who has been convicted upon an indictment containing several counts, each charging a distinct offense, or who is under conviction at the same time for several distinct offenses; each sentence is to run consecutively, beginning at the expiration of the previous sentence.
Accusation	A formal criminal charge against a person alleged to have committed an offense punishable by law, which is presented before a court or a magistrate having jurisdiction to inquire into the alleged crime.
Accusatory body	Body such as a grand jury whose duty it is to hear evidence to determine whether a person should be accused of (charged with) a crime; to be distinguished from a traverse or petit jury, which is charged with the duty of determining guilt or innocence.
Accused	The generic name for the defendant in a criminal case. A person becomes accused within the meaning of a guarantee of speedy trial only at the point at which either formal indictment or information has been returned against him or her, or when he or she becomes subject to actual restraints on liberty imposed by arrest, whichever occurs first.
Acknowledgment	To *acknowledge* is to admit, affirm, declare, testify, avow, confess, or own as genuine. Admission or affirmation of obligation or responsibility. Most states have adopted the Uniform Acknowledgment Act.
Acquiescence	Conduct recognizing the existence of a transaction and intended to permit the transaction to be carried into effect; a tacit agreement; consent inferred from silence.
Acquisition charge	A fee imposed upon a borrower who satisfies a loan prior to the date of payment specified in the loan agreement.
Acquit	To set free, release or discharge as from an obligation, burden or accusation. To absolve one from an obligation or a liability; or to legally certify the innocence of one charged with a crime.
Acquittal	The legal and formal certification of the innocence of a person who has been charged with a crime.
Act	Something done; usually, something done intentionally or voluntarily or with a purpose.
Action	Conduct; behavior; something done; a series of acts. A case or lawsuit; a legal and formal demand for enforcement of one's rights against another party asserted in a court of justice.

Actionable
Giving sufficient legal grounds for a lawsuit; giving rise to a cause of action.

Actionable per se
Legally sufficient to support a lawsuit in itself.

Act of God
An event that directly and exclusively results from the occurrence of natural causes that could not have been prevented by the exercise of foresight or caution; an inevitable accident.

Actual cash value
The fair or reasonable cash price for which a property could be sold in the market in the ordinary course of business, and not at forced sale. The price it will bring in a fair market after reasonable efforts to find a purchaser who will give the highest price. What property is worth in money, allowing for depreciation. Ordinarily, *actual cash value*, *fair market value*, and *market value* are synonymous terms.

Actual notice
Conveying facts to a person with the intention to apprise that person of a proceeding in which his or her interests are involved, or informing a person of some fact that he or she has a right to know and which the informer has a legal duty to communicate.

Actuary
A statistician who computes insurance and pension rates and premiums on the basis of experience of people sharing similar age and health characteristics.

Adaptation
The act or process of modifying an object to render it suitable for a particular or new purpose or situation.

Ad damnum
[*Latin, To the loss.*] The clause in a complaint that sets a maximum amount of money that the plaintiff can recover under a default judgment if the defendant fails to appear in court.

Addict
Any individual who habitually uses any narcotic drug so as to endanger the public morals, health, safety, or welfare, or who is so drawn to the use of such narcotic drugs as to have lost the power of self-control with reference to his or her drug use.

Additional extended coverage
A provision added to an insurance policy to extend the scope of coverage to include further risks to dwellings.

Additional instructions
A charge given to a jury by a judge after the original instructions to explain the law and guide the jury in its decision making.

Additur
The power of the trial court to assess damages or increase the amount of an inadequate award made by jury verdict, as a condition of a denial of a motion for a new trial, with the consent of the defendant whether or not the plaintiff consents to such action. This is not allowed in the federal system.

Add-on
A purchase of additional goods before payment is made for goods already purchased.

Adduce To present, offer, bring forward, or introduce.

Ademption The failure of a gift of personal property—a bequest—or of real property—a devise—to be distributed according to the provisions of a decedent's will because the property no longer belongs to the testator at the time of his or her death or because the property has been substantially changed.

Adequate Sufficient; equal to what is required; suitable to the case or occasion.

Adequate remedy at law Sufficient compensation by way of monetary damages.

Adhesion contract A type of contract, a legally binding agreement between two parties to do a certain thing, in which one side has all the bargaining power and uses it to write the contract primarily to his or her advantage.

Ad hoc [*Latin, For this; for this special purpose.*] An attorney ad hoc, or a guardian or curator ad hoc, is one appointed for a special purpose, generally to represent the client or infant in the particular action in which the appointment is made.

Ad hominem [*Latin, To the person.*] A term used in debate to denote an argument made personally against an opponent, instead of against the opponent's argument.

Ad interim [*Latin, In the meantime.*] An officer *ad interim* is a person appointed to fill a position that is temporarily open, or to perform the functions of a particular position during the absence or temporary incapacity of the individual who regularly fulfills those duties.

Adjacent Lying near or close to; neighboring.

Adjective law The aggregate of rules of procedure or practice. Also called adjectival law, as opposed to that body of law that the courts are established to administer (called substantive law), it means the rules according to which the substantive law is administered, e.g., Rules of Civil Procedure. That part of the law that provides a method for enforcing or maintaining rights, or obtaining redress for their invasion. Pertains to and prescribes the practice, method, procedure, or legal machinery by which substantive law is enforced or made effective.

Adjoining landowners Those persons, such as next-door and backyard neighbors, who own lands that share common boundaries and therefore have mutual rights, duties, and liabilities.

Adjourned term A continuance of a previous or regular court session that results from postponement.

Adjournment A putting off or postponing of proceedings; an ending or dismissal of further business by a court, legislature, or public official—either temporarily or permanently.

Adjudge   To determine by a judge; to pass on and decide judicially.

Adjudication   The legal process of resolving a dispute. The formal giving or pronouncing of a judgment or decree in a court proceeding; also the judgment or decision given. The entry of a decree by a court in respect to the parties in a case. It implies a hearing by a court, after notice, of legal evidence on the factual issue(s) involved. The equivalent of a determination. It indicates that the claims of all the parties thereto have been considered and set at rest.

Adjudicative facts   Factual matters concerning the parties to an administrative proceeding as contrasted with legislative facts, which are general and usually do not touch individual questions of particular parties to a proceeding. Facts that concern a person's motives and intent, as contrasted with general policy issues. Those facts that must be found beyond a reasonable doubt by the trier of fact before there can be a conviction.

Adjudicative facts, of which a trial court may take notice if a fact is not subject to reasonable dispute, are those to which law is applied in the process of adjudication; they are facts that, in a jury case, normally go to the jury.

Adjunction   Attachment or affixing to another. Something attached as a dependent or auxiliary part.

Adjuration   A swearing; taking an oath to be truthful.

Adjust   To settle or arrange; to free from differences or discrepancies. To bring to a satisfactory state so that parties are agreed, as to adjust amount of loss by fire or controversy regarding property or estate. To bring to proper relations. To determine and apportion an amount due. The term is sometimes used in the sense of pay, when used in reference to a liquidated claim. Determination of an amount to be paid to insured by insurer to cover loss or damage sustained.

Adjusted gross income   The term used for income tax purposes to describe gross income less certain allowable deductions such as trade and business deductions, moving expenses, alimony paid, and penalties for premature withdrawals from term savings accounts, in order to determine a person's taxable income.

Adjuster   A person appointed or employed to settle or arrange matters that are in dispute; one who determines the amount to be paid on a claim.

Adjustment securities   Stocks and bonds of a new corporation that are issued to stockholders during a corporate reorganization in exchange for stock held in the original corporation before it was reorganized.

Ad litem   [*Latin, For the suit; for the purposes of the suit; pending the suit.*] A guardian ad litem is a guardian appointed to prosecute or defend a suit on behalf of a party who is legally incapable of doing so, such as an infant or an insane person.

Administer   To give an oath, as to administer the oath of office to the president at the inauguration. To direct the transactions of business or government. Immigration laws are administered largely by the Immigration and Naturalization Service. To take care of affairs, as an executor administers the estate of a deceased person. To directly cause the ingestion of medications or poisons. To apply a court decree, enforce its provisions, or resolve disputes concerning its meaning.

Administration The performance of executive duties in an institution or business. The Small Business Administration is responsible for administration of some disaster-relief loans. In government, the practical management and direction of some department or agency in the executive branch; in general, the entire class of public officials and employees managing the executive department. The management and distribution of the estate of a decedent performed under the supervision of the surrogate's or probate court by a person duly qualified and legally appointed. If the decedent made a valid will designating someone called an executor to handle this function, the court will issue that person letters testamentary as authority to do so. If a person dies intestate or did not name an executor in his or her will, the court will appoint an administrator and grant him or her letters of administration to perform the duties of administration.

Administrative acts Whatever actions are necessary to carry out the intent of statutes; those acts required by legislative policy as it is expressed in laws enacted by the legislature.

Administrative adjudication The process by which an administrative agency issues an order, such order being affirmative, negative, injunctive, or declaratory in form.

Administrative agency An official governmental body empowered with the authority to direct and supervise the implementation of particular legislative acts. In addition to *agency*, such governmental bodies may be called commissions, corporations (e.g., FDIC), boards, departments, or divisions.

Administrative board A comprehensive phrase that can refer to any administrative agency but usually means a public agency that holds hearings.

Administrative discretion The exercise of professional expertise and judgment, as opposed to strict adherence to regulations or statutes, in making a decision or performing official acts or duties.

Administrative law and procedure *Administrative law* is the body of law that allows for the creation of public regulatory agencies and contains all the statutes, judicial decisions, and regulations that govern them. It is the body of law created by administrative agencies to implement their powers and duties in the form of rules, regulations, orders, and decisions. *Administrative procedure* constitutes the methods and processes before administrative agencies, as distinguished from judicial procedure, which applies to courts.

Administrator A person appointed by the court to manage and take charge of the assets and liabilities of a decedent who has died without making a valid will.

Admiralty and maritime law A field of law relating to, and arising from, the practice of the admiralty courts (tribunals that exercise jurisdiction over all contracts, torts, offenses, or injuries within maritime law) that regulates and settles special problems associated with sea navigation and commerce.

Admissible   A term used to describe information that is relevant to a determination of issues in any judicial proceeding so that such information can be properly considered by a judge or jury in making a decision.

Admission   A voluntary acknowledgment made by a party to a lawsuit or in a criminal prosecution that certain facts that are inconsistent with the party's claims in the controversy are true.

Admission to the bar   The procedure that governs the authorization of attorneys to practice law before the state and federal courts.

Admonition   Any formal verbal statement made during a trial by a judge to advise and caution the jury on their duty as jurors, on the admissibility or nonadmissibility of evidence, or on the purpose for which any evidence admitted may be considered by them. A reprimand directed by the court to an attorney appearing before it cautioning the attorney about the unacceptability of his or her conduct before the court. If the attorney continues to act in the same way, ignoring the admonition, the judge will find him or her in contempt of court, punishable by a fine, imprisonment, or both. In criminal prosecution, before the court receives and records the plea of the accused, a statement made by a judge informing the accused on the effect and consequences of a plea of guilty to criminal charges.

Adopt   To accept, appropriate, choose, or select, as to adopt a child. To consent to and put into effect, as to adopt a constitution or a law.

Adoption   A two-step judicial process in conformance to state statutory provisions in which the legal obligations and rights of a child toward the biological parents are terminated and new rights and obligations are created in the acquired parents.

Adult   A person who by virtue of attaining a certain age, generally eighteen, is regarded in the eyes of the law as being able to manage his or her own affairs.

Adulteration   Mixing something impure with something genuine, or an inferior article with a superior one of the same kind.

Adultery   Voluntary sexual relations between an individual who is married and someone who is not the individual's spouse.

Ad valorem   According to value.

Advance   To pay money or give something of value before the date designated to do so; to provide capital to help a planned enterprise, expecting a return from it; to give someone an item before payment has been made for it.

Advancement   A gift of money or property made by a person while alive to his or her child or other legally recognized heir, the value of which the person intends to be deducted from the child's or heir's eventual share in the estate after the giver's death.

Advance sheets   Pamphlets containing recently decided opinions of federal courts or state courts of a particular region.

Adversary proceeding   Any action, hearing, investigation, inquest, or inquiry brought by one party against another in which the party seeking relief has given legal notice to and provided the other party with an opportunity to contest the claims that have been made against him or her.

Adversary system   The scheme of American jurisprudence wherein a judge renders a decision in a controversy between parties who assert contradictory positions during a judicial examination such as a trial or hearing.

Adverse interest   The legal right or liability of a person called to testify as a witness in a lawsuit that might be lost or impaired if the party who called him or her to testify wins the case.

Adverse possession   A method of gaining legal title to real property by the actual, open, hostile, and continuous possession of it to the exclusion of its true owner for the period prescribed by state law. Personal property may also be acquired by adverse possession.

Advise   To give an opinion or recommend a plan or course of action; to give notice; to encourage, inform, or acquaint.

Advisement   Deliberation; consultation.

Advisory opinion   An opinion by a court as to the legality of proposed legislation or conduct, given in response to a request by the government, legislature, or some other interested party.

Advocacy   The act of pleading or arguing a case or a position; forceful persuasion.

Advocate   To support or defend by argument; to recommend publicly. An individual who presents or argues another's case; one who gives legal advice and pleads the cause of another before a court or tribunal; a counselor. A person admitted to the practice of law who advises clients of their legal rights and argues their cases in court.

Aeronautics   The science and art of flight, encompassing the functioning and ownership of aircraft vehicles from balloons to those that travel into space.

Affidavit   A written statement of facts voluntarily made by an affiant under an oath or affirmation administered by a person authorized to do so by law.

Affiliation proceeding   A court hearing to determine whether a man against whom the action is brought is the father of an illegitimate child and thus legally bound to provide financial support for the child.

Affinity   The relationship that a person has to the blood relatives of a spouse by virtue of the marriage.

Affirm   To ratify, establish, or reassert. To make a solemn and formal declaration, as a substitute for an oath, that the statements contained in an affidavit are true or that a witness will tell the truth. In the practice of appellate courts, to declare a judgment, decree, or order valid and to concur in its correctness so that it must stand as rendered in the lower court. As a matter of pleading, to allege or aver a matter of fact.

Affirmance   A declaration by an appellate court that a judgment, order, or decree of a lower court that has been brought before it for review is valid and will be upheld.

Affirmation   A solemn and formal declaration of the truth of a statement, such as an affidavit or the actual or prospective testimony of a witness or a party, that is in place of an oath.

Affirmative action   Employment programs required by federal statutes and regulations designed to remedy discriminatory practices in hiring minority group members; i.e., positive steps designed to eliminate existing and continuing discrimination, to remedy lingering effects of past discrimination, and to create systems and procedures to prevent future discrimination; commonly based on population percentages of minority groups in a particular area. Factors considered are race, color, sex, creed, and age.

Affirmative defense   A new fact or set of facts that operates to defeat a claim even if the facts supporting that claim are true.

Affray   A criminal offense generally defined as the fighting of two or more persons in a public place that disturbs others.

Aforesaid   Before, already said, referred to, or recited.

Aforethought   In criminal law, intentional, deliberate, planned, or premeditated.

A fortiori   [*Latin, With stronger reason.*] This phrase is used in logic to denote an argument to the effect that because one ascertained fact exists, therefore another which is included in it or analogous to it and is less improbable, unusual, or surprising must also exist.

After-acquired property clause   A phrase in a mortgage (an interest in land that furnishes security for payment of a debt or performance of an obligation) that provides that any holdings obtained by the borrower subsequent to the date of the loan and mortgage will automatically constitute additional security for the loan.

After-acquired title   A legal doctrine under which, if a grantor conveys what is mistakenly believed to be good title to land that he or she did not own, and the grantor later acquires that title, it vests automatically in the grantee.

After-born child   A child born after a will has been executed by either parent or after the time in which a class gift made according to a trust arrangement expires.

Agent	One who agrees and is authorized to act on behalf of another, a principal, to legally bind an individual in particular business transactions with third parties pursuant to an agency relationship.
Age of consent	The age at which a person may marry without parental approval. The age at which a female is legally capable of agreeing to sexual intercourse, so that a male who engages in sex with her cannot be prosecuted for statutory rape.
Age of majority	The age at which a person, formerly a minor or an infant, is recognized by law to be an adult, capable of managing his or her own affairs and responsible for any legal obligations created by his or her actions.
Age of reason	The age at which a child is considered capable of acting responsibly.
Aggravated assault	A person is guilty of aggravated assault if he or she attempts to cause serious bodily injury to another or causes such injury purposely, knowingly, or recklessly under circumstances manifesting extreme indifference to the value of human life; or attempts to cause or purposely or knowingly causes bodily injury to another with a deadly weapon. In all jurisdictions statutes punish such aggravated assaults as assault with intent to murder (or rob or kill or rape) and assault with a dangerous (or deadly) weapon more severely than "simple" assaults.
Aggravation	Any circumstances surrounding the commission of a crime that increase its seriousness or add to its injurious consequences.
Aggression	Unjustified planned, threatened, or carried out use of force by one nation against another.
Aggressive collection	Various legal methods used by a creditor to force a debtor to repay an outstanding obligation.
Aggrieved party	An individual who is entitled to commence a lawsuit against another because his or her legal rights have been violated.
Agreement	A meeting of minds with the understanding and acceptance of reciprocal legal rights and duties as to particular actions or obligations, which the parties intend to exchange; a mutual assent to do or refrain from doing something; a contract. The writing or document that records the meeting of the minds of the parties. An oral compact between two parties who join together for a common purpose intending to change their rights and duties.
Agricultural law	The body of law governing the cultivation of various crops and the raising and management of livestock to provide a food and fabric supply for human and animal consumption.
Aid and abet	To assist another in the commission of a crime by words or conduct.
Aid and comfort	To render assistance or counsel.

Alderman or alderwoman   A public officer of a town or city council or a local legislative body who is elected to the position by the persons he or she represents.

Aleatory contract   A mutual agreement between two parties in which the performance of the contractual obligations of one or both parties depends upon a fortuitous event.

Alias   [*Latin, Otherwise called.*] A term used to indicate that a person is known by more than one name.

Alias writ   A second writ, or court order, issued in the same case after an earlier writ of that kind has been issued but has not been effective.

Alienable   The character of property that makes it capable of sale or transfer.

Alienate   To voluntarily convey or transfer title to real property by gift, disposition by will or the laws of descent and distribution, or by sale.

Alienation clause   A provision in a document permitting or forbidding a person from transferring property that is the subject of the document.

Alienation of affection   The removal of love, companionship, or aid of an individual's spouse.

Alien enemy   In international law, a foreign-born citizen or subject of a nation or power that is hostile to the United States.

Aliens   Foreign-born persons who have not been naturalized to become U.S. citizens under federal law and the Constitution.

Alimony   Payment that a family court may order one person in a couple to make to the other person when that couple separates or divorces.

Allegation   The assertion, claim, declaration, or statement of a party to an action, setting out what he or she expects to prove.

Allege   To state, recite, assert, or charge the existence of particular facts in a pleading or an indictment; to make an allegation.

Allegiance   In English law, the duty of loyalty and obedience owed by all persons born within the king's realm that attaches immediately upon their birth and that they cannot be relieved of by their own actions.

   In U.S. law, the obligation of fidelity and obedience that is owed by native born and naturalized American citizens to the United States that cannot be relinquished without the consent of the government expressed by a statutory enactment.

All fours   Identical; similar.

Allocation   The apportionment or designation of an item for a specific purpose or to a particular place.

Allocution   The formal inquiry by a judge of an accused person, convicted of a crime, as to whether the person has any legal cause to show why judgment should not be pronounced against him or her or as to whether the person has anything to say to the court before being sentenced.

Allodial Free; not subject to the rights of any lord or superior; owned without obligation of vassalage or fealty; the opposite of feudal.

A description given to the outright ownership of land that did not impose upon its owner the performance of feudal duties.

Allograph A writing or signature made by one person for another.

Allonge Additional paper firmly attached to commercial paper, such as a promissory note, to provide room to write endorsements.

Allotment A portion, share, or division. The proportionate distribution of shares of stock in a corporation. The partition and distribution of land.

Alteration Modification; changing a thing without obliterating it.

Alteration of instruments A change in the meaning or language of a legal document, such as a contract, deed, lease, or commercial paper, that is made by one party to the document without the consent of the other after it has been signed or completed.

Alter ego A doctrine used by the courts to ignore the corporate status of a group of stockholders, officers, and directors of a corporation in reference to their limited liability in order to hold them personally liable for their actions when they have acted fraudulently or unjustly, or when to refuse to do so will deprive an innocent victim of redress for an injury caused by them.

Alternative dispute resolution Procedures for settling disputes by means other than litigation; e.g., by arbitration, mediation, or minitrials. Such procedures, which are usually less costly and more expeditious than litigation, are increasingly being used in commercial and labor disputes, divorce actions, in resolving motor vehicle and medical malpractice tort claims, and in other disputes that would likely otherwise involve court litigation.

Alternative relief Remedies sought in a lawsuit in various forms or in the alternative, such as a demand for specific performance of a contract or monetary damages to compensate for the failure to perform the obligation, or both.

Alternative writ An order, issued originally by the king in England but more recently by a court, commanding a person to do a specific thing or to appear and explain why he or she should not be compelled to do it.

Ambassadors and consuls An *ambassador* is the foreign diplomatic representative of a nation who is authorized to handle political negotiations between his or her country and the country where the ambassador has been assigned. A *consul* is the commercial agent of a nation, who is empowered only to engage in business transactions, and not political matters in the country where he or she is stationed.

Ambiguity Uncertainty or doubtfulness of the meaning of language.

Ambit   A boundary line that indicates ownership of a parcel of land as opposed to other parcels; an exterior or enclosing line. The limits of a power or jurisdiction. The delineation of the scope of a particular subject matter.

Ambulance chaser   A colloquial phrase that is used derisively for a person who is hired by an attorney to seek out negligence cases at the scenes of accidents or in hospitals where injured parties are treated, in exchange for a percentage of the damages that will be recovered in the case.

    Also used to describe attorneys who, upon learning of a personal injury that might have been caused by the negligence or the wrongful act of another, immediately contact the victim for consent to represent him or her in a lawsuit in exchange for a contingent fee, a percentage of the judgment recovered.

Ambulatory   Movable; revocable; subject to change; capable of alteration.

Amendment   The modification of materials by the addition of supplemental information; the deletion of unnecessary, undesirable, or outdated information; or the correction of errors existing in the text.

A mensa et thoro   [*Latin, From table and bed.*] More commonly translated as "from bed and board."

Amicable action   An action commenced and maintained by the mutual consent and arrangement of the parties to obtain a judgment of a court on a doubtful question of law that is based upon facts that both parties accept as being correct and complete.

Amicus curiae   [*Latin, Friend of the court.*] A person with strong interest in or views on the subject matter of an action, but not a party to the action, may petition the court for permission to file a brief, ostensibly on behalf of a party but actually to suggest a rationale consistent with its own views. Such amicus curiae briefs are commonly filed in appeals concerning matters of a broad public interest; e.g., civil rights cases. They may be filed by private persons or the government. In appeals to the U.S. courts of appeals, an amicus brief may be filed only if accompanied by written consent of all parties, or by leave of court granted on motion or at the request of the court, except that consent or leave shall not be required when the brief is presented by the United States or an officer or agency thereof.

Amnesty   The action of a government by which all persons or certain groups of persons who have committed a criminal offense—usually of a political nature that threatens the sovereignty of the government (such as sedition or treason)—are granted immunity from prosecution.

Amortization   The reduction of a debt incurred, for example, in the purchase of stocks or bonds, by regular payments consisting of interest and part of the principal made over a specified time period upon the expiration of which the entire debt is repaid. A mortgage is amortized when it is repaid with periodic payments over a particular term. After a certain portion of each payment is applied to the interest on the debt, any balance reduces the principal.

The allocation of the cost of an intangible asset, for example, a patent or copyright, over its estimated useful life that is considered an expense of doing business and is used to offset the earnings of the asset by its declining value. If an intangible asset has an indefinite life, such as good will, it cannot be amortized.

Amotion Putting out; removal; taking away; dispossession of lands.

Amount in controversy The value of the relief demanded or the amount of monetary damages claimed in a lawsuit.

Analogy The inference that two or more things that are similar to each other in some respects are also similar in other respects.

Anarchism The theory espousing a societal state in which there is no structured government or law or in which there is resistance to all current forms of government.

Ancient lights A doctrine of English common law that gives a landowner an easement or right by prescription to the unobstructed passage of light and air from adjoining land if the landowner has had uninterrupted use of the lights for twenty years.

Ancient writing An original document affecting the transfer of real property, which can be admitted as evidence in a lawsuit because its aged condition and its location upon discovery sufficiently establish its authenticity.

Ancillary Subordinate; aiding. A legal proceeding that is not the primary dispute but which aids the judgment rendered in or the outcome of the main action. A descriptive term that denotes a legal claim, the existence of which is dependent upon or reasonably linked to a main claim.

Ancillary administration The settlement and distribution of a decedent's property in the state where it is located and which is other than the state in which the decedent was domiciled.

Animus [*Latin, Mind, soul, or intention.*] A tendency or an inclination toward a definite, sometimes unavoidable, goal; an aim, objective, or purpose.

Annexation The act of attaching, uniting, or joining together in a physical sense; consolidating.

Annotation A note, summary, or commentary on some section of a book or a statute that is intended to explain or illustrate its meaning.

Annual percentage rate The actual cost of borrowing money, expressed in the form of a yearly measure to allow consumers to compare the cost of borrowing money among several lenders.

Annuity A right to receive periodic payments, usually fixed in size, for life or a term of years that is created by a contract or other legal document.

Annulment A judgment by a court that retroactively invalidates a marriage to the date of its formation.

Anon.   An abbreviation for anonymous, nameless, or name unknown.

Answer   The first responsive pleading filed by the defendant in a civil action; a formal written statement that admits or denies the allegations in the complaint and sets forth any available affirmative defenses.

Antarctica   The polar land adjacent to the South Pole.

Ante   [*Latin, Before.*] A reference to a previous portion of a report or textbook.

Antecedent debt   A legally enforceable obligation, which has been in existence prior to the time in question, to reimburse another with money or property.

Anticipation   The performance of an act or obligation before it is legally due. In patent law, the publication of the existence of an invention that has already been patented or has a patent pending, which are grounds for denying a patent to an invention that has substantially the same structure and function as the earlier invention.

Anticipatory repudiation   The unjustifiable denial by a party to a contract of any intention to perform contractual duties, which occurs prior to the time performance is due.

Antinomy   An expression in law and logic to indicate that two authorities, laws, or propositions are inconsistent with each other.

Antitrust law   Legislation enacted by the federal and various state governments to regulate trade and commerce by preventing unlawful restraints, price-fixing, and monopolies, to promote competition, and to encourage the production of quality goods and services at the lowest prices, with the primary goal of safeguarding public welfare by ensuring that consumer demands will be met by the manufacture and sale of goods at reasonable prices.

A posteriori   [*Latin, From the effect to the cause.*]

Apparent   That which is clear, plain, and evident.

Appeal   Timely resort by an unsuccessful party in a lawsuit or administrative proceeding to an appropriate superior court empowered to review a final decision on the ground that it was based upon an erroneous application of law.

Appear   To come before a court as a party or a witness in a lawsuit.

Appearance   A coming into court by a party to a suit, either in person or through an attorney, whether as plaintiff or defendant. The formal proceeding by which a defendant submits to the jurisdiction of the court. The voluntary submission to a court's jurisdiction.

Appellant   A person who, dissatisfied with the judgment rendered in a lawsuit decided in a lower court or the findings from a proceeding before an administrative agency, asks a superior court to review the decision.

Appellate   Relating to appeals; reviews by superior courts of decisions of inferior courts or administrative agencies and other proceedings.

Appellate court   A court having jurisdiction to review decisions of a trial-level or other lower court.

Appellee   A party who has won a judgment in a lawsuit or favorable findings in an administrative proceeding, which judgment or findings the losing party, the appellant, seeks to have a higher court reverse or set aside.

Appoint   To designate, select, or assign authority to a position or an office.

Apportionment   The process by which legislative seats are distributed among units entitled to representation. Determination of the number of representatives that a state, county, or other subdivision may send to a legislative body. The U.S. Constitution provides for a census every ten years, on the basis of which Congress apportions representatives according to population; but each state must have at least one representative. *Districting* is the establishment of the precise geographical boundaries of each such unit or constituency. Apportionment by state statute that denies the rule of one-person, one-vote is violative of equal protection of laws.

   Also, the allocation of a charge or cost such as real estate taxes between two parties, often in the same ratio as the respective times that the parties are in possession or ownership of property during the fiscal period for which the charge is made or assessed.

Appraisal   A valuation or an approximation of value by impartial, properly qualified persons; the process of determining the value of an asset or liability, which entails expert opinion rather than express commercial transactions.

Appraiser   A person selected or appointed by a competent authority or an interested party to evaluate the financial worth of property.

Appreciation   The fair and reasonable estimation of the value of an item. The increase in the financial worth of an asset as compared to its value at a particular earlier date as a result of inflation or greater market demand.

Apprehension   The seizure and arrest of a person who is suspected of having committed a crime.

   A reasonable belief of the possibility of imminent injury or death at the hands of another that justifies a person acting in self-defense against the potential attack.

Apprentice   A person who agrees to work for a specified time in order to learn a trade, craft, or profession in which the employer, traditionally called the master, assents to instruct him or her.

Appropriation   The designation by the government or an individual of the use to which a fund of money is to be applied. The selection and setting apart of privately owned land by the government for public use, such as a military reservation or public building. The diversion of water flowing on public domain from its natural course by means of a canal or ditch for a private beneficial use of the appropriator.

Approval   The present confirmation, ratification, or assent to some action or thing done by another, which is submitted to an individual, group, or governmental body for judgment. The acceptance by a judge of a bond, security, or other document that is required by law to meet with the judge's satisfaction before it becomes legally effective.

Appurtenance   An accessory or adjunct that is attached and incidental to something that has greater importance or value. As applied to real property, an object attached to or a right to be used with land as an incidental benefit but which is necessary to the complete use and enjoyment of the property.

A priori   [*Latin, From the cause to the effect.*]

Arbiter   [*Latin, One who attends something to view it as a spectator or witness.*] Any person who is given an absolute power to judge and rule on a matter in dispute.

Arbitrage   The simultaneous purchase in one market and sale in another of a security or commodity in hope of making a profit on price differences in the different markets.

Arbitrary   Irrational; capricious.

Arbitration   The submission of a dispute to an unbiased third person designated by the parties to the controversy, who agree in advance to comply with the award—a decision to be issued after a hearing at which both parties have an opportunity to be heard.

Architect   A person who prepares the plan and design of a building or other structure and sometimes supervises its construction.

Arguendo   In the course of the argument.

Argument   A form of expression consisting of a coherent set of reasons presenting or supporting a point of view; a series of reasons given for or against a matter under discussion that is intended to convince or persuade the listener.

Argumentative   Controversial; subject to argument.

Armistice   A suspending or cessation of hostilities between belligerent nations or forces for a considerable time. An armistice differs from a mere suspension of arms in that the latter is concluded for very brief periods and for local military purposes only, whereas an armistice not only covers a longer period, but is agreed upon for political purposes. It is said to be general if it relates to the whole area of the war, and partial if it relates to only a portion of that area. Partial armistices are sometimes called truces but there is no hard and fast distinction.

Array	The entire group of jurors selected for a trial from which a smaller group is subsequently chosen to form a petit jury or a grand jury; the list of potential jurors.
Arrears	A sum of money that has not been paid or has only been paid in part at the time it is due.
Arrest of judgment	The postponement or stay of an official decision of a court, or the refusal to render such a determination, after a verdict has been reached in an action at law or a criminal prosecution, because some defect appears on the face of the record that, if a decision is made, would make it erroneous or reversible.
Arrest warrant	A written order issued by authority of the state and commanding the seizure of the person named.
Arrogation	Claiming or seizing something without justification; claiming something on behalf of another. In civil law, the adoption of an adult who was legally capable of acting for himself or herself.
Arson	At common law, the malicious burning or exploding of the dwelling house of another, or the burning of a building within the curtilage, the immediate surrounding space, of the dwelling of another.
Articles	Series or subdivisions of individual and distinct sections of a document, statute, or other writing, such as the Articles of Confederation. Codes or systems of rules created by written agreements of parties or by statute that establish standards of legally acceptable behavior in a business relationship, such as articles of incorporation or articles of partnership. Writings that embody contractual terms of agreements between parties.
Articles of confederation	The document that set forth the terms under which the original thirteen states agreed to participate in a centralized form of government, in addition to their self-rule, and that was in effect from March 1, 1781, to March 4, 1789, prior to the adoption of the Constitution.
Articles of impeachment	Formal written allegations of the causes that warrant the criminal trial of a public official before a quasi-political court.
Articles of incorporation	The document that must be filed with an appropriate government agency, commonly the office of the secretary of state, if the owners of a business want it to be given legal recognition as a corporation.
Articles of partnership	A written compact by which parties agree to pool their money, labor, or skill, or all three, to carry on a business for profit. The parties sign the compact with the understanding that they will share proportionally the losses and profits according to the provisions and conditions that they have mutually assented would govern their business relationship.
Articles of war	Codes created to prescribe the manner in which the armed services of a nation are to be governed.

Artificial insemination The process by which a woman is medically impregnated using semen from her husband or from a third-party donor.

Artificial person A legal entity that is not a human being but for certain purposes is considered by virtue of statute to be a natural person.

As is A term used to describe a sales transaction in which the seller offers goods in their present, existing condition to prospective buyers.

As per A phrase commonly recognized to mean "in accordance with the terms of" a particular document—such as a contract, deed, or affidavit—or "as authorized by the contract."

Asportation The removal of items from one place to another, such as carrying things away illegally.

Assassination Murder committed by a perpetrator without the personal provocation of the victim, who is usually a government official.

Assault At common law, an intentional act by one person that creates an apprehension in another of an imminent harmful or offensive contact.

Assault and battery Two separate offenses against the person that when used in one expression may be defined as any unlawful and unpermitted touching of another. *Assault* is an act that creates an apprehension in another of an imminent, harmful, or offensive contact. The act consists of a threat of harm accompanied by an apparent, present ability to carry out the threat. *Battery* is a harmful or offensive touching of another.

Assembly The congregation of a number of persons at the same location.

Assent An intentional approval of known facts that are offered by another for acceptance; agreement; consent.

Assess To determine financial worth. To ascertain the amount of damages. To fix and adjust the individual shares to be contributed by several persons toward a common beneficial objective in proportion to the benefit each person will receive. To tax by having qualified experts estimate the value of property by considering the nature of the property, its size, the value of other comparable property, and the proportionate share of services that is used by that property. To levy a charge on the owner of property that has been improved at the expense of the local government unit, such as when sewers or sidewalks are installed.

Assessed valuation The financial worth assigned to property by taxing authorities that is used as a basis or factor against which the tax rate is applied.

Assessment The process by which the financial worth of property is determined. The amount at which an item is valued. A demand by the board of directors of a corporation for the payment of any money that is still owed on the purchase of capital stock. The determination of the amount of damages to be awarded to a plaintiff who has been successful in a lawsuit. The ascertainment of the pro rata share of taxes to be paid by members of a group of taxpayers who have directly benefited from a particular common goal or project according to the benefit conferred upon the individual or his or her property. This is known as a special assessment. The listing and valuation of property for purposes of fixing a tax upon it for which its owner will be liable. The procedure by which the Internal Revenue Service, or other government department of taxation, declares that a taxpayer owes additional tax because, for example, the individual has understated personal gross income or has taken deductions to which he or she is not entitled. This process is also known as a deficiency assessment.

Asset   Real or personal property, whether tangible or intangible, that has financial value and can be used for the payment of its owner's debts.

Assign   To transfer to another, as to assign one's right to receive rental income from property to another. To designate for a particular function, as to assign an attorney to defend an indigent in a criminal prosecution. To specify or point out, as to assign errors in a lower court proceeding on a writ of error that is submitted to request a court to reverse the judgment of the lower court.

Assigned account   A type of secured transaction whereby an account receivable is pledged to a bank, factor, or other lender to secure the repayment of a loan.

Assigned risk   A danger or hazard of loss or injury that an insurer will not normally accept for coverage under a policy issued by the insurer, but that the insurance company is required by state law to offer protection against by participating in a pool of insurers who are also compelled to provide coverage.

Assigned risk plan   An insurance plan created and imposed by state statute under which persons who normally would be denied insurance coverage as bad risks are permitted to purchase insurance from a pool of insurers who must offer coverage to such individuals.

Assignment   A transfer of rights in real property or personal property to another that gives the recipient—the transferee—the rights that the owner or holder of the property—the transferor—had prior to the transfer.

Assignment for benefit of creditors   The voluntary transfer of all or most of a debtor's property to another person in trust so that he or she will collect any money that is owed to the debtor, sell the debtor's property, and apply the money received to the payment of the debts, returning any surplus to the debtor.

Assigns   Individuals to whom property is, will, or may be transferred by conveyance, will, descent and distribution, or statute; assignees.

Assistance, writ of   A court order issued to enforce an existing judgment.

Assize, or assise   A judicial procedure in early England whereby a certain number of men in a community were called together to hear and decide a dispute; a type of court. A type of writ, commanding the convening of such a tribunal in order to determine disputed rights to possess land. An edict or statute issued by an ancient assembly.

Associate justice The designation given to a judge who is not the chief or presiding justice of the court on which he or she sits.

Assumpsit [*Latin, He undertook or he promised.*] A promise by which someone assumes or undertakes an obligation to another person. The promise may be oral or in writing, but it is not under seal. It is express when the person making the promise puts it into distinct and specific language, but it may also be implied because the law sometimes imposes obligations based on the conduct of the parties or the circumstances of their dealings.

Assumption The undertaking of the repayment of a debt or the performance of an obligation owed by another.

Assumption of risk A defense, facts offered by a party against whom proceedings have been instituted to diminish a plaintiff's cause of action or defeat recovery to an action in negligence, which entails proving that the plaintiff knew of a dangerous condition and voluntarily exposed himself or herself to it.

Assured A person protected by insurance coverage against loss or damage stipulated by the provisions of a policy purchased from an insurance company or an underwriter.

Asylums Establishments that exist for the aid and protection of individuals in need of assistance due to disability, such as insane persons, those who are physically handicapped, or persons who are unable to properly care for themselves, such as orphans.

At issue A phrase that describes the status of parties in a lawsuit when they make contradictory statements about a point specified in their pleadings.

At large Not limited to any place, person, or topic; for example, a representative at large is elected by the voters of the state as a whole rather than voters of a particular district. Free from control or restraint, such as a criminal at large.

At law According to law; by, for, or in the law, as in the professional title *attorney at law*. Within or arising from the traditions of the common law as opposed to equity, the system of law that developed alongside the common law and emphasized fairness and justice rather than enforcement of technical rules.

Attachment The legal process of seizing property to ensure satisfaction of a judgment.

Attainder At common law, that extinction of civil rights and capacities that took place whenever a person who had committed treason or a felony received a sentence of death for the crime.

The effect of attainder upon a felon was, in general terms, that all estate, real and personal, was forfeited. In common law, attainder resulted in three ways: by confession, by verdict, and by process or outlawry. The first case was where the prisoner pleaded guilty at the bar, or having fled, confessed guilt and abjured the realm to save his or her life. The second was where the prisoner pleaded not guilty at the bar, and the jury brought in a verdict against him or her. The third, when the person accused made his or her escape and was outlawed.

In England, by statute 33 & 34 Vict. c. 23, attainder upon conviction, with consequent corruption of blood, forfeiture, or escheat, was abolished. In the United States, the doctrine of attainder is now scarcely known, although during and shortly after the Revolution acts of attainder were passed by several of the states. The passage of such bills is expressly forbidden by the Constitution (Art. I, Sec. 9).

Bills of attainder are special acts of the legislature that inflict capital punishments upon persons supposed to be guilty of high offenses, such as treason and felony, without any conviction in the ordinary course of judicial proceedings. If an act inflicts a milder degree of punishment than death, it is called a bill of pains and penalties, but both are included in the prohibition in the Constitution (Art. I, Sec. 9).

Attempt An undertaking to do an act that entails more than mere preparation but does not result in the successful completion of the act.

Attenuate To reduce the force or severity; to lessen a relationship or connection between two objects.

Attest To solemnly declare verbally or in writing that a particular document or testimony about an event is a true and accurate representation of the facts; to bear witness to. To formally certify by a signature that the signer has been present at the execution of a particular writing so as to rebut any potential challenges to its authenticity.

Attestation The act of attending the execution of a document and bearing witness to its authenticity, by signing one's name to it to affirm that it is genuine. The certification by a custodian of records that a copy of an original document is a true copy that is demonstrated by his or her signature on a certificate.

Attorn To turn over money, rent, or goods to another. To assign to a specific function or service.

Attorney A person admitted to practice law in at least one jurisdiction and authorized to perform criminal and civil legal functions on behalf of clients. These functions include providing legal counsel, drafting legal documents, and representing clients before courts, administrative agencies, and other tribunals.

Attorney-client privilege In law of evidence, client's privilege to refuse to disclose and to prevent any other person from disclosing confidential communications between the client and his or her attorney. Such privilege protects communications between attorney and client made for the purpose of furnishing or obtaining professional legal advice or assistance. That privilege that permits an attorney to refuse to testify as to communications from the client though it belongs to the client, not the attorney, and hence the client may waive it. In federal courts, state law is applied with respect to such privilege.

Attorney misconduct   Behavior by an attorney that conflicts with established rules of professional conduct and is punishable by disciplinary measures.

Attorney's lien   The right of a lawyer to hold a client's property or money until payment has been made for legal aid and advice given.

Auctions   A sale open to the general public and conducted by an auctioneer, a person empowered to conduct such a sale, at which property is sold to the highest bidder.

Audit   A systematic examination of financial or accounting records by a specialized inspector, called an auditor, to verify their accuracy and truthfulness. A hearing during which financial data are investigated for purposes of authentication.

Authentication   The confirmation rendered by an officer of a court that a certified copy of a judgment is what it purports to be, an accurate duplicate of the original judgment. In the law of evidence, the act of establishing a statute, record, or other document, or a certified copy of such an instrument as genuine and official so that it can be used in a lawsuit to prove an issue in dispute.

Authorities   Legal powers. Governmental agencies created by statute for specific public purposes, such as a county highway authority. References to statutes, precedents, judicial decision, and legal textbooks that support the position of a party to a lawsuit made in the briefs submitted by the attorneys for the parties to the court that is to hear the case or during the trial in the oral arguments.

Authorize   To empower another with the legal right to perform an action.

Autopsy   The dissection of a dead body by a medical examiner or physician authorized by law to do so in order to determine the cause and time of a death that appears to have resulted from other than natural causes.

Auxiliary   Aiding; ancillary; subordinate; subsidiary.

Aver   To specifically allege certain facts or claims in a pleading.

Averment   The allegation of facts or claims in a pleading.

Avoidable consequences   The doctrine that places the responsibility of minimizing damages upon the person who has been injured.

Avoidance   An escape from the consequences of a specific course of action through the use of legally acceptable means. Cancellation; the act of rendering something useless or legally ineffective.

Avowal An open declaration by an attorney representing a party in a lawsuit, made after the jury has been removed from the courtroom, that requests the admission of particular testimony from a witness that would otherwise be inadmissible because it has been successfully objected to during the trial.

Avulsion The immediate and noticeable addition to land caused by its removal from the property of another, by a sudden change in a water bed or in the course of a stream.

Award To concede; to give by judicial determination; to rule in favor of after an evaluation of the facts, evidence, or merits. The decision made by a panel of arbitrators or commissioners, a jury, or other authorized individuals in a controversy that has been presented for resolution. A document that memorializes the determination reached in a dispute.

Backdating Predating a document or instrument prior to the date it was actually drawn. The negotiability of an instrument is not affected by the fact that it is backdated.

Back pay award A legally enforceable decree ordering an employer to pay to an employee retroactively a designated increase in his or her salary that occurred during a particular period of employment. A decision rendered by a judicial or quasi-judicial body that an employee has a legal right to collect accrued salary that has not been paid out to him or her.

Back to work agreement The accord reached between an employer and a union to which his or her employees belong that establishes the terms and conditions governing the return of striking employees to work.

Bad faith The fraudulent deception of another person; the intentional or malicious refusal to perform some duty or contractual obligation.

Bail The system that governs the status of individuals charged with committing crimes, from the time of their arrest to the time of their trial, and pending appeal, with the major purpose of ensuring their presence at trial.

Bail bond A written promise signed by a defendant or a surety (one who promises to act in place of another) to pay an amount fixed by a court should the defendant named in the document fail to appear in court for the designated criminal proceeding at the date and time specified.

Bailee   One to whom personal property is entrusted for a particular purpose by another, the bailor, according to the terms of an express or implied agreement.

Bailiff   An individual who is entrusted with some authority, care, guardianship, or jurisdiction over designated persons or property. One who acts in a managerial or ministerial capacity or takes care of land, goods, and chattels of another in order to make the best profit for the owner. A minor officer of a court serving primarily as a messenger or usher. A low-level court official or sheriff's deputy whose duty is to preserve and protect orderly conduct in court proceedings.

Bailment   The temporary placement of control over, or possession of, personal property by one person, the bailor, into the hands of another, the bailee, for a designated purpose upon which the parties have agreed.

Bailor   One who places control over or possession of personal property in the hands of another, a bailee, for its care, safekeeping, or use, in accordance to the terms of a mutual agreement.

Bait and switch   A deceptive sales technique that involves advertising a low-priced item to attract customers to a store, then persuading them to buy more expensive goods by failing to have a sufficient supply of the advertised item on hand or by disparaging its quality.

Balance sheet   A comprehensive financial statement that is a summarized assessment of a company's accounts specifying its assets and liabilities. A report, usually prepared by independent auditors or accountants, which includes a full and complete statement of all receipts and disbursements of a particular business. A review that shows a general balance or summation of all accounts without showing the particular items that make up the several accounts.

Balancing   A process sometimes used by the Supreme Court in deciding between the competing interests represented in a case.

Balloon payment   The final installment of a loan to be paid in an amount that is disproportionately larger than the regular installment.

Banc   [*French, Bench.*] The location where a court customarily or permanently sits.

Banker's lien   An enforceable right of a bank to hold in its possession any money or property belonging to a customer and to apply it to the repayment of any outstanding debt owed to the bank, provided that, to the bank's knowledge, such property is not part of a trust fund or is not already burdened with other debts.

Bankruptcy   A federally authorized procedure by which a debtor—an individual, corporation, or municipality—is relieved of total liability for its debts by making court-approved arrangements for their partial repayment.

Banks and banking	Authorized financial institutions and the business in which they engage, which encompasses the receipt of money for deposit, to be payable according to the terms of the account; collection of checks presented for payment; issuance of loans to individuals who meet certain requirements; discount of commercial paper; and other money-related functions.
Bar association	An organization of lawyers established to promote professional competence, enforce standards of ethical conduct, and encourage a spirit of public service among members of the legal profession.
Bar examination	A written test that an individual must pass before becoming licensed to practice law as an attorney.
Bargain	A reciprocal understanding, contract, or agreement of any sort usually pertaining to the loan, sale, or exchange of property between two parties, one of whom wants to dispose of an item that the other wants to obtain. To work out the terms of an agreement; to negotiate in good faith for the purpose of entering into an agreement.
Bargaining agent	A union that possesses the sole authority to act on behalf of all the employees of a particular type in a company.
Barratry	In criminal law, the frequent incitement of lawsuits and quarrels that is a punishable offense.
Barrister	In English law, an attorney who has an exclusive right of argument in all the superior courts.
Barter	The exchange of goods or services without the use of money as currency.
Base fee	An interest in real property that has the potential to last forever, provided a specific contingency does not occur.
Base line	Survey line used in the government survey to establish township lines. Horizontal elevation line used as a centerline in a highway survey.
Basis	The minimum, fundamental constituents, foundation, or support of a thing or a system without which the thing or system would cease to exist. In accounting, the value assigned to an asset that is sold or transferred so that it can be determined whether a gain or loss has resulted from the transaction. The amount that property is estimated to be worth at the time it is received for tax purposes.
Bastardy action	An archaic name given to a court proceeding in which the paternity of an illegitimate child is determined in order to impose and enforce support obligations upon the father.
Battel	Physical combat engaged in by an accuser and accused to resolve their differences, usually involving a serious crime or ownership of land. It was recognized by the English king from the eleventh to seventeenth centuries.

Battery   At common law, an intentional unpermitted act causing harmful or offensive contact with the person of another.

Bearer   One who is the holder or possessor of an instrument that is negotiable—for example, a check, a draft, or a note—and upon which a specific payee is not designated.

Belief   Mental reliance on or acceptance of a particular concept, which is arrived at by weighing external evidence, facts, and personal observation and experience.

Below   In an inferior, subordinate, or lower place in regard to any entity.

Bench   A forum of justice comprised of the judge or judges of a court. The seat of the court occupied by the judges.

Bench trial   A trial conducted before a judge presiding without a jury.

Bench warrant   A process that is initiated by the court pro se in order to attach or arrest a person. An order that a judge, or group of judges, issues directly to the police with the purpose of directing a person's arrest.

Beneficial association   An incorporated or voluntary nonprofit organization that has been created primarily to protect and aid its members and their dependents.

Beneficial interest   Profits or advantages from property derived from the terms of a trust agreement.

Beneficial use   A right to utilize real property, including light, air, and access to it, in any lawful manner to gain a profit, advantage, or enjoyment from it. A right to enjoy real or personal property held by a person who has equitable title to it while legal title is held by another.

Beneficiary   An organization or a person for whom a trust is created and who thereby receives the benefits of the trust. One who inherits under a will. A person entitled to a beneficial interest or a right to profits, benefit, or advantage from a contract.

Benefit of clergy   In old England, the privilege of clergy that allowed them to avoid trial by all courts of the civil government.

Bequeath   To dispose of personal property owned by a decedent at the time of death as a gift under the provisions of the decedent's will.

Bequest   A gift of personal property, such as money, stock, bonds, or jewelry, owned by a decedent at the time of death which is directed by the provisions of the decedent's will; a legacy.

Best evidence   An original document or object offered as proof of a fact in a lawsuit as opposed to a photocopy of, or other substitute for, the item or the testimony of a witness describing it.

Bestiality   Sexual relations between a human being and an animal.

Beyond a reasonable doubt	The standard that must be met by the prosecution's evidence in a criminal prosecution: that no other logical explanation can be derived from the facts except that the defendant committed the crime, thereby overcoming the presumption that a person is innocent until proven guilty.
Bias	A predisposition or a preconceived opinion that prevents a person from impartially evaluating facts that have been presented for determination; a prejudice.
Bicameral	The division of a legislative or judicial body into two components or chambers.
Bifurcated trial	One judicial proceeding that is divided into two stages in which different issues are addressed separately by the court.
Bigamy	The offense of willfully and knowingly entering into a second marriage while validly married to another individual.
Bilateral contract	An agreement formed by an exchange of promises in which the promise of one party is consideration supporting the promise of the other party.
Bill	A declaration in writing. A document listing separate items. An itemized account of charges or costs. In equity practice, the first pleading in the action, the paper in which the plaintiff sets out his or her case and demands relief from the defendant.
Bill of attainder	A special legislative enactment that imposes a death sentence without a judicial trial upon a particular person or class of persons suspected of committing serious offenses, such as treason or a felony.
Bill of exchange	A three-party negotiable instrument in which the first party, the drawer, presents an order for the payment of a sum certain on a second party, the drawee, for payment to a third party, the payee, on demand or at a fixed future date.
Bill of indictment	A formal written document that is drawn up by a government prosecutor accusing a designated person of having committed a felony or misdemeanor and which is presented to a grand jury so that it may take action upon it.
Bill of lading	A document signed by a carrier (a transporter of goods) or the carrier's representative and issued to a consignor (the shipper of goods) that evidences the receipt of goods for shipment to a specified designation and person.
Bill of particulars	A written statement used in both civil and criminal actions that is submitted by a plaintiff or a prosecutor at the request of a defendant, giving the defendant detailed information concerning the claims or charges made against him or her.
Bill of review	In the practice of equity courts, a paper filed with a court after expiration of the time for filing a petition for a rehearing in order to

request, due to exceptional circumstances, the correction or reversal of a final judgment or decree.

Bill of rights The first ten amendments to the U.S. Constitution, ratified in 1791, which set forth and guarantee certain fundamental rights and privileges of individuals, including freedom of religion, speech, press, and assembly; guarantee of a speedy jury trial in criminal cases; and protection against excessive bail and cruel and unusual punishment.

A list of fundamental rights included in each state constitution.

A declaration of individual rights and freedoms, usually issued by a national government.

Bill of sale In the law of contracts, a written agreement, previously required to be under seal, by which one person transfers to another a right to, or interest in, personal property and goods, a legal instrument that conveys title in property from seller to purchaser.

Bills and notes An archaic term that designated the body of law currently known as the law of commercial paper, which governs the methods by which commercial transactions are financed and facilitated by the execution and transfer of documents that contain promises to repay debts according to the terms specified in the documents.

Bills of credit Non-interest-bearing promissory notes issued by the government and backed by its faith and credit to be paid when presented by their holders, which are in the form of currency and are intended to be circulated and exchanged in the community as money.

Binder A written document that records the essential provisions of a contract of insurance and temporarily protects the insured until an insurance company has investigated the risks to be covered, or until a formal policy is issued.

A receipt for cash or for a check that is deposited by a prospective buyer with the seller to secure the right to purchase real estate at terms that have been agreed upon by both buyer and seller.

Binding authority Source of law that a judge must examine or evaluate in a decision of a case.

Binding over The requirement imposed by a court or a magistrate upon a person to enter into a recognizance or to post bail to ensure that he or she will appear for trial. The transfer of a case from a lower court to a higher court or to a grand jury after probable cause to believe that the defendant committed the crime has been established.

Birth control A measure or measures undertaken to prevent conception.

Blackacre A fictitious designation that legal writers use to describe a piece of land.

Black letter law A term used to describe basic principles of law that are accepted by a majority of judges in most states.

Blacklist	A list of individuals or organizations designated for special discrimination or boycott; also to put a person or organization on such a list.
Blackmail	The crime involving a threat for purposes of compelling a person to do an act against his or her will, or for purposes of taking the person's money or property.
Blackstone's commentaries	A series of lectures delivered by the English jurist Sir William Blackstone at Oxford in 1753 and published as *Commentaries on the Laws of England* in four volumes between 1765 and 1769, which systematized and clarified the amorphous body of English law.
Blank	Lacking something essential to fulfillment or completeness; unrestricted or open. A space left empty for the insertion of one or more words or marks in a written document that will effectuate its meaning or make it legally operative. A printed legal form in which the standard or necessary words are printed in their proper order with spaces left open, to be filled with names, dates, figures, and additional clauses.
Blank endorsement	The writing of the name of a person who holds a negotiable instrument on the back of the document without specifically designating to whom the paper is to be paid, which transfers the rights that the signer had in the instrument to the person who presents it for payment.
Blasphemy	The malicious or wanton reproach of God, either written or oral. In English law, the offense of speaking disparaging words about God, Jesus Christ, the Bible, or the Book of Common Prayer with the intent to undermine religious beliefs and promote contempt and hatred for the church as well as general immorality. In U.S. law, any maliciously intended written or oral accusation made against God or religion with the purpose of dishonoring the divine majesty and alienating mankind from the love and reverence of God.
Block	A segment of a town or city surrounded by streets and avenues on at least three sides and usually occupied by buildings, though it may be composed solely of vacant lots. The section of a city enclosed by streets that is described by a map which indicates how a portion of land will be subdivided.
Blockbusting	The practice of illegally frightening homeowners by telling them that people who are members of a particular race, religion, or national origin are moving into their neighborhood and that they should expect a decline in the value of their property. The purpose of this scheme is to get the homeowners to sell out at a deflated price.
Blood feud	The act of avenging the wrongful death of a person's kin by killing the murderer or by receiving compensation from the murderer's possessions.
Blotter	A written record of arrests and other occurrences maintained by the police. The report kept by the police when a suspect is booked, which

involves the written recording of facts about the person's arrest and the charges against him or her.

Blue Book A publication that establishes the correct form of case citations or of references to a legal authority showing where information can be found. A volume that explains the organization of a state government and provides the names of state officials.

Blue ribbon jury A group of highly qualified persons selected by a court on the request of either party to a lawsuit to decide complex and specialized disputes.

Blue sky law A popular name for state statutes providing for the regulation and supervision of securities offerings and sales, to protect citizen-investors from investing in fraudulent companies. Most blue sky laws require the registration of new issues of securities with a state agency that reviews selling documents for accuracy and completeness. Blue sky laws also often regulate securities brokers and salespeople.

Board of directors A group of people comprising the governing body of a corporation.

Body The principal part of anything as distinguished from its subordinate parts, as in the main part of an instrument. An individual, an organization, or an entity given legal recognition, such as a corporation or body corporate. A compilation of laws known as a body of laws.

Body execution An arrest; a seizure of a defendant.

Boilerplate A description of uniform language used normally in legal documents that has a definite, unvarying meaning in the same context that denotes that the words have not been individually fashioned to address the legal issue presented.

Bona fide [*Latin, In good faith.*] Honest; genuine; actual; authentic; acting without the intention of defrauding.

Bonds Written documents by which a government, corporation, or individual—the obligor—promises to perform a certain act, usually the payment of a definite sum of money, to another—the obligee—on a certain date.

Booking The procedure by which law enforcement officials record facts about the arrest of and charges against a suspect such as the crime for which the arrest was made, together with information concerning the identification of the suspect and other pertinent facts.

Bookkeeping The process of systematically and methodically recording the financial accounts and transactions of an entity.

Book value The current value of an asset. The book value of an asset at any time is its cost minus its accumulated depreciation. (Depreciation reflects the decrease in the useful life of an asset due to use of the asset.) Companies use book value to determine the point at which they have recovered the cost of an asset.

The net asset value of a company's securities. This is calculated by subtracting from the company's total assets the following items: intangible assets (such as goodwill), current liabilities, and long-term liabilities and equity issues. This figure, divided by the total number of bonds or of shares of stock, is the book value per bond or per share of stock.

Bottomry A contract, in maritime law, by which money is borrowed for a specified term by the owner of a ship for its use, equipment, or repair for which the ship is pledged as collateral. If the ship is lost in the specified voyage or during the limited time, the lender will lose his or her money according to the provisions of the contract. A contract by which a ship or its freight is pledged as security for a loan, which is to be repaid only in the event that the ship survives a specific risk, voyage, or period.

Boundaries Natural or artificial separations or divisions between adjoining properties to show their limits.

Bounty A subsidy paid to a category of persons who have performed a public service.

Boycott A lawful concerted attempt by a group of people to express displeasure with, or obtain concessions from, a particular person or company by refusing to do business with them. An unlawful attempt that is prohibited by the Sherman Anti-Trust Act (15 U.S.C.A. § 1 et seq.), to adversely affect a company through threat, coercion, or intimidation of its employees, or to prevent others from doing business with said company. A practice utilized in labor disputes whereby an organized group of employees bands together and refrains from dealing with an employer, the legality of which is determined by applicable provisions of statutes governing labor-management relations.

Bracket The category of the percentage of income tax found on the tax tables set by the Internal Revenue Code, within which a taxpayer falls based upon his or her taxable income.

Breach of marriage promise A common–law right of action for breaking a commitment to enter into matrimony.

Breach of the peace A comprehensive term encompassing acts or conduct that seriously endanger or disturb public peace and order.

Breaking To use physical force to separate or damage a solid object.

Bribery The offering, giving, receiving, or soliciting of something of value for the purpose of influencing the action of an official in the discharge of his or her public or legal duties.

Bridges Structures constructed over obstructions to highways or waterways, such as canals or rivers, in order to provide continuous and convenient passages for purposes of transportation.

Brief   A summary of the important points of a longer document. An abstract of a published judicial opinion prepared by a law student as part of an assignment in the case method study of law. A written document drawn up by an attorney for a party in a lawsuit or by a party himself or herself appearing pro se that concisely states the (1) issues of a lawsuit; (2) facts that bring the parties to court; (3) relevant laws that can affect the subject of the dispute; and (4) arguments that explain how the law applies to the particular facts so that the case will be decided in the party's favor.

Bring suit   To initiate legal proceedings; to start an action for judicial relief.

Broker   An individual or firm employed by others to plan and organize sales or negotiate contracts for a commission.

Buggery   The criminal offense of anal or oral copulation by penetration of the male organ into the anus or mouth of another person of either sex or copulation between members of either sex with an animal.

Building and loan association   An organization that exists to accumulate a fund, composed of subscriptions and savings of its members, to help facilitate the purchase or construction of real estate by such members by lending them the necessary funds.

Building line   A line that a municipal corporation establishes, beyond which no building may extend to ensure that its streets will appear uniform.

Bulk transfer   A sale of all or most of the materials, supplies, merchandise, or other inventory of a business at one time that is not normally done in the ordinary course of the seller's business.

Bulletin   A printing of public notices and announcements that discloses the progress of matters affecting the general public and which usually includes provisions for public comment. A summarized report of a newsworthy item for immediate release to the public. The official publication of an association, business, or institution.

Burden of going forward   The onus on a party to a case to refute or to explain.

Burden of persuasion   The onus on the party with the burden of proof to convince the trier of fact of all elements of his or her case. In a criminal case the burden of the government to produce evidence of all the necessary elements of the crime beyond a reasonable doubt.

Bureaucracy   A system of administration wherein there is a specialization of functions, objective qualifications for office, action according to the adherence to fixed rules, and a hierarchy of authority and delegated power.

Burglary   The criminal offense of breaking and entering a building illegally for the purpose of committing a crime therein.

Business affected with a public interest   A commercial venture or an occupation that has become subject to governmental regulation by virtue of its offering essential services or products to the community at large.

Business judgment rule   A legal principle that makes officers, directors, managers, and other agents of a corporation immune from liability to the corporation for loss incurred in corporate transactions that are within their authority and power to make when sufficient evidence demonstrates that the transactions were made in good faith.

Business record exception   A rule of evidence that allows routine entries made customarily in financial records, or business logs or files kept in the regular course of business, to be introduced as proof in a lawsuit when the person who made such notations is not available to testify.

Business trust   An unincorporated business organization created by a legal document, a declaration of trust, and used in place of a corporation or partnership for the transaction of various kinds of business with limited liability.

"But for" rule   In the law of negligence, a principle that provides that the defendant's conduct is not the cause of an injury to the plaintiff, unless that injury would not have occurred except for ("but for") the defendant's conduct.

Bylaws   The rules and regulations enacted by an association or a corporation to provide a framework for its operation and management.

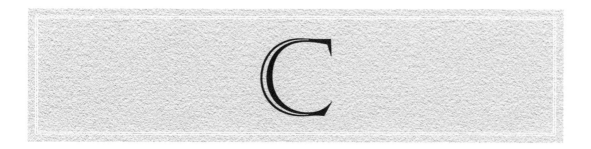

Cabinet   The counsel or group of advisers of a king or other chief executive of a government. A group of individuals who advise the president of the United States.

Calendar   A list of cases that are awaiting trial or other settlement, often called a trial list or docket.

Call   To convoke or summon by public announcement; to request the appearance and participation of several people—such as a call of a jury to serve, a roll call, a call of public election, or a call of names of the members of a legislative body.

In contract law, the demand for the payment of money according to the contract terms, usually by formal notice.

As applied to corporation law, the demand of the board of directors that subscribers pay an installment or portion of the amount that is still owed on shares that they have agreed to buy. A call price is the price paid by a corporation for the redemption of its own securities.

In securities, a contract that gives a person the right to demand payment of a certain specified number of shares of stock at a stated price or upon a fixed date.

Calvo clause   A provision in an agreement between a private individual and a foreign state that says, in effect, that "aliens are not entitled to rights and privileges not accorded to nationals, and that, therefore, they may seek redress for grievances only before local authorities."

Calvo doctrine   The principle set forth by an Argentine jurist, Carlos Calvo, that a government has no duty to compensate aliens for losses or injuries that they incur as a result of domestic disturbances or a civil war, in cases where the state is not at fault, and, therefore, no justification exists for foreign nations to intervene to secure the settlements of the claims made by their citizens due to such losses or injuries.

Camera   A chamber, room, or apartment in old English law. A judge's chamber. Treasury, chest, or coffer.

Canals   Artificial channels for the conveyance of water, used for navigation, transportation, drainage, or irrigation of land.

Cancellation of an instrument   An equitable remedy by which a court relieves both parties to a legal document of their obligations under it due to fraud, duress, or other grounds.

Canon law   Any church's or religion's laws, rules, and regulations; more commonly, the written policies that guide the administration and religious ceremonies of the Roman Catholic Church.

Canons of construction   The system of basic rules and maxims applied by a court to aid in its interpretation of a written document, such as a statute or contract.

Canons of ethics   Rules that govern the practice of law.

Capacity   The ability, capability, or fitness to do something; a legal right, power, or competency to perform some act. An ability to comprehend both the nature and consequences of one's acts.

Capias   [*Latin, That you take.*] The name for several different kinds of writs, or court orders, all of which require an officer to take the defendant into custody.

Capital asset   Property held by a taxpayer, such as houses, cars, stocks, bonds, and jewelry, or a building owned by a corporation to furnish facilities for its employees.

Capitalize   To regard the cost of an improvement or other purchase as a capital asset for purposes of determining income tax liability. To calculate the net worth upon which an investment is based. To issue company stocks or bonds to finance an investment.

Capital punishment The lawful infliction of death as a punishment; the death penalty.

Capital stock All shares constituting ownership of a business, including common stock and preferred stock. The amount of shares that a corporate charter requires to be subscribed and paid, or secured to be paid, by shareholders. The amount of stock that a corporation may issue; the amount actually contributed, subscribed, or secured to be paid on. The liability of the corporation to its shareholders after creditors' claims have been settled. The valuation of the corporation as a business enterprise.

Capitation tax An assessment levied by the government upon a person at a fixed rate regardless of income or worth.

Caption The standardized heading of a legal instrument, such as a motion or a complaint, which sets forth the names of the parties in controversy, the name of the court, the docket number, and the name of the action.

Care Watchful attention; custody; diligence; concern; caution; as opposed to negligence or carelessness.

Car-jacking The criminal taking of a motor vehicle from its driver by force, violence, or intimidation.

Carnal knowledge Copulation; the act of a man having sexual relations with a woman.

Carriers Individuals or businesses that are employed to deliver people or property to an agreed destination.

Carrier's lien The right of an individual or organization that publicly advertises itself for hire for the transportation of goods to keep possession of the cargo it has delivered to a destination until the person who is liable to pay the freight charges plus any other expenses incurred by its shipment has done so.

Carrington report A report delineating proposed changes in legal education submitted by Professor Paul D. Carrington of the University of Michigan School of Law, chairman of the Curriculum Study Project Committee of the Association of American Law Schools (AALS), to the AALS on September 7, 1971.

Carry-back The name given to the method provided under federal tax law that allows a taxpayer to apply net operating losses incurred during one year to the recomputation of income tax owed to the government for three preceding taxable years.

Carrying charges Payments made to satisfy expenses incurred as a result of ownership of property, such as land taxes and mortgage payments. Disbursements paid to creditors, in addition to interest, for extending credit.

Carry-over   The designation of the process by which net operating loss for one year may be applied, as provided by federal tax law, to each of several taxable years following the taxable year of such loss.

Cartel   A combination of producers of any product joined together to control its production, sale, and price, so as to obtain a monopoly and restrict competition in any particular industry or commodity. Cartels exist primarily in Europe, being illegal in the United States by virtue of antitrust laws. Also, an association by agreement of companies or sections of companies having common interests, designed to prevent extreme or unfair competition and allocate markets, and to promote the interchange of knowledge resulting from scientific and technical research, exchange of patent rights, and standardization of products.

In war, an agreement between two hostile powers for the delivery of prisoners or deserters, or authorizing certain nonhostile intercourse between each other that would otherwise be prevented by the state of war, for example, agreements between enemies for intercommunication by post, telegraph, telephone, or railway.

Case   A general term for any action, cause of action, lawsuit, or controversy. All the evidence and testimony compiled and organized by one party in a lawsuit to prove that party's version of the controversy at a trial in court.

Case, action on the   One of the old common-law forms of action that provided a remedy for the invasion of personal or property interests.

Case agreed on   An action in which the parties submit a formal written enumeration of facts that they both accept as correct and complete so that a judge can render a decision based upon conclusions of law that can be drawn from the stated facts.

Casebook   A printed compilation of judicial decisions illustrating the application of particular principles of a specific field of law, such as torts, that is used in legal education to teach students under the case method system.

Case law   Legal principles enunciated and embodied in judicial decisions that are derived from the application of particular areas of law to the facts of individual cases.

Case method   A system of instruction or study of law focused upon the analysis of court opinions rather than lectures and textbooks; the predominant method of teaching in U.S. law schools today.

Case or controversy   A term used in Article III, Section 2, of the Constitution to describe the structure by which actual, conflicting claims of individuals must be brought before a federal court for resolution if the court is to exercise its jurisdiction to consider the questions and provide relief.

Case stated   An action that is brought upon the agreement of the parties who submit a statement of undisputed facts to the court but who take adversary positions as to the legal ramifications of the facts, thereby requiring a judge to decide the question of law presented.

Cash basis A method of accounting that considers only money actually received as income and only money actually paid out as expense.

Cash surrender value The amount of money that an insurance company pays an insured upon cancellation of a life insurance policy before death and which is a specific figure assigned to the policy at that particular time, reduced by a charge for administrative expenses.

Casual Irregular, occasional, or accidental; happening without being planned or foreseen.

Casual ejector A fictitious and nominal defendant in an action of ejectment.

Casualty A serious or fatal accident. A person or thing injured, lost, or destroyed. A disastrous occurrence due to sudden, unexpected, or unusual cause. Accident; misfortune or mishap; that which comes by chance or without design. A loss from such an event or cause, as by fire, shipwreck, lightning, etc.

Casus belli [*Latin, Cause of war.*] A term used in international law to describe an event or occurrence giving rise to or justifying war.

Categorical That which is unqualified or unconditional.

Causa mortis [*Latin, In contemplation of approaching death.*] A phrase sometimes used in reference to a deathbed gift, or a gift *causa mortis*, since the giving of the gift is made in expectation of approaching death. A gift causa mortis is distinguishable from a gift inter vivos, which is a gift made during the donor's (the giver's) lifetime.

Cause Each separate antecedent of an event. Something that precedes and brings about an effect or a result. A reason for an action or condition. A ground of a legal action. An agent that brings something about. That which in some manner is accountable for a condition that brings about an effect or that produces a cause for the resultant action or state.

A suit, litigation, or action. Any question, civil or criminal, litigated or contested before a court of justice.

Cause of action The fact or combination of facts that gives a person the right to seek judicial redress or relief against another. Also, the legal theory forming the basis of a lawsuit.

Caveat [*Latin, Let him beware.*] A warning; admonition. A formal notice or warning given by an interested party to a court, judge, or ministerial officer in opposition to certain acts within his or her power and jurisdiction.

Caveat emptor [*Latin, Let the buyer beware.*] A warning that notifies a buyer that the goods he or she is buying are "as is," or subject to all defects.

Cease and desist order An order issued by an administrative agency or a court proscribing a person or a business entity from continuing a particular course of conduct.

Cede To yield up; to assign; to grant; to surrender; to withdraw. Generally used to designate the transfer of territory from one government to another.

Celebration of marriage A colloquial phrase that refers to the solemnization or formalization of a marriage.

Cemeteries Areas that are set aside by public authority or private persons for the burial of the dead.

Censorship The suppression or proscription of speech or writing that is deemed obscene, indecent, or unduly controversial.

Census An official count of the population of a particular area, such as a district, state, or nation.

Century Digest® A volume of the American Digest System that arranges by subject summaries of court opinions reported chronologically in the various units of the National Reporter System during the period from 1658 to 1896.

Certificate A written document that is official verification that a condition or requirement has, or has not, been met.

A written assurance issued from a court that is notification to another officer, judge, or court of procedures practiced therein.

A document (such as a birth certificate) prepared by an official during the course of his or her regular duties, and which may be used as evidence for certain purposes.

A document certifying that one has fulfilled certain requirements and may practice in a field.

Certificate of deposit A written recognition by a bank of a deposit, coupled with a pledge to pay the deposited amount plus interest, if any, to the depositor or to his or her order, or to another individual or to his or her order.

A form of commercial paper that serves as documentary evidence that a savings account exists.

Certificate of occupancy A document issued by a local building or zoning authority to the owner of premises attesting that the premises have been built and maintained according to the provisions of building or zoning ordinances, such as those that govern the number of fire exits or the safety of electrical wiring.

Certification proceeding An administrative hearing before the National Labor Relations Board (NLRB), pursuant to the federal Wagner Act (29 U.S.C.A. § 151 et seq. [1935]) to determine whether a group of employees is an appropriate bargaining unit, and if so, to decide whether a particular union should be declared its bargaining agent.

Certified check A written order made by a depositor to a bank to pay a certain sum to the person designated—the payee—which is marked by the bank as "accepted" or "certified," thereby unconditionally promising that the bank will pay the order upon its presentation by the payee.

Certified copy A photocopy of a document, judgment, or record that is signed and attested to as an accurate and a complete reproduction of the original document by a public official in whose custody the original has been placed for safekeeping.

Certiorari [*Latin, To be informed of.*] At common law, an original writ or order issued by the Chancery or King's Bench, commanding officers of inferior courts to submit the record of a cause pending before them to give the party more certain and speedy justice.

A writ that a superior appellate court issues on its discretion to an inferior court, ordering it to produce a certified record of a particular case it has tried, in order to determine whether any irregularities or errors occurred that justify review of the case.

A device by which the Supreme Court of the United States exercises its discretion in selecting the cases it will review.

Cession The act of relinquishing one's right.

A surrender, relinquishment, or assignment of territory by one state or government to another.

The territory of a foreign government gained by the transfer of sovereignty.

Cestui que [*French, He or she who.*] The person for whom a benefit exists.

CF. An abbreviation for the Latin word *confer*, meaning "compare."

C.F.&I. An abbreviation for cost, freight, and insurance that is used in a sales contract to indicate that the purchase price quoted for the goods by the seller includes the expense incurred by the seller for shipment of such goods and for insurance of the goods against loss or destruction until their arrival at the destination named by the buyer.

Chain of title A list of successive owners of a parcel of land, beginning from the government, or original owner, to the person who currently owns the land.

Chain referral A type of sales plan that convinces individuals to make purchases based upon the promise that their payment will be reduced for each new purchaser they recommend to the seller.

Chambers A judge's private room or office wherein he or she hears motions, signs papers, and performs other tasks pertaining to his or her office when a session of the court, such as a trial, is not being held.

Chamizal tract A description of the 1895 title dispute between the United States and Mexico that arose over a tract of land in El Paso, Texas, known as "El Chamizal."

Champerty and maintenance Champerty is the process whereby one person bargains with a party to a lawsuit to obtain a share in the proceeds of the suit. Maintenance is the support or promotion of another person's suit initiated by intermeddling for personal gain.

Chancellor A secretary, secretary of state, or minister of a king or other high nobleman.

Chancery The old English court in which the monarch's secretary, or Chancellor, began hearing lawsuits during the fourteenth century.

Character evidence Proof or attestations about an individual's moral standing, general nature, traits, and reputation in the general community.

Charge To impose a burden, duty, obligation, or lien; to create a claim against property; to assess; to demand; to accuse; to instruct a jury on matters of law. To impose a tax, duty, or trust. To entrust with responsibilities and duties (e.g., care of another). In commercial transactions, to bill or invoice; to purchase on credit. In criminal law, to indict or formally accuse.

An encumbrance, lien, or claim; a burden or load; an obligation or duty; a liability; an accusation. A person or thing committed to the care of another. The price of, or rate for, something.

Charge-off Eliminate or write off.

Charitable trust The arrangement by which real or personal property given by one person is held by another to be used for the benefit of a class or the general public.

Charities Organizations created for the purpose of philanthropic rather than pecuniary pursuits.

Charter A grant from the government of ownership rights in land to a person, a group of people, or an organization such as a corporation.

A basic document of law of a municipal corporation granted by the state, defining its rights, liabilities, and responsibilities of self-government.

A document embodying a grant of authority from the legislature or the authority itself, such as a corporate charter.

The leasing of a mode of transportation, such as a bus, ship, or plane. A *charter-party* is a contract formed to lease a ship to a merchant in order to facilitate the conveyance of goods.

Chattel An item of personal property that is movable; it may be animate or inanimate.

Chattel mortgage A transfer of some legal or equitable right in personal property as security for the payment of money or performance of some other act. Chattel mortgages have generally been superseded by other types of secured transactions under the Uniform Commercial Code (UCC), a body of law adopted by the states that governs commercial transactions.

Chattel paper A writing or writings that evidence both a monetary obligation and a security interest in, or a lease of, specific goods. In many instances chattel paper will consist of a negotiable instrument coupled with a security agreement. When a transaction is evidenced both by such a security agreement or a lease and by an instrument or a series of instruments, the group of writings taken together constitutes chattel paper.

Check A written order instructing a bank to pay upon its presentation to the person designated in it, or to the person possessing it, a certain sum of money from the account of the person who draws it.

Checkoff A system whereby an employer regularly deducts a portion of an employee's wages to pay union dues or initiation fees.

Chief justice The presiding, most senior, or principal judge of a court.

Child abuse Physical, sexual, or emotional mistreatment or neglect of a child.

Child care The supervision and nurturing of a child, including casual and informal services provided by a parent as well as more formal services provided by an organized child care center.

Child custody The care, control, and maintenance of a child, which a court may award to one of the parents following a divorce or separation proceeding.

Child labor laws Federal and state legislation that protects children by restricting the type and hours of work they perform.

Children's rights The opportunity for children to participate in political and legal decisions that affect them; in a broad sense, the rights of children to live free from hunger, abuse, neglect, and other inhumane conditions.

Child support A payment that a noncustodial parent makes as a contribution to the costs of raising her or his child.

Chilling effect doctrine In constitutional law, any practice or law that has the effect of seriously dissuading the exercise of a constitutional right, such as freedom of speech.

Choate Perfected, complete, or certain.

Chose [*French, Thing.*] Chattel; item of personal property.

Chose in action The right to bring a lawsuit to recover chattels, money, or a debt.

Churning The practice whereby a broker dealing in securities abuses the confidence of a client for personal gain by unnecessarily trading stocks to earn more commissions.

Circuit A territorial or geographical division of a country or state.

Circuit court A specific tribunal that possesses the legal authority to hear cases within its own geographical territory.

Circumstantial evidence Information and testimony presented by a party in a civil or criminal action that permit conclusions that indirectly establish the existence or nonexistence of a fact or event that the party seeks to prove.

Citation
A paper commonly used in various courts—such as a probate, matrimonial, or traffic court—that is served upon an individual to notify him or her that he or she is required to appear at a specific time and place.

Reference to a legal authority—such as a case, constitution, or treatise—where particular information may be found.

Citator
A volume or set of volumes that is a record of the status of cases or statutes.

Cite
To notify a person of a proceeding against him or her or to call a person forth to appear in court.

To make reference to a legal authority, such as a case, in a citation.

Citizens
Those who, under the Constitution and laws of the United States, or of a particular community or of a foreign country, owe allegiance and are entitled to the enjoyment of all civil rights that accrue to those who qualify for that status.

Civil action
A lawsuit brought to enforce, redress, or protect rights of private litigants (the plaintiffs and the defendants); not a criminal proceeding.

Civil death
The forfeiture of rights and privileges of an individual who has been convicted of a serious crime.

Civil law
Legal system derived from the Roman *Corpus Juris Civilus* of Emperor Justinian I; differs from a common-law system, which relies on prior decisions to determine the outcome of a lawsuit. Most European and South American countries have a civil law system. England and most of the countries it dominated or colonized, including Canada and the United States, have a common-law system. However, within these countries, Louisiana, Quebec, and Puerto Rico exhibit the influence of French and Spanish settlers in their use of civil law systems.

A body of rules that delineate private rights and remedies and govern disputes between individuals in such areas as contracts, property, and family law; distinct from criminal or public law.

Civil procedure
The methods, procedures, and practices used in civil cases.

Civil rights
Personal liberties that belong to an individual owing to his or her status as a citizen or resident of a particular country or community.

Civil rights acts
Federal legislation enacted by Congress over the course of a century beginning with the post–Civil War era that implemented and extended the fundamental guarantees of the Constitution to all citizens of the United States, regardless of their race, color, age, or religion.

Civil Rights cases
A landmark decision, which was a consolidation of several cases brought before the Supreme Court of the United States in 1883 that declared the Civil Rights Act of 1875 (18 Stat. 336) unconstitutional and ultimately led to the enactment of state laws, such as Jim Crow Laws, which codified what had previously been individual adherence to the practice of racial segregation. The cases were *United States v. Stanley, United States v. Ryan, United States v. Nichols,* and *United States v. Singleton,* 109 U.S. 3, 3 S. Ct. 18, 27 L. Ed. 835.

Civil service	The designation given to government employment for which a person qualifies on the basis of merit rather than political patronage or personal favor.
C.J.	An abbreviation for chief justice, the principal presiding judge or the judge with most seniority on a particular court, as well as an abbreviation for circuit judge, the judge of a particular judicial circuit.
C.J.S.®	The abbreviation for *Corpus Juris Secundum®*, which is a comprehensive encyclopedia of the principles of American law.
Claim	To demand or assert as a right. Facts that combine to give rise to a legally enforceable right or judicial action. Demand for relief.
Claim for relief	The section of a modern complaint that states the redress sought from a court by a person who initiates a lawsuit.
Clarendon, Constitutions of	Statutes—enacted by a parliament convened at Clarendon, England, in 1164 during the reign of King Henry II—that restricted the authority of the pope and his clergy by subjecting them to the secular jurisdiction of the king's court.
Class action	A lawsuit that allows a large number of people with a common interest in a matter to sue or be sued as a group.
Clause	A section, phrase, paragraph, or segment of a legal document, such as a contract, deed, will, or constitution, that relates to a particular point.
Clause paramount	In admiralty law, a statement required by federal law to be included in any bill of lading, which evinces a contract for the transportation of goods by sea from U.S. ports in foreign trade.
Clayton Act	A federal law enacted in 1914 as an amendment to the Sherman Anti-Trust Act (15 U.S.C.A. § 1 et seq. [1890]), prohibiting undue restriction of trade and commerce by designated methods.
Clear	Free from doubt, burden, or obstacle; without limitation; plain or unencumbered.
Clear and convincing proof	A standard applied by a jury or by a judge in a nonjury trial to measure the probability of the truthfulness of particular facts alleged during a civil lawsuit.
Clear title	Unencumbered or unrestricted legal ownership that is free from doubt as to its validity.
Clemency	Leniency or mercy. A power given to a public official, such as a governor or the president, to in some way lower or moderate the harshness of punishment imposed upon a prisoner.
Clerical error	A mistake made in a letter, paper, or document that changes its meaning, such as a typographical error or the unintentional addition or omission of a word, phrase, or figure.

Clerk A person employed in an office or government agency who performs various tasks such as keeping records or accounts, filing, letter writing, or transcribing. One who works in a store and whose job might include working as a cashier, selling merchandise, or waiting on customers.

Client A person who employs or retains an attorney to represent him or her in any legal business; to assist, to counsel, and to defend the individual in legal proceedings; and to appear on his or her behalf in court.

Close A parcel of land that is surrounded by a boundary of some kind, such as a hedge or a fence. To culminate, complete, finish, or bring to an end. To seal up. To restrict to a certain class. A narrow margin, as in a close election.

Closed account A detailed statement of the mutual debit and credit demands between parties to which no further changes can be made on either side.

Closed corporation A type of business corporation that is owned and operated by a small group of people.

Closed shop A business in which persons are required to join a particular union as a precondition to employment and to remain union members for the duration of their employment.

Closely held A phrase used to describe the ownership, management, and operation of a corporation by a small group of people.

Close writ In English law, a certain kind of letter issued by the sovereign that is sealed with the great seal indicating his or her office and directed to a particular person and for a special purpose.

Closing The final transaction between a buyer and seller of real property.

Closing argument The final factual and legal argument made by each attorney on all sides of a case in a trial prior to a verdict or judgment.

Cloture The procedure by which debate is formally ended in a meeting or legislature so that a vote may be taken.

Cloud on title An apparent claim or encumbrance, such as a lien, that, if true, impairs the right of the owner to transfer his or her property free and clear of the interests of any other party.

Club An organization comprised of people who voluntarily meet on a regular basis for a mutual purpose other than educational, religious, charitable, or financial pursuits.

Co A prefix that denotes jointness or the state of being conjunct or united. To be together, with, or not separate from; conjoint or combined.

Code A systematic and comprehensive compilation of laws, rules, or regulations that are consolidated and classified according to subject matter.

Code of Federal Regulations	A set of books published by the federal government and containing the regulations of federal agencies currently in effect.
Code of Hammurabi	A comprehensive set of laws, considered by many scholars to be the oldest established, that were handed down four thousand years ago by King Hammurabi of Babylon.
Code of Judicial Conduct	A collection of rules governing the conduct of judges while they serve in their professional capacity.
Code pleading	A statutory scheme that abolished the ancient common-law forms of action and replaced the overly technical system of common-law pleading with simplified provisions for a plaintiff to bring a lawsuit and a defendant to answer the claims alleged against him or her.
Codicil	A document that is executed by a person who had previously made his or her will, to modify, delete, qualify, or revoke provisions contained in it.
Codification	The collection and systematic arrangement, usually by subject, of the laws of a state or country, or the statutory provisions, rules, and regulations that govern a specific area or subject of law or practice.
Coercion	The intimidation of a victim to compel the individual to do some act against his or her will by the use of psychological pressure, physical force, or threats. The crime of intentionally and unlawfully restraining another's freedom by threatening to commit a crime, accusing the victim of a crime, disclosing any secret that would seriously impair the victim's reputation in the community, or by performing or refusing to perform an official action lawfully requested by the victim, or by causing an official to do so. A defense asserted in a criminal prosecution that a person who committed a crime did not do so of his or her own free will, but only because the individual was compelled by another through the use of physical force or threat of immediate serious bodily injury or death.
Cognizance	The power, authority, and ability of a judge to determine a particular legal matter. A judge's decision to take note of or deal with a cause.
Cognovit actionem	[*Latin, He has confessed the action.*] The written confession made by a defendant admitting the merits of the action brought against him or her by a plaintiff. The confession is usually based upon designated conditions, given in court, and by implication empowers the plaintiff's attorney to sign judgment and issue execution for its enforcement.
Cognovit note	An extraordinary document by which a debtor authorizes his or her creditor's attorney to enter a confession in court that allows judgment against the debtor.
Cohabitation	A living arrangement in which an unmarried couple live together in a long-term relationship that resembles a marriage.
Coinsurance	A provision of an insurance policy that provides that the insurance company and the insured will apportion between them any loss

covered by the policy according to a fixed percentage of the value for which the property, or the person, is insured.

Collateral   Related; indirect; not bearing immediately upon an issue. The property pledged or given as a security interest, or a guarantee for payment of a debt, that will be taken or kept by the creditor in case of a default on the original debt.

Collateral attack   An attempt to impeach or overturn a judgment rendered in a judicial proceeding, made in a proceeding other than within the original action or an appeal from it.

Collateral estoppel   A doctrine by which an earlier decision rendered by a court in a lawsuit between parties is conclusive as to the issues or controverted points so that they cannot be relitigated in subsequent proceedings involving the same parties.

Collateral heir   A successor to property—either by will or descent and distribution—who is not directly descended from the deceased but comes from a parallel line of the deceased's family, such as a brother, sister, uncle, aunt, niece, nephew, or cousin.

Collateral warranty   In real estate transactions, an assurance or guaranty of title made by the holder of the title to the person to whom the property is conveyed.

Collective bargaining   The process through which a labor union and an employer negotiate the scope of the employment relationship.

Collective bargaining agreement   The contractual agreement between an employer and a labor union that governs wages, hours, and working conditions for employees and which can be enforced against both the employer and the union for failure to comply with its terms.

Collision   The violent contact of one vehicle—such as an automobile, ship, or boat—with another vehicle.

Collusion   An agreement between two or more people to defraud a person of his or her rights or to obtain something that is prohibited by law.

   A secret arrangement wherein two or more people whose legal interests seemingly conflict conspire to commit fraud upon another person; a pact between two people to deceive a court with the purpose of obtaining something that they would not be able to get through legitimate judicial channels.

Color   The appearance or semblance of a thing, as distinguished from the thing itself.

Colorable   False; counterfeit; something that is false but has the appearance of truth.

Color of law   The appearance of a legal right.

Color of office   A description of an act by an officer done without authority under the pretext that he or she has an official right to do the act by reason of the officer's position.

Color of title The appearance of a legally enforceable right of possession or owner-ship. A written instrument that purports to transfer ownership of property but, due to some defect, does not have that effect. A document purporting to pass title to land, such as a deed that is defective due to a lack of title in the grantor, passes only color of title to the grantee.

Co-maker One who becomes obligated, an obligor, under a negotiable instru-ment—such as a check or promissory note—by signing his or her name along with the name of the original obligor, thereby promising to pay on it in full.

Combination In criminal law, an agreement between two or more people to act jointly for an unlawful purpose; a conspiracy. In patent law, the joining together of several separate inventions to produce a new invention.

Combination in restraint of trade An illegal compact between two or more persons to unjustly restrict competition and monopolize commerce in goods or services by controlling their production, distribution, and price or through other unlawful means.

Comity Courtesy; respect; a disposition to perform some official act out of goodwill and tradition rather than obligation or law. The acceptance or adoption of decisions or laws by a court of another jurisdiction, either foreign or domestic, based on public policy rather than legal mandate.

Commerce The exchange of goods, products, or any type of personal property. Trade and traffic carried on between different peoples or states and its inhabitants, including not only the purchase, sale, and exchange of commodities but also the instrumentalities, agencies, and means by which business is accomplished. The transportation of persons and goods, by air, land, and sea. The exchange of merchandise on a large scale between different places or communities.

Commerce Clause The provision of the U.S. Constitution that gives Congress exclusive power over trade activities between the states and with foreign countries and Indian tribes.

Commerce Department An agency of the executive branch of the federal government that promotes international trade, economic growth, and technological advancement.

Commercial Code A colloquial designation for the body of law known as the Uniform Commercial Code (UCC), which governs the various business trans-actions that are integral parts of the U.S. system of commerce.

Commercial paper A written instrument or document such as a check, draft, promissory note, or a certificate of deposit, that manifests the pledge or duty of one individual to pay money to another.

Commingling Combining things into one body.

Commissioner A person charged with the management or direction of a board, a court, or a government agency.

Commitment
Proceedings directing the confinement of a mentally ill or incompetent person for treatment.

Commitment fee
Compensation paid to a lender by a borrower for the lender's promise to give a mortgage at some future time.

Committee
An individual or group of people to whom authority has been delegated by a larger group to perform a particular function or duty. A part of a legislative body made up of one or more individuals who have been assigned the task of investigating a certain issue and reporting their observations and recommendations to the legislature. The Senate has various committees, such as the Committee on Nuclear Energy. The name given to the person or group of people appointed by a court and charged with the responsibility of acting as the guardian of an incompetent person.

Commodity
A tangible item that may be bought or sold; something produced for commerce.

Common
Belonging to or pertaining to the general public. Common lands, also known as public lands, are those that are set aside for use by the community at large, such as parks and public recreation areas. Common also means habitual or recurring, such as offenses that are committed frequently or repeatedly. A *common thief* is one who has been repeatedly convicted of larceny. Something that is common is owned equally by two or more people, such as a piece of land. A tenancy in common is an interest in land wherein at least two people share ownership.

Common carrier
An individual or business that advertises to the public that it is available for hire to transport people or property in exchange for a fee.

Common Council
In English legal history, the name given to Parliament. In the U.S. legal system, the legislative body of a city or of a municipal corporation.

Common count
A traditional type of common-law pleading that is used in actions to recover a debt of money of the defendant based upon an express or implied promise to pay after performance had been rendered. In a common-count pleading, the plaintiff sets forth in account form the facts that constitute the basis of his or her claim, such as money had and received and goods sold and delivered.

Common disaster
A set of circumstances in which two individuals die apparently simultaneously.

Common lands
An archaic designation of property set aside and regulated by the local, state, or federal government for the benefit of the public for recreational purposes.

Common law
The ancient law of England based upon societal customs and recognized and enforced by the judgments and decrees of the courts. The general body of statutes and case law that governed England and the American colonies prior to the American Revolution.

The principles and rules of action, embodied in case law rather than legislative enactments, applicable to the government and protection of persons and property that derive their authority from the community customs and traditions that evolved over the centuries as interpreted by judicial tribunals.

A designation used to denote the opposite of statutory, equitable, or civil; for example, a common-law action.

Common-law action	A lawsuit governed by the general principles of law derived from court decisions, as opposed to the provisions of statutes.
Common-law courts	The early royal courts in England that administered the law common to all.
Common-law marriage	A union of two people not formalized in the customary manner as prescribed by law but created by an agreement to marry followed by cohabitation.
Common-law pleading	The system of rules and principles that governed the forms into which parties cast their claims or defenses in order to set an issue before the court.
Common-law trust	A business organization for investment purposes by which trustees manage and control property for the benefit of beneficiaries who are protected against personal liability for any losses incurred.
Common pleas	Trial-level courts of general jurisdiction. One of the royal common-law courts in England existing since the beginning of the thirteenth century and developing from the Curia Regis, or the King's Court.
Common scold	A person who frequently or habitually causes public disturbances or breaks the peace by brawling or quarreling.
Common stock	Evidence of participation in the ownership of a corporation that takes the form of printed certificates.
Communism	A system of social organization in which goods are held in common.
Community property	The holdings and resources owned in common by a husband and wife.
Commutation	Modification, exchange, or substitution.
Compact	An agreement, treaty, or contract.
Compact Clause	A provision contained in Article I, Section 10, Clause 3, of the U.S. Constitution, which states that "No State shall, without the consent of Congress . . . enter into any Agreement or Compact with another State . . ."
Company	An organization of individuals conducting a commercial or industrial enterprise. A corporation, partnership, association, or joint stock company.

Comparable worth   The idea that men and women should receive equal pay when they perform work that involves comparable skills and responsibility or that is of comparable worth to the employer; also known as pay equity.

Comparative rectitude   The principle by which a divorce is awarded to the party whose fault is less serious in cases where both spouses allege grounds that would justify a divorce.

Compensation   A pecuniary remedy that is awarded to an individual who has sustained an injury in order to replace the loss caused by said injury, such as workers' compensation. Wages paid to an employee or, generally, fees, salaries, or allowances. The payment a landowner is given to make up for the injury suffered as a result of the seizure when his or her land is taken by the government through eminent domain.

Compensatory damages   A sum of money awarded in a civil action by a court to indemnify a person for the particular loss, detriment, or injury suffered as a result of the unlawful conduct of another.

Competent   Possessing the necessary reasoning abilities or legal qualifications; qualified; capable; sufficient.

Competent evidence   Information that proves a point at issue in a lawsuit.

Complainant   A plaintiff; a person who commences a civil lawsuit against another, known as the defendant, in order to remedy an alleged wrong. An individual who files a written accusation with the police charging a suspect with the commission of a crime and providing facts to support the allegation and which results in the criminal prosecution of the suspect.

Complaint   The pleading that initiates a civil action; in criminal law, the document that sets forth the basis upon which a person is to be charged with an offense.

Compliance   Observance; conformity; obedience.

Composition with creditors   A contract made by an insolvent or financially pressed debtor with two or more creditors in which the creditors agree to accept one specific partial payment of the total amount of their claims, which is to be divided pro rata among them in full satisfaction of their claims.

Compounding a felony   A criminal offense consisting of the acceptance of a reward or other consideration in exchange for an agreement not to prosecute or reveal a felony committed by another.

Compounding offense   A criminal act in which a person agrees not to report the occurrence of a crime or not to prosecute a criminal offender in exchange for money or other consideration.

Compound interest   Interest generated by the sum of the principal and any accrued interest.

Comprise   To embrace, cover, or include; to confine within; to consist of.

Compromise and settlement	Settlement of a dispute by mutual agreement to avoid a lawsuit.
Compromise of 1850	A program of legislative measures enacted by Congress to reconcile the differences existing between the North and South concerning the issue of slavery in newly formed territories of the United States.
Comptroller	An officer who conducts the fiscal affairs of a state or municipal corporation.
Compulsory process	The method employed by which a person wanted as a witness, or for some other purpose, in a civil or criminal action is forced to appear before the court hearing the proceeding.
Compurgator	In early legal practice, one of several character witnesses produced by someone accused of a crime or by a defendant in a civil suit to attest, in court, that he or she believed the defendant on his or her oath.
Computer-assisted legal research	Technology that allows lawyers and judges to bypass the traditional law library and locate statutes, court cases, and other legal references in minutes using a personal computer, research software, and a modem.
Computer crime	The use of a computer to take or alter data, or to gain unlawful use of computers or services.
Con	A prefix meaning with or together. A slang abbreviation for confidence, as in *con man* or *con game*. To con someone is to deceive or take advantage of a person through fraud or trickery after winning the person's confidence. Con is also used as a slang abbreviation for convict, as in *ex-con*, to mean someone previously incarcerated. An abbreviation for contra, which means against. To show the pros and cons of a particular issue means to present arguments or evidence on both sides.
Concealment of birth or death	The crime of refusing to disclose the birth or death of a newborn child.
Conciliation	The process of adjusting or settling disputes in a friendly manner through extrajudicial means. Conciliation means bringing two opposing sides together to reach a compromise in an attempt to avoid taking a case to trial. Arbitration, in contrast, is a contractual remedy used to settle disputes out of court. In arbitration the two parties in controversy agree in advance to abide by the decision made by a third party called in as a mediator, whereas conciliation is less structured.
Conciliation, international	A method by which the differences between nations may be settled by means of a commission employed to consider and report upon such differences.
Conclusion of law	The rule by which the rights of parties in a lawsuit are determined by a judge's application of relevant statutes or legal principles to the facts of the case that have been found to be true by the jury. The final judgment or decree rendered by a court based upon the verdict

reached by the jury. Legal principles that provide the basis for the decision rendered by a judge in a case tried without a jury or with an advisory jury after certain facts have been established.

Conclusive   Determinative; beyond dispute or question. That which is conclusive is manifest, clear, or obvious. It is a legal inference made so peremptorily that it cannot be overthrown or contradicted.

Concur   To agree; coincide; act together. To concur is to evidence consent in an affirmative or concrete manner as opposed to merely acquiescing or silently submitting to a decision.

Concurrent   Simultaneous; converging; of equal or joint authority.

Concurrent estates   Ownership or possession of real property by two or more individuals simultaneously.

Concurrent jurisdiction   The authority of several different courts, each of which is authorized to entertain and decide cases dealing with the same subject matter.

Concurrent resolution   An action of Congress passed in the form of an enactment of one house, with the other house in agreement, which expresses the ideas of Congress on a particular subject.

Concurrent writs   Court orders issued in duplicate originals; several orders issued at the same time for the same purpose.

Condemn   To adjudge or find guilty of a crime and sentence. To declare a building or ship unsafe for use or occupancy. To decide that a navigable vessel is a prize or is unfit for service. To take privately owned land for public use in exchange for just compensation by virtue of the power of eminent domain.

Condemnation   The process of implementing eminent domain, whereby the government takes private property for public use.

Condition   A future and uncertain event upon the happening of which certain rights or obligations will be either enlarged, created, or destroyed.

Conditional   Subject to change; dependent upon or granted based on the occurrence of a future, uncertain event.

Condominium, international   A non-self-governing territory over which two states share administrative control. In this context the term *coimperium* is sometimes used interchangeably with the term *condominium*.

Condominiums and cooperatives   Two common forms of multiple-unit dwellings, with independent owners or lessees of the individual units comprising the multiple-unit dwelling who share various costs and responsibilities of areas they use in common.

Condonation   In marriage, the voluntary pardoning by an innocent spouse of an offense committed by his or her partner conditioned upon the promise that it will not recur.

Confederacy	The association or banding together of two or more persons for the purpose of committing an act or furthering an enterprise that is forbidden by law, or that, though lawful in itself, becomes unlawful when made the object of the confederacy. More commonly called a conspiracy. The union of two or more independent states for the purpose of common safety or a furtherance of their mutual goals.
Confederation	A union of states in which each member state retains some independent control over internal and external affairs. Thus, for international purposes, there are separate states, not just one state. A federation, in contrast, is a union of states in which external affairs are controlled by a unified, central government.
Confession	A statement made by an individual that acknowledges his or her guilt in the commission of a crime.
Confession and avoidance	A form of plea that served as the formal answer to a plaintiff's complaint or declaration.
Confession of judgment	A procedure whereby a defendant did not enter a plea, the usual response to a plaintiff's declaration in common-law pleading, but instead either confessed to the accuracy of the plaintiff's claim or withdrew a plea already entered.
Confidential communication	A form of privileged communication passed from one individual to another, intended to be heard only by the individual addressed.
Confidential relation	Any connection between two individuals in which one of the parties has an obligation to act with extreme good faith for the benefit of the other party.
Confiscate	To expropriate private property for public use without compensating the owner under the authority of the police power of the government. To seize property.
Conflict of interest	A term used to describe the situation in which a public official or fiduciary who, contrary to the obligation and absolute duty to act for the benefit of the public or a designated individual, exploits the relationship for personal benefit, typically pecuniary.
Conformed copy	A duplicate of a document that includes handwritten notations of items incapable of reproduction, such as a signature, which must be inscribed upon the duplicate with the explanation that it was placed there by the person whose signature appears on the original document.
Conforming use	When land is employed in compliance with zoning ordinances in a particular area.
Confrontation	A fundamental right of a defendant in a criminal action to come face to face with an adverse witness in the court's presence so the defendant has a fair chance to object to the testimony of the witness and the opportunity to cross-examine the witness.
Confusion	The combination or mixture of two things; the process of commingling.

Confusion of goods	A blending together of property individually owned by two or more people so as to make it impossible to distinguish who owns what.
Conglomerate	A corporation operating in several different and unrelated enterprises, such as the movie industry, baking, and oil refining.
Congressional-executive agreement	An accord made by joint authority of the Congress and the president covering areas of international law that are not within the ambit of treaties.
Congressional Record	A daily publication of the federal government that details the legislative proceedings of Congress.
Congress of the United States	The legislative branch of the U.S. government, consisting of the Senate and the House of Representatives.
Conjugal	Pertaining or relating to marriage; suitable or applicable to married people.
Connecting up doctrine	A term relating to the admissibility of evidence which means that a fact may be admitted into evidence provided that its relevance will subsequently become apparent when it is linked to other facts presented later.
Connivance	The furtive consent of one person to cooperate with another in the commission of an unlawful act or crime—such as an employer's agreement not to withhold taxes from the salary of an employee who wants to evade federal income tax. The false consent that a plaintiff gave to a defendant's past conduct during their marriage which the plaintiff presently alleges as a ground for divorce.
Conquest	A term used in feudal law to designate land acquisition by purchase; or any method other than descent or inheritance by which an individual obtains ownership of an estate. A term used in international law for the process whereby a sovereign nation is, by force of arms, made to submit to another nation; the defeated country thus becomes part of the empire of the conqueror.
Consanguinity	Blood relationship; the relation of people who descend from the same ancestor.
Conscientious objector	A person who, because of principles of religious training and moral belief, is opposed to all war regardless of its cause.
Conscription	Compulsory enrollment and induction into the military service.
Consensual alteration	A change in a legal document agreed to by the parties and binding upon them.
Consent	Voluntary acquiescence to the proposal of another; the act or result of reaching an accord; a concurrence of minds; actual willingness that an act or an infringement of an interest shall occur.

Consequential damages	Injury or harm that does not ensue directly and immediately from the act of a party, but only from some of the results of such act, and that is compensable by a monetary award after a judgment has been rendered in a lawsuit. Detriment that arises from the interposition of special, unpredictable circumstances. Harm to a person or property directly resulting from any breach of warranty or from a false factual statement, concerning the quality or nature of goods sold, made by the seller to induce the sale and relied on by the buyer.
Conservator of the peace	An officer of the government authorized by law to act in such a manner that will preserve and maintain the order and safety of the community and the general public.
Consideration	Something of value given by both parties to a contract that induces them to enter into the agreement to exchange mutual performances.
Consignment	The delivery of goods to a carrier to be shipped to a designated person for sale. A bailment of goods for sale.
Consortium	The marital alliance between a husband and wife and their respective right to each other's support, cooperation, aid, and companionship.
Conspiracy	An agreement between two or more persons to engage jointly in an unlawful or criminal act, or an act that is innocent in itself but becomes unlawful when done by the combination of actors.
Constable	An official of a municipal corporation whose primary duties are to protect and preserve the peace of the community.
Constitute	To comprise or put together. That which is *duly constituted* is properly made up and formally correct and valid.
Constitution	The fundamental law, written or unwritten, that establishes the character of a government by defining the basic principles to which society must conform; by describing the organization of the government and regulation, distribution, and limitations on the functions of different government departments; and by prescribing the extent and manner of the exercise of its sovereign powers. A legislative charter by which a government or group derives its authority to act.
Constitutional	That which is consistent with or dependent upon the fundamental law that defines and establishes government in society and basic principles to which society is to conform.
Constitutional amendment	The means by which an alteration to the U.S. Constitution, whether a modification, deletion, or addition, is accomplished.
Constitutional law	The written text of the state and federal constitutions. The body of judicial precedent that has gradually developed through a process in which courts interpret, apply, and explain the meaning of particular constitutional provisions and principles during a legal proceeding.

Executive, legislative, and judicial actions that conform with the norms prescribed by a constitutional provision.

Constitution of the United States A written document executed by representatives of the people of the United States as the absolute rule of action and decision for all branches and officers of the government, and with which all subsequent laws and ordinances must be in accordance unless it has been changed by a constitutional amendment by the authority that created it.

Construction The process by which the meaning of an ambiguous provision of a statute, written document, or oral agreement is determined.

Constructive That which exists, not in fact, but as a result of the operation of law. That which takes on a character as a consequence of the way it is treated by a rule or policy of law, as opposed to its actual character.

Constructive desertion The end of marital cohabitation brought about when one spouse, by his or her conduct, forces the other to leave home.

Constructive eviction The disturbance, by a landlord, of a tenant's possession of premises that the landlord makes uninhabitable and unsuitable for the purposes for which they were leased, causing the tenant to surrender possession.

Constructive trust A relationship by which a person who has obtained title to property has an equitable duty to transfer it to another, to whom it rightfully belongs, on the basis that the acquisition or retention of it is wrongful and would unjustly enrich the person if he or she were allowed to retain it.

Consular court A tribunal convened by public officials who reside in a foreign country to protect the interests of their country for the settlement of civil cases based upon situations that happened in the foreign nation and which is held pursuant to authority granted by treaty.

Consuls Public officials stationed in a foreign country who are responsible for developing and securing the economic interests of their government and safeguarding the welfare of their government's citizens who might be traveling or residing within their jurisdiction.

Consumer An individual who purchases and uses products and services in contradistinction to manufacturers who produce the goods or services and wholesalers or retailers who distribute and sell them. A member of the general category of persons who are protected by state and federal laws regulating price policies, financing practices, quality of goods and services, credit reporting, debt collection, and other trade practices of U.S. commerce. A purchaser of a product or service who has a legal right to enforce any implied or express warranties pertaining to the item against the manufacturer who has introduced the goods or services into the marketplace or the seller who has made them a term of the sale.

Consumer credit Short-term loans made to enable people to purchase goods or services primarily for personal, family, or household purposes.

Consumer Credit Protection Act A federal statute designed to protect borrowers of money by mandating complete disclosure of the terms and conditions of finance charges in transactions by limiting the garnishment of wages and by regulating the use of charge accounts.

Consumer price index A computation made and issued monthly by the Bureau of Labor Statistics of the federal Labor Department that attempts to track the price level of designated goods and services purchased by the average consumer.

Consumer protection Consumer protection laws are federal and state statutes governing sales and credit practices involving consumer goods. Such statutes prohibit and regulate deceptive or unconscionable advertising and sales practices, product quality, credit financing and reporting, debt collection, leases, and other aspects of consumer transactions.

Consummate To carry into completion; to fulfill; to accomplish.

Contemner An individual who intentionally acts to hinder or obstruct the administration of justice by a court, either by refusing to comply with its orders or by disrupting its orderly proceedings, thereby committing contempt.

Contemplation of death The apprehension of an individual that his or her life will be ended in the immediate future by a particular illness the person is suffering from or by an imminent known danger which the person faces.

Contempt An act of deliberate disobedience or disregard for the laws, regulations, or decorum of a public authority, such as a court or legislative body.

Contest To defend against an adverse claim made in a court by a plaintiff or a prosecutor; to challenge a position asserted in a judicial proceeding, as to contest the probate of a will.

Context The language that precedes and follows a series of words, such as a particular sentence or clause.

Continental Congress The first national legislative assembly in the United States, existing from 1774 to 1789.

Contingent Fortuitous; dependent upon the possible occurrence of a future event, the existence of which is not assured.

Contingent fee Payment to an attorney for legal services that depends, or is contingent, upon there being some recovery or award in the case. The payment is then a percentage of the amount recovered—such as 25 percent if the matter is settled, 30 percent if it proceeds to trial.

Continuance The adjournment or postponement of an action pending in a court to a later date of the same or another session of the court, granted by a court in response to a motion made by a party to a lawsuit. The entry into the trial record of the adjournment of a case for the purpose of formally evidencing it.

Contra   Against; conflicting; opposite.

Contraband   Any property that it is illegal to produce or possess. Smuggled goods that are imported into or exported from a country in violation of its laws.

Contracts   Agreements between two or more persons that create an obligation to do, or refrain from doing, a particular thing.

Contravention   A term of French law meaning an act violative of a law, a treaty, or an agreement made between parties; a breach of law punishable by a fine of fifteen francs or less and by an imprisonment of three days or less. In the U.S. legal system, a breach or violation of the provisions of a contract, statute, or treaty.

Contribution   In maritime law, where the property of one of several parties with interests in a vessel and cargo has been voluntarily sacrificed for the common safety of the vessel—as by casting goods overboard to lighten the vessel—such loss must be made up by the contribution of the others, which is labeled "general average." In civil law, a partition by which the creditors of an insolvent debtor divide among themselves the proceeds of the debtor's property in proportion to the amount of their respective credits. The right of a defendant who has paid an entire debt, or common liability, to recoup a proportionate share of the payment from another defendant who is equally responsible for the payment of that debt or liability.

Controller   The key financial officer of a state, private, or municipal corporation, who is charged with certain specific responsibilities related to its financial affairs. See also comptroller.

Controversy   An actual dispute between individuals who seek judicial resolution of their grievances that have arisen from a conflict of their alleged legal rights.

Controvert   To contest, deny, or take issue with.

Contumacy   Willful disobedience. The intentional failure of an individual to obey a summons to appear in court to defend against a charge or to obey an order rendered by the court.

Convention   An agreement or compact, particularly an international agreement, such as the Geneva Convention. An accord between states or nations, which resembles a treaty: ordinarily applied to agreements prior to an execution of an official treaty or which serve as its foundation; or to international agreements for the regulation of international affairs of common interest not within the ambit of commercial transactions or politics, such as international postage. An agreement between states concerning finance, trade, or other matters considered less significant than those usually governed by a treaty. An assembly or meeting of representatives or members of legislative, political, or fraternal organizations.

Conventional   Derived from or contingent upon the mutual agreement of the parties, as opposed to that created by or dependent upon a statute or other act of the law.

Conversion Any unauthorized act that deprives an owner of personal property without his or her consent.

Conveyance The transfer of ownership or interest in real property from one person to another by a document, such as a deed, lease, or mortgage.

Convict To adjudge an accused person guilty of a crime at the conclusion of a criminal prosecution, or after the entry of a plea of guilty or a plea of nolo contendere. An individual who has been found guilty of a crime and, as a result, is serving a sentence as punishment for the act; a prisoner.

Conviction The outcome of a criminal prosecution which concludes in a judgment that the defendant is guilty of the crime charged. The juncture of a criminal proceeding during which the question of guilt is ascertained. In a case where the perpetrator has been adjudged guilty and sentenced, a record of the summary proceedings brought pursuant to any penal statute before one or more justices of the peace or other properly authorized persons.

Cooling-off period An interval of time during which no action of a specific type can be taken by either side in a dispute. An automatic delay in certain jurisdictions, apart from ordinary court delays, between the time when divorce papers are filed and the divorce hearing takes place. An amount of time within which a buyer is permitted to cancel a contract for the purchase of consumer goods—designed to effect consumer protection. A number of states require that a three-day cancellation period must be allowed purchasers following door-to-door sales.

Cooperative An association or corporation established for the purpose of providing services on a nonprofit basis to its shareholders or members who own and control it.

Copyright An intangible right granted by statute to the author or originator of certain literary or artistic productions, whereby, for a limited period, the exclusive privilege is given to the person to make copies of the same for publication and sale.

Copyright, international The manner in which the exclusive right to print and publish copies of various intellectual productions may be obtained in foreign countries.

Coram [*Latin, Before; in the presence of.*]

Coram nobis [*Latin, In our presence; before us.*] The designation of a remedy for setting aside an erroneous judgment in a civil or criminal action that resulted from an error of fact in the proceeding.

Coram rege [*Latin, In the presence of the king himself.*]

Corespondent One of two or more parties against whom a lawsuit is commenced. A person named with others who must answer claims alleged in a bill, petition, or libel in a judicial proceeding. An individual who is accused of adultery with another's spouse who is being sued for divorce on that ground, and who thereby becomes a defendant in the action.

Corner   For surveying purposes, the designation given to a particular location formed by the intersection of two boundary lines of real property.

The process by which a group of investors or dealers in a particular commodity exploit its market by purchasing it in large quantities and removing it from general sale for a time, thereby dramatically increasing its market price because its limited supply is greatly exceeded by the demand for it. The condition created when a commitment is made to sell at a special time of delivery in the future, a much greater quantity of a commodity than is available in the present market.

Corollary   A consequence or result that can be logically drawn from the existence of a set of facts by the exercise of common sense and reason.

Coroner   An official of a municipal corporation whose responsibilities include the performance of designated functions, the most important of which is the investigation of the cause of any violent or suspicious death that takes place within the geographical boundaries of his or her municipality.

Corporal punishment   Physical punishment, as distinguished from pecuniary punishment or a fine; any kind of punishment inflicted on the body.

Corporate   Pertaining to or possessing the qualities of a corporation, a legal entity created—pursuant to state law—to serve the purposes set out in its certificate of incorporation.

Corporate personality   The distinct status of a business organization that has complied with law for its recognition as a legal entity and that has an independent legal existence from that of its officers, directors, and shareholders.

Corporations   Artificial entities that are created by state statute, and that are treated much like individuals under the law, having legally enforceable rights, the ability to acquire debt and pay out profits, the ability to hold and transfer property, the ability to enter into contracts, the requirement to pay taxes, and the ability to sue and be sued.

Corporeal   Possessing a physical nature; having an objective, tangible existence; being capable of perception by touch and sight.

Corpus   [*Latin, Body, aggregate, or mass.*]

Corpus delicti   [*Latin, The body of the crime.*] The foundation or material substance of a crime.

Corpus juris   [*Latin, A body of law.*] A phrase used to designate a volume encompassing several collections of law, such as the Corpus Juris Civilis. The name of an American legal encyclopedia, the most recent edition of which is known as *Corpus Juris Secundum*®.

Corpus juris civilis   [*Latin, The body of the civil law.*] The name given in the early seventeenth century to the collection of civil law based upon the compilation and codification of the Roman system of jurisprudence directed by the Emperor Justinian I during the years from 528 to 534 A.D.

Correlative Having a reciprocal relationship in that the existence of one relationship normally implies the existence of the other.

Correspondence audit An examination of the accuracy of a taxpayer's income tax return conducted through the mail by the Internal Revenue Service, which sends the taxpayer a request for proof of a particular deduction or exemption taken. The taxpayer may either complete a special form or send in photocopies of relevant financial records.

Correspondent A bank, securities firm, or other financial institution that regularly renders services for another in an area or market to which the other party lacks direct access. A bank that functions as an agent for another bank and carries a deposit balance for a bank in another city.

Corroborate To support or enhance the believability of a fact or assertion by the presentation of additional information that confirms the truthfulness of the item.

Corruption of blood In English law, the result of attainder, in that the attainted person lost all rights to inherit land or other hereditaments from an ancestor, to retain possession of such property and to transfer any property rights to anyone, including heirs, by virtue of his or her conviction for treason or a felony punishable by death, because the law considered the person's blood tainted by the crime.

Cosigner An obligor—a person who becomes obligated, under a commercial paper, such as a promissory note or check—by signing the instrument in conjunction with the original obligor, thereby promising to pay it in full.

Costs Fees and charges required by law to be paid to the courts or their officers, the amount of which is specified by court rule or statute. A monetary allowance, granted by the court to a prevailing party and recoverable from the unsuccessful party, for expenses incurred in instituting or defending an action or a separate proceeding within an action.

Council A legislative body of local government. A group of persons who, whether elected or appointed, serve as representatives of the public to establish state or municipal policies and to assist the chief executive of the government unit in the performance of duties.

Counsel An attorney or lawyer. The rendition of advice and guidance concerning a legal matter, contemplated form of argument, claim, or action.

Counsellor One engaged in the practice of law; lawyer; advocate.

Count In common-law pleading or code pleading, the initial statements made by a plaintiff that set forth a cause of action to commence a civil lawsuit; the different points of a plaintiff's declaration, each of which constitute a basis for relief. In criminal procedure, one of several parts or charges of an indictment, each accusing the defendant of a different offense.

Counterclaim   A claim by a defendant opposing the claim of the plaintiff and seeking some relief from the plaintiff for the defendant.

Counterclaims and setoffs against sovereigns   A comprehensive term for the vulnerability of a foreign government to retaliatory suits against it arising out of a lawsuit that it commences against a party.

Counterfeit   To falsify, deceive, or defraud. A copy or imitation of something that is intended to be taken as authentic and genuine in order to deceive another.

Counterfeiting   The process of fraudulently manufacturing, altering, or distributing a product that is of lesser value than the genuine product.

Counteroffer   In contract law, a proposal made in response to an original offer modifying its terms, but which has the legal effect of rejecting it.

Countersign   The inscription of one's name at the end of a writing, done by a secretary or a subordinate, to attest to the fact that such a writing has been signed by a principal or a superior, thereby vouching for the genuineness of the signature. To write one's name at the end of a document—in addition to the inscription of a name by another—to attest to the authenticity of the signature.

County   A political subdivision of a state, the power and importance of which varies from one state to another.

Coupon   A certificate evidencing the obligation to pay an installment of interest or a dividend that must be cut and presented to its issuer for payment when it is due.

Course of dealing   A clearly recognizable pattern of previous conduct between parties to a business transaction.

Course of employment   As set forth in workers' compensation acts, the time, place, and conditions under which an on-the-job accident occurs. The performance of an act that an employee might prudently do while in the appropriate area during working hours.

Course of performance   Evidence of the conduct of parties concerning the execution of obligations under a contract requiring more than one performance that is used for the purpose of interpreting the contract's provisions.

Court   A legislative assembly; a deliberative body, such as the General Court of Massachusetts, which is its legislature. An entity in the government to which the administration of justice is delegated.

Court administrator   An officer of the judicial system who performs administrative and clerical duties essential to the proper operation of the business of a court, such as tracking trial dates, keeping records, entering judgments, and issuing process.

Court commissioners   Persons appointed by a judge to find facts, to hear testimony, or to perform a specific function connected with certain types of cases.

Court hand In old English practice, the peculiar style and form of writing in which court records were transcribed from the earliest period to the reign of George II, circa 1760.

Court-martial A tribunal that tries violations of military criminal law. Often, the entire military justice process, from actual court proceedings to punishment.

Court of appeal An intermediate federal judicial tribunal of review that is found in thirteen judicial districts, called circuits, in the United States.

    A state judicial tribunal that reviews a decision rendered by an inferior tribunal to determine whether it made errors that warrant the reversal of its judgment.

Court of claims A state judicial tribunal established as the forum in which to bring certain types of lawsuits against the state or its political subdivisions, such as a county. The former designation given to a federal tribunal created in 1855 by Congress with original jurisdiction—initial authority—to decide an action brought against the United States that is based upon the Constitution, federal law, any regulation of the executive department, or any express or implied contracts with the federal government.

Court of probate A judicial body that exercises jurisdiction over the acceptance of wills as valid documents and over the management and settlement of the estates of minors or of spendthrifts, of mentally incompetent persons, and of habitual drunkards.

Court opinion A statement that is prepared by a judge or court announcing the decision after a case is tried; includes a summary of the facts, a recitation of the applicable law and how it relates to the facts, the rationale supporting the decision, and a judgment; and is usually presented in writing, though occasionally an oral opinion is rendered.

Courts Judicial tribunals established to administer justice.

Courts of request Inferior judicial tribunals in England, created by special enactments of Parliament, that possessed local jurisdiction to determine actions involving claims for small debts. These courts were abolished in 1846 and replaced by county courts.

Covenant An agreement, contract, or written promise between two individuals that frequently constitutes a pledge to do or refrain from doing something.

Covenant, action of One of the old common-law forms of action by which the plaintiff claimed damages for breach of a covenant, that is, a contract under seal.

Cover To protect or shelter; to make good; to insure. *To cover a check* means to deposit sufficient funds in a bank account to pay the amount written on a check or checks.

    The right of a purchaser to buy goods other than those that were originally contracted for as a remedy in the event of a breach of contract by the seller.

Coverage   The risks that are included in the terms of an insurance contract for protection under the policy; the amount and type of insurance.

Coverture   An archaic term that refers to the legal status of a married woman.

CPA   An abbreviation for certified public accountant. A CPA is a trained accountant who has been examined and licensed by the state. He or she is permitted to perform all the tasks of an ordinary accountant in addition to examining the books and records of various business organizations, such as corporations.

Craft union   An association of laborers wherein all the members do the same type of work.

Credibility   Believability. The major legal application of the term *credibility* relates to the testimony of a witness or party during a trial. Testimony must be both competent and credible if it is to be accepted by the trier of fact as proof of an issue being litigated.

Credit   A term used in accounting to describe either an entry on the righthand side of an account or the process of making such an entry. A credit records the increases in liabilities, owners' equity, and revenues as well as the decreases in assets and expenses.

A sum in taxation that is subtracted from the computed tax, as opposed to a deduction that is ordinarily subtracted from gross income to determine adjusted gross income or taxable income. Claim for a particular sum of money.

The ability of an individual or a company to borrow money or procure goods on time, as a result of a positive opinion by the particular lender concerning such borrower's solvency and reliability. The right granted by a creditor to a debtor to delay satisfaction of a debt, or to incur a debt and defer the payment thereof.

Credit bureau   A privately owned, profit-making establishment that—as a regular business—collects and compiles data regarding the solvency, character, responsibility, and reputation of a particular individual or business in order to furnish such information to subscribers, in the form of a report allowing them to evaluate the financial stability of the subject of the report.

Creditor   An individual to whom an obligation is owed because he or she has given something of value in exchange. One who may legally demand and receive money, either through the fulfillment of a contract or due to injury sustained as a result of another's negligence or intentionally wrongful act. The term *creditor* is also used to describe an individual who is engaged in the business of lending money or selling items for which immediate payment is not demanded but an obligation of repayment exists as of a future date.

Creditor's bill   An equitable proceeding initiated by a person who has obtained—and is entitled to enforce—a money judgment against a debtor to collect the payment of a debt that cannot be reached through normal legal procedures.

Credit union A corporation formed under special statutory provisions to further thrift among its members while providing credit for them at more favorable rates of interest than those offered by other lending institutions. A credit union is a cooperative association that utilizes funds deposited by a small group of people who are its sole borrowers and beneficiaries. It is ordinarily subject to regulation by state banking boards or commissions. When formed pursuant to the Federal Credit Union Act (12 U.S.C.A. § 1751 et seq. [1934]), credit unions are chartered and regulated by the National Credit Union Administration.

Crimes Acts or omissions that are in violation of law.

Criminal Pertaining to, or involving, crimes or the administration of penal justice. An individual who has been found guilty of the commission of conduct that causes social harm and that is punishable by law; a person who has committed a crime.

Criminal action The procedure by which a person accused of committing a crime is charged, brought to trial, and judged.

Criminal conversation A tort under common law that involved the seduction of another person's spouse.

Criminal forfeiture The loss of a criminal defendant's rights to property which is confiscated by the government when the property was used in the commission of a crime. The seizure by law enforcement officers of an automobile used in the transportation of illegal narcotics is a criminal forfeiture.

Criminal law A body of rules and statutes that defines conduct prohibited by the government because it threatens and harms public safety and welfare and that establishes punishment to be imposed for the commission of such acts.

Criminal negligence The failure to use reasonable care to avoid consequences that threaten or harm the safety of the public and that are the foreseeable outcome of acting in a particular manner.

Criminal procedure The framework of laws and rules that govern the administration of justice in cases involving an individual who has been accused of a crime, beginning with the initial investigation of the crime and concluding either with the unconditional release of the accused by virtue of acquittal (a judgment of not guilty) or by the imposition of a term of punishment pursuant to a conviction for the crime.

Criminology The scientific study of the causation, correction, and prevention of crime.

Critical legal studies An intellectual movement whose members argue that law is neither neutral nor value free but is in fact inseparable from politics.

Crop insurance A contract of indemnity by which, for a specified premium, one party promises to compensate another for the financial loss incurred by the destruction of agricultural products from the forces of nature, such as rain, hail, frost, or insect infestation.

Crops   Commodities produced from the earth which are planted, raised, and gathered within the course of a single season.

Cross-action   A separate and independent lawsuit brought by the defendant against a plaintiff for some reason arising from the same transaction or event that is the basis for the plaintiff's lawsuit.

Cross-claim   A demand made in a pleading against another party on the same side of the lawsuit.

Cross-complaint   A type of pleading that asserts a claim against any of the parties suing the person making the complaint, or against anyone else involved in the same controversy or having an interest in the same property that is the subject of the lawsuit.

Cross-demand   A claim made against someone who has already made a demand of the person asserting that claim.

Cross-examination   The questioning of a witness or party during a trial, hearing, or deposition by the party opposing the one who asked the person to testify in order to evaluate the truth of that person's testimony, to develop the testimony further, or to accomplish any other objective. The interrogation of a witness or party by the party opposed to the one who called the witness or party, upon a subject raised during direct examination—the initial questioning of a witness or party—on the merits of that testimony.

Cruel and inhuman treatment   Another name for cruelty, or for the intentional, hostile infliction of physical or mental suffering upon another individual, which is a ground for divorce in many states.

Cruel and unusual punishment   Such punishment as would amount to torture or barbarity, any cruel and degrading punishment not known to the common law, or any fine, penalty, confinement, or treatment so disproportionate to the offense as to shock the moral sense of the community.

Cruelty   The deliberate and malicious infliction of mental or physical pain upon persons or animals.

CTA   An abbreviation for cum testamento annexo, Latin for "with the will attached."

Culpa   [*Latin, Fault, blame, or neglect.*] A civil law term that implies that certain conduct is actionable.

Culpable   Blameworthy; involving the commission of a fault or the breach of a duty imposed by law.

Culprit   An individual who has been formally charged with a criminal offense but who has not yet been tried and convicted.

Cum testamento annexo
[*Latin, With the will annexed.*] A phrase that describes an administrator named by a probate or surrogate court to settle and distribute an estate according to the terms of a will in which the testator, its maker, has failed to name an executor, or in which the one named refuses to act or is legally incapable of acting.

Cumulative evidence
Facts or information that proves what has previously been established by other information concerning the same issue.

Cumulative sentence
Separate consecutive terms of imprisonment imposed upon a defendant who has been convicted of two or more distinct offenses; any term of imprisonment that becomes effective subsequent to the expiration of a prior one.

Cumulative voting
A method of election of the board of directors used by corporations whereby a stockholder may cast as many votes for directors as he or she has shares of stock, multiplied by the number of directors to be elected.

A plan used for the election of members to the lower house of the Illinois legislature by which voters, each of whom is given three votes, may cast all of the votes for one candidate or allocate them among two or three candidates.

Cunnilingus
An act in which the female sexual organ is orally stimulated.

Cure
The act of restoring health after injury or illness. Care, including medical and nursing services rendered to a sailor throughout a period of duty, pursuant to the principle that the owner of a vessel must furnish maintenance and cure to a sailor who becomes ill or is injured during service.

The right of a seller, under the Uniform Commercial Code (UCC), a body of law governing commercial transactions, to correct a delivery of goods that do not conform to contractual terms made to a buyer within the period specified by the contract in order to avoid a breach of contract action.

The actual payment of all amounts that are past due in regard to a default in such payments.

Curia
[*Latin, Court.*] A judicial tribunal or court convened in the sovereign's palace to dispense justice. A court that exercised jurisdiction over civil matters, as distinguished from religious matters, which were determined by ecclesiastical courts, a system of courts in England that were held by authority of the sovereign and had jurisdiction over matters concerning the religion and ritual of the established church.

Curia regis
[*Latin, The King's Court.*]

Current account
A detailed financial statement representing the debit and credit relationship between two parties that has not been finally settled or paid because of the continuous, ongoing dealings of the parties.

Curtesy
An estate to which a man is entitled by common-law right on the death of his wife, in all the lands that his wife owned at any time

during their marriage, provided a child is born of the marriage who could inherit the land.

Curtilage   The area, usually enclosed, encompassing the grounds and buildings immediately surrounding a home that is used in the daily activities of domestic life.

Custodial interrogation   Questioning initiated by law enforcement officers after a person is taken into custody or otherwise deprived of his or her freedom in any significant way, thus requiring that the person be advised of his or her constitutional rights.

Custody   The care, possession, and control of a thing or person. The retention, inspection, guarding, maintenance, or security of a thing within the immediate care and control of the person to whom it is committed. The detention of a person by lawful authority or process.

Customs duties   Tariffs or taxes payable on merchandise imported or exported from one country to another.

Cy pres   Abbreviated form of *cy pres comme possible*, French for "as near as possible." The name of a rule employed in the construction of such instruments as trusts and wills, by which the intention of the person who executes the instrument is effectuated as nearly as possible when circumstances make it impossible or illegal to give literal effect to the document.

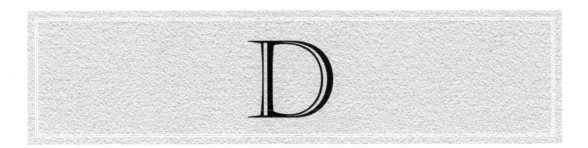

Damages   Monetary compensation that is awarded by a court in a civil action to an individual who has been injured through the wrongful conduct of another party.

Damnum   [*Latin, Damage.*] The loss or reduction in the value of property, life, or health of an individual as a consequence of fraud, carelessness, or accident.

Danelage   A system of law introduced into England as a result of its invasion and conquest by the Danes during the eighth and ninth centuries, which occurred primarily in some of the midland counties and on the eastern coast.

Dangerous instrumentality   Any article that is inherently hazardous or has the potential for harming people through its careless use.

Davis-Bacon Act	A federal law that governs the minimum wage rate to be paid to laborers and mechanics employed on federal public works projects.
Day certain	A specified date. A term used in the rules of civil and criminal procedure to designate a particular time by which all motions for a new trial must be submitted to the court.
Day in court	The opportunity afforded an individual to have a claim litigated in a judicial setting.
Days of grace	An extension of the time originally scheduled for the performance of an act, such as payment for a debt, granted merely as a gratuitous favor by the person to whom the performance is owed.
Dead body	A corpse; the physical remains of expired human beings prior to complete decomposition.
Deadly force	An amount of force that is likely to cause either serious bodily injury or death to another person.
Dead man's statutes	State rules of evidence that make the oral statements of a decedent inadmissible in a civil lawsuit against the executor or administrator of the decedent's estate when presented by persons to bolster their claims against the estate.
Death and dying	*Death* is the end of life. *Dying* is the process of approaching death, including the choices and actions involved in that process.
Death warrant	An order from the executive, the governor of a state, or the president directing the warden of a prison or a sheriff or other appropriate officer to carry into execution a sentence of death; an order commanding that a named person be put to death in a specified manner at a specific time.
Debenture	[*Latin, Are due.*] A promissory note or bond offered by a corporation to a creditor in exchange for a loan, the repayment of which is backed only by the general creditworthiness of the corporation and not by a mortgage or a lien on any specific property.
Debit	A sum charged as due or owing. An entry made on the asset side of a ledger or account. The term is used in bookkeeping to denote the left side of the ledger, or the charging of a person or an account with all that is supplied to or paid out for that person or for the subject of the account. Also, the balance of an account where it is shown that something remains due to the party keeping the account. As a noun, an entry on the left-hand side of an account. As a verb, to make an entry on the left-hand side of an account. A term used in accounting or bookkeeping that results in an increase to an asset and an expense account and a decrease to a liability, revenue, or owner's equity account.
De bonis non administratis	[*Latin, Of the goods not administered.*] When an administrator is appointed to succeed another who has left the estate partially un-

settled, the administrator is said to be granted "administration *de bonis non*," that is, of the goods not already administered.

Debt A sum of money that is owed or due to be paid because of an express agreement; a specified sum of money that one person is obligated to pay and that another has the legal right to collect or receive.

A fixed and certain obligation to pay money or some other valuable thing or things, either in the present or in the future. In a still more general sense, that which is due from one person to another, whether money, goods, or services. In a broad sense, any duty to respond to another in money, labor, or service; it may even mean a moral or honorary obligation, unenforceable by legal action. Also, sometimes an aggregate of separate debts, or the total sum of the existing claims against a person or company. Thus we speak of the "national debt," the "bonded debt" of a corporation, and so on.

Debt, action of One of the oldest common-law forms of action available to private litigants seeking to collect what is owed to them because of a harm done to them by another.

Debtor One who owes a debt or the performance of an obligation to another, who is called the creditor; one who may be compelled to pay a claim or demand; anyone liable on a claim, whether due or to become due.

In bankruptcy law, a person who files a voluntary petition or person against whom an involuntary petition is filed. A person or municipality concerning which a bankruptcy case has been commenced.

Debt poolers Individuals or organizations who receive and apply monthly funds from a person owing money to several creditors and who make arrangements to pay these creditors less than what is actually owed.

Decedent An individual who has died. The term literally means "one who is dying," but it is commonly used in the law to denote one who has died, particularly someone who has recently passed away.

Deceit A misrepresentation made with the express intention of defrauding someone, which subsequently causes injury to that person.

Decennial Digest® One of the volumes of the American Digest System that classifies by topic the summaries of court decisions that were reported chronologically in the various units of the National Reporter System.

Decision A conclusion reached after an evaluation of facts and law.

Decision on the merits An ultimate determination rendered by a court in an action that concludes the status of legal rights contested in a controversy and precludes a later lawsuit on the same cause of action by the parties to the original lawsuit.

Declaration The first pleading in a lawsuit governed by the rule of common-law pleading. In the law of evidence, a statement or narration made not under oath but simply in the middle of things, as a part of what is happening. Also, a proclamation.

Declaration of Independence	A formal announcement executed by the Continental Congress on July 4, 1776, on behalf of the people living in the American colonies, that asserted and proclaimed their freedom from Britain.
Declaration of trust	An assertion by a property owner that he or she holds the property or estate for the benefit of another person, or for particular designated objectives.
Declaratory judgment	Statutory remedy for the determination of a justiciable controversy where the plaintiff is in doubt as to his or her legal rights. A binding adjudication of the rights and status of litigants even though no consequential relief is awarded.
Decree	A judgment of a court that announces the legal consequences of the facts found in a case and orders that the court's decision be carried out. A decree in equity is a sentence or order of the court, pronounced on hearing and understanding all the points in issue, and determining the rights of all the parties to the suit, according to equity and good conscience. It is a declaration of the court announcing the legal consequences of the facts found. With the procedural merger of law and equity in the federal and most state courts under the Rules of Civil Procedure, the term *judgment* has generally replaced *decree*.
Dedication	In copyright law the first publication of a work that does not comply with the requirements relating to copyright notice and which therefore permits anyone to legally republish it. The gift of land—or an easement, that is, a right of use of the property of another—by the owner to the government for public use, and accepted for such use by or on behalf of the public.
Deductible	That which may be taken away or subtracted. In taxation, an item that may be subtracted from gross income or adjusted gross income in determining taxable income (e.g., interest expenses, charitable contributions, certain taxes).
	The portion of an insured loss to be borne by the insured before he or she is entitled to recovery from the insurer.
Deduction	That which is deducted; the part taken away; abatement; as in deductions from gross income in arriving at net income for tax purposes.
	In civil law, a portion or thing that an heir has a right to take from the mass of the succession before any partition takes place.
Deed	A written instrument, which has been signed and delivered, by which one individual, the grantor, conveys title to real property to another individual, the grantee; a conveyance of land, tenements, or hereditaments, from one individual to another.
Deed of trust	A document that embodies the agreement between a lender and a borrower to transfer an interest in the borrower's land to a neutral third party, a trustee, to secure the payment of a debt by the borrower.
Deem	To hold; consider; adjudge; believe; condemn; determine; treat as if; construe.

De facto   [*Latin, In fact.*] In fact, in deed, actually.

Defalcation   The misappropriation or embezzlement of money.

Defamation   Any intentional false communication, either written or spoken, that harms a person's reputation; decreases the respect, regard, or confidence in which a person is held; or induces disparaging, hostile, or disagreeable opinions or feelings against a person.

Default   An omission; a failure to do that which is anticipated, expected, or required in a given situation.

Default judgment   Judgment entered against a party who has failed to defend against a claim that has been brought by another party. Under rules of civil procedure, when a party against whom a judgment for affirmative relief is sought has failed to plead (i.e., answer) or otherwise defend, the party is in default and a judgment by default may be entered either by the clerk or the court.

Defeasance clause   A provision of a mortgage—an interest in land given to a mortgagee-lender to secure the payment of a debt—which promises that the mortgagor-borrower will regain title to the mortgaged property when all the terms of the mortgage have been met.

Defeasible   Potentially subject to defeat, termination, or annulment upon the occurrence of a future action or event, or the performance of a condition subsequent.

Defect   Imperfection, flaw, or deficiency.

Defendant   The person defending or denying; the party against whom relief or recovery is sought in an action or suit, or the accused in a criminal case.

Defense   The forcible repulsion of an unlawful and violent attack, such as the defense of one's person, property, or country in time of war.

The totality of the facts, law, and contentions presented by the party against whom a civil action or ciminal prosecution is instituted in order to defeat or diminish the plaintiff's cause of action or the prosecutor's case. A reply to the claims of the other party, which asserts reasons why the claims should be disallowed. The defense may involve an absolute denial of the other party's factual allegations or may entail an affirmative defense, which sets forth completely new factual allegations. Pursuant to the rules of federal civil procedure, numerous defenses may be asserted by motion as well as by answer, while other defenses must be pleaded affirmatively.

Deficiency   A shortage or insufficiency. The amount by which federal income tax due exceeds the amount reported by the taxpayer on his or her return; also, the amount owed by a taxpayer who has not filed a return. The outstanding balance of a debt secured by a mortgage after the mortgaged property has been sold to satisfy the obligation at a price less than the debt.

Deficiency judgment An assessment of personal liability against a mortgagor, a person who pledges title to property to secure a debt, for the unpaid balance of the mortgage debt when the proceeds of a foreclosure sale are insufficient to satisfy the debt.

Deficit A deficiency, misappropriation, or defalcation; a minus balance; something wanting.

Definitive Conclusive; ending all controversy and discussion in a lawsuit.

Deforcement The common-law name given to the wrongful possession of land to which another person is rightfully entitled; the detention of dower from a widow.

Defraud To make a misrepresentation of an existing material fact, knowing it to be false or making it recklessly without regard to whether it is true or false, intending for someone to rely on the misrepresentation and under circumstances in which such person does rely on it to his or her damage. To practice fraud; to cheat or trick. To deprive a person of property or any interest, estate, or right by fraud, deceit, or artifice.

Degree Extent, measure, or scope of an action, condition, or relation. Legal extent of guilt or negligence. Title conferred on graduates of school, college, or university. The state or civil condition of a person.

The grade or distance one thing may be removed from another; i.e., the distance, or number of removes that separate two persons who are related by consanguinity. Thus, a sibling is in the second degree of kinship but a parent is in the first degree of kinship.

De jure [*Latin, In law.*] Legitimate; lawful, as a matter of law. Having complied with all the requirements imposed by law.

Del credere [*Italian, Of belief or trust.*] An arrangement in which an agent or factor—an individual who takes possession and agrees to sell goods for another—consents for an additional fee to guarantee that the purchaser, to whom credit has been extended, is financially solvent and will perform the contract.

Delectus personae [*Latin, Choice of the person.*] By this term is understood the right of partners to exercise their choice and preference as to the admission of any new members to the partnership, and as to the persons to be so admitted, if any. The doctrine is equally applicable to close and family corporations and is exemplified in the use of restrictions for the transfer of shares of stock.

Delegate A person who is appointed, authorized, delegated, or commissioned to act in the place of another. Transfer of authority from one to another. A person to whom affairs are committed by another.

A person elected or appointed to be a member of a representative assembly. Usually spoken of one sent to a special or occasional assembly or convention. Person selected by a constituency and authorized to act for it at a party or state political convention.

As a verb, it means to transfer authority from one person to another; to empower one to perform a task in behalf of another, e.g., a landlord may delegate an agent to collect rents.

Delegation   A sending away; a putting into commission; the assignment of a debt to another; the entrusting of another with a general power to act for the good of those who depute him or her; a body of delegates. The transfer of authority by one person to another.

The body of delegates from a state to a national nominating convention or from a county to a state or other party convention. The whole body of delegates or representatives sent to a convention or assembly from one district, place, or political unit is collectively spoken of as a *delegation*.

Deliberate   Willful; purposeful; determined after thoughtful evaluation of all relevant factors; dispassionate. To act with a particular intent, which is derived from a careful consideration of factors that influence the choice to be made.

Delictum   [*Latin, A fault.*] An injury, an offense, or a tort—a wrong done to the property or person of another that does not involve breach of contract.

Culpability; blameworthiness of a criminal nature, as in the Latin phrase *in pari delicto*—in equal fault or equally criminal—used to describe accomplices to a crime.

Delivery   The transfer of possession of real property or personal property from one person to another.

Demand   Peremptory allegation or assertion of a legal right.

Demeanor   The outward physical behavior and appearance of a person.

De minimis   An abbreviated form of the Latin maxim *de minimis non curat lex*, "the law cares not for small things." A legal doctrine by which a court refuses to consider trifling matters.

Demise   Death. A conveyance of property, usually of an interest in land.

Demonstrative evidence   Evidence other than testimony that is presented during the course of a civil or criminal trial.

Demonstrative legacy   A gift by will of money or other personal property that is to be paid to an heir from a fund designated in the provisions of the will but, in any event, is to be paid if there are sufficient available assets in the estate.

Demur   To dispute a legal pleading or a statement of the facts being alleged through the use of a demurrer.

Demurrage   A separate freight charge, in addition to ordinary shipping costs, which is imposed according to the terms of a carriage contract upon the person responsible for unreasonable delays in loading or unloading cargo.

In maritime law, demurrage is the amount identified in a charter contract as damages payable to a shipowner as compensation for the detention of a ship beyond the time specified by a charter party for loading and unloading or for sailing.

Demurrer An assertion by the defendant that although the facts alleged by the plaintiff in the complaint may be true, they do not entitle the plaintiff to prevail in the lawsuit.

De novo [*Latin, Anew.*] A second time; afresh. A trial or a hearing that is ordered by an appellate court that has reviewed the record of a hearing in a lower court and sent the matter back to the original court for a new trial, as if it had not been previously heard nor decided.

Deny To refuse to acknowledge something; to disclaim connection with or responsibility for an action or statement. To deny someone of a legal right is to deprive him or her of that right.

Dependent A person whose support and maintenance is contingent upon the aid of another. Conditional.

Dependent relative revocation The doctrine that regards as mutually interrelated the acts of a testator destroying a will and executing a second will. In such cases, if the second will is either never made or improperly executed, there is a rebuttable presumption that the testator would have preferred the former will to no will at all, which allows the possibility of probate of the destroyed will.

Depletion allowance A tax deduction authorized by federal law for the exhaustion of oil and gas wells, mines, timber, mineral deposits or reserves, and other natural deposits.

Deponent An individual who, under oath or affirmation, gives out-of-court testimony in a deposition. A deponent is someone who gives evidence or acts as a witness. The testimony of a deponent is written and carries the deponent's signature.

Deportation Banishment to a foreign country, attended with confiscation of property and deprivation of civil rights.

The transfer of an alien, by exclusion or expulsion, from the United States to a foreign country. The removal or sending back of an alien to the country from which he or she came because his or her presence is deemed inconsistent with the public welfare, and without any punishment being imposed or contemplated. The grounds for deportation are set forth at 8 U.S.C.A. § 1251, and the procedures are provided for in §§ 1252-1254.

Depose To make a deposition; to give evidence in the shape of a deposition; to make statements that are written down and sworn to; to give testimony that is reduced to writing by a duly qualified officer and sworn to by the deponent.

To deprive an individual of a public employment or office against his or her will. The term is usually applied to the deprivation of all authority of a sovereign.

In ancient usage, to testify as a witness; to give evidence under oath.

Deposition   The testimony of a party or witness in a civil or criminal proceeding taken before trial, usually in an attorney's office.

Depository   The place where a deposit is placed and kept, e.g., a bank, savings and loan institution, credit union, or trust company. A place where something is deposited or stored as for safekeeping or convenience, e.g., a safety deposit box.

Deposits in court   The payments of funds or property to an officer of the court as a precautionary measure during the pendency of litigation.

Depreciation   The gradual decline in the financial value of property used to produce income due to its increasing age and eventual obsolescence, which is measured by a formula that takes into account these factors in addition to the cost of the property and its estimated useful life.

Deputy   A person duly authorized by an officer to serve as his or her substitute by performing some or all of the officer's functions.

Derivative action   A lawsuit brought by a shareholder of a corporation on its behalf to enforce or defend a legal right or claim, which the corporation has failed to do.

Derivative evidence   Facts, information, or physical objects that tend to prove an issue in a criminal prosecution but which are excluded from consideration by the trier of fact because they were learned directly from information illegally obtained in violation of the constitutional guarantee against unreasonable searches and seizures.

Derogation   The partial repeal of a law, usually by a subsequent act that in some way diminishes its original intent or scope.

Descent   Hereditary succession. Succession to the ownership of an estate by inheritance, or by any act of law, as distinguished from *purchase*. Title by descent is the title by which one person, upon the death of another, acquires the real estate of the latter as an heir at law. The title by inheritance is in all cases called descent, although by statute law the title is sometimes made to ascend. The division among those legally entitled thereto of the real property of intestates.

Descent and distribution   The area of law that pertains to the transfer of real property or personal property of a decedent who failed to leave a will or make a valid will and the rights and liabilities of heirs, next of kin, and distributees who are entitled to a share of the property.

Descriptive word index   An alphabetically arranged aid used in legal research to locate cases that have discussed a particular topic.

Desertion   The act by which a person abandons and forsakes, without justification, a condition of public, social, or family life, renouncing its responsibilities and evading its duties. A willful abandonment of an employment or duty in violation of a legal or moral obligation.

Criminal desertion is a husband's or wife's abandonment or willful failure without just cause to provide for the care, protection, or support of a spouse who is in ill health or necessitous circumstances.

Desk audit   An evaluation of a particular civil service position to determine whether its duties and responsibilities correspond to its job classification and salary grade.

Destroy   In general, to ruin completely; may include a taking. To ruin the structure, organic existence, or condition of a thing; to demolish; to injure or mutilate beyond possibility of use; to nullify.

Detainer   The act (or the juridical fact) of withholding from a lawfully entitled person the possession of land or goods, or the restraint of a person's personal liberty against his or her will; detention. The wrongful keeping of a person's goods is called an unlawful detainer although the original taking may have been lawful.

A request filed by a criminal justice agency with the institution in which a prisoner is incarcerated asking the institution either to hold the prisoner for the agency or to notify the agency when release of the prisoner is imminent.

Detectives   Individuals whose business it is to observe and provide information about alleged criminals or to discover matters of secrecy for the protection of the public.

Detention   The act of keeping back, restraining, or withholding, either accidentally or by design, a person or thing.

Determinable   Liable to come to an end upon the happening of a certain contingency. Susceptible of being determined, found out, definitely decided upon, or settled.

Determinate sentence   A sentence to confinement for a fixed or minimum period that is specified by statute.

Determination   The final resolution or conclusion of a controversy.

Detinue   One of the old common-law forms of action used to recover personal property from a person who refuses to give it up. Also used to collect money damages for losses caused by the wrongful detention.

Detriment   Any loss or harm to a person or property; relinquishment of a legal right, benefit, or something of value.

Deviance   Conspicuous dissimilarity with, or variation from, customarily acceptable behavior.

Devise   A testamentary disposition of land or realty; a gift of real property by the last will and testament of the donor. When used as a noun, it means a testamentary disposition of real or personal property, and when used as a verb, it means to dispose of real or personal property by will.

To contrive; plan; scheme; invent; prepare.

Dewey Decimal System   A numerical classification system of books employed by libraries.

Dicta   Opinions of a judge that do not embody the resolution or determination of the specific case before the court. Expressions in a court's opinion that go beyond the facts before the court and therefore are individual views of the author of the opinion and not binding in subsequent cases as legal precedent. The plural of *dictum*.

Dictum   [*Latin, A remark.*] A statement, comment, or opinion. An abbreviated version of obiter dictum, "a remark by the way," which is a collateral opinion stated by a judge in the decision of a case concerning legal matters that do not directly involve the facts or affect the outcome of the case, such as a legal principle that is introduced by way of illustration, argument, analogy, or suggestion.

Digest   A collection or compilation that embodies the chief matter of numerous books, articles, court decisions, and so on, disposed under proper heads or titles, and usually by an alphabetical arrangement, for facility in reference.

An index to reported cases, providing brief statements of court holdings or facts of cases, which is arranged by subject and subdivided by jurisdiction and courts.

Dilatory   Tending to cause a delay in judicial proceedings.

Dilatory plea   In common-law-pleading, any of several types of defenses that could be asserted against a plaintiff's cause of action, delaying the time when the court would begin consideration of the actual facts in the case.

Diligence   Vigilant activity; attentiveness; or care, of which there are infinite shades, from the slightest momentary thought to the most vigilant anxiety. Attentive and persistent in doing a thing; steadily applied; active; sedulous; laborious; unremitting; untiring. The attention and care required of a person in a given situation; the opposite of negligence.

Diminished capacity   This doctrine recognizes that although, at the time the offense was committed, an accused was not suffering from a mental disease or defect sufficient to exonerate him or her from all criminal responsibility, the accused's mental capacity may have been diminished by intoxication, trauma, or mental disease so that he or she did not possess the specific mental state or intent essential to the particular offense charged.

Diminution   Taking away; reduction; lessening; incompleteness.

Diplomatic agents   Government representatives sent by one country to live and work in another to serve as intermediaries for the two countries.

Diplomatic immunity   A principle of international law that provides foreign diplomats with protection from legal action in the country in which they work.

Direct   As a verb, to point to; guide; order; command; instruct. To advise; suggest; request. As an adjective, immediate; proximate; by the shortest course; without circuity; operating by an immediate connection or relation, instead of operating through an intermediary; the opposite of *indirect*. In the usual or regular course or order, as distinguished from that which diverts, interrupts, or opposes. The opposite of cross, contrary, collateral, or remote. Without any intervening medium, agency, or influence; unconditional.

Directed verdict A procedural device whereby the decision in a case is taken out of the hands of the jury by the judge.

Direct evidence Evidence in the form of testimony from a witness who actually saw, heard, or touched the subject of questioning. Evidence that, if believed, proves existence of the fact in issue without inference or presumption. That means of proof which tends to show the existence of a fact in question, without the intervention of the proof of any other fact, and which is distinguished from circumstantial evidence, often called *indirect*.

Evidence that directly proves a fact, without an inference or presumption, and which in itself, if true, conclusively establishes that fact.

Direct examination The primary questioning of a witness during a trial that is conducted by the side for which that person is acting as a witness.

Director One who supervises, regulates, or controls.

Directory A provision in a statute, rule of procedure, or the like, that is a mere direction or instruction of no obligatory force and involves no invalidating consequence for its disregard, as opposed to an imperative or mandatory provision, which must be followed. The general rule is that the prescriptions of a statute relating to the performance of a public duty are so far directory that, though neglect of them may be punishable, it does not affect the validity of the acts done under them, as in the case of a statute requiring an officer to prepare and deliver a document to another officer on or before a certain day.

Direct tax A charge levied by the government upon property, which is determined by its financial worth.

Disability The lack of competent physical and mental faculties; the absence of legal capability to perform an act.

The term *disability* usually signifies an incapacity to exercise all the legal rights ordinarily possessed by an average person. Convicts, minors, and incompetents are regarded to be under a disability. The term is also used in a more restricted sense when it indicates a hindrance to marriage or a deficiency in legal qualifications to hold office.

The impairment of earning capacity; the loss of physical function resulting in diminished efficiency; the inability to work.

Disabled persons Persons who have a physical or mental impairment that substantially limits one or more major life activities. Some laws also include in their definition of disabled persons those people who have a record of or are regarded as having such an impairment.

Disaffirm Repudiate; revoke consent; refuse to support former acts or agreements.

Disallow To exclude; reject; deny the force or validity of.

Disaster relief   Monies or services made available to individuals and communities that have experienced losses due to disasters such as floods, hurricanes, earthquakes, drought, tornadoes, and riots.

Disbar   To revoke an attorney's license to practice law.

Discharge   To liberate or free; to terminate or extinguish. A discharge is the act or instrument by which a contract or agreement is ended. A mortgage is discharged if it has been carried out to the full extent originally contemplated or terminated prior to total execution.

Discharge also means to release, as from legal confinement in prison or the military service, or from some legal obligation such as jury duty, or the payment of debts by a person who is bankrupt. The document that indicates that an individual has been legally released from the military service is called a discharge.

Disciplinary rules   Precepts, such as the Code of Professional Responsibility, that proscribe an attorney from taking certain actions in the practice of law.

Disclaimer   The denial, refusal, or rejection of a right, power, or responsibility.

Discontinuance   Cessation; ending; giving up. The discontinuance of a lawsuit, also known as a dismissal or a nonsuit, is the voluntary or involuntary termination of an action.

Discovery   A category of procedural devices employed by a party to a civil or criminal action, prior to trial, to require the adverse party to disclose information that is essential for the preparation of the requesting party's case and that the other party alone knows or possesses.

Discretionary trust   An arrangement whereby property is set aside with directions that it be used for the benefit of another, the beneficiary, and which provides that the trustee (one appointed or required by law to administer the property) has the right to accumulate, rather than pay out to the beneficiary, the annual income generated by the property or a portion of the property itself.

Discretion in decision making   Discretion is the power or right to make official decisions using reason and judgment to choose from among acceptable alternatives.

Discrimination   In constitutional law, the grant by statute of particular privileges to a class arbitrarily designated from a sizable number of persons, where no reasonable distinction exists between the favored and disfavored classes. Federal laws, supplemented by court decisions, prohibit discrimination in such areas as employment, housing, voting rights, education, and access to public facilities. They also proscribe discrimination on the basis of race, age, sex, nationality, disability, or religion. In addition, state and local laws can prohibit discrimination in these areas and in others not covered by federal laws.

Disfranchisement   The removal of the rights and privileges inherent in an association with some group; the taking away of the rights of a free citizen, especially the right to vote. Sometimes called disenfranchisement.

The relinquishment of a person's right to membership in a corporation is distinguishable from amotion, which is the act of removing an officer from an office without depriving him or her of membership in the corporate body.

Dishonor   To refuse to accept or pay a draft or to pay a promissory note when duly presented. An instrument is dishonored when a necessary or optional presentment is made and due acceptance or payment is refused, or cannot be obtained within the prescribed time, or in case of bank collections, the instrument is seasonably returned by the midnight deadline; or presentment is excused and the instrument is not duly accepted or paid. Includes the insurer of a letter of credit refusing to pay or accept a draft or demand for payment.

As respects the flag, to deface or defile, imputing a lively sense of shaming or an equivalent acquiescent callousness.

Disinherit   To cut off from an inheritance. To deprive someone, who would otherwise be an heir to property or another right, of his or her right to inherit.

Disinterested   Free from bias, prejudice, or partiality.

Dismissal   A discharge of an individual or corporation from employment. The disposition of a civil or criminal proceeding or a claim or charge made therein by a court order without a trial or prior to its completion which, in effect, is a denial of the relief sought by the commencement of the action.

Disorderly conduct   A broad term describing conduct that disturbs the peace or endangers the morals, health, or safety of a community.

Disorderly house   A place where individuals reside or which they frequent for purposes that pose a threat to public health, morals, convenience, or safety, and that may create a public nuisance. *Disorderly house* is an all-inclusive term that may be used to describe such places as a house of prostitution, an illegal gambling casino, or a site where drugs are constantly bought and sold. It is any place where unlawful practices are habitually carried on by the public.

Disparagement   In old English law, an injury resulting from the comparison of a person or thing with an individual or thing of inferior quality; to discredit oneself by marriage below one's class. A statement made by one person that casts aspersions on another person's goods, property, or intangible things.

Disposable earnings   That portion of one's income that a person is free to spend or invest as he or she sees fit, after payment of taxes and other obligations.

Disposition   Act of disposing; transferring to the care or possession of another. The parting with, alienation of, or giving up of property. The final settlement of a matter and, with reference to decisions announced by a court, a judge's ruling is commonly referred to as disposition, regardless of level of resolution. In criminal procedure, the sentencing or other final settlement of a criminal case. With respect to a mental state, denotes an attitude, prevailing tendency, or inclination.

Dispositive fact   Information or evidence that unqualifiedly brings a conclusion to a legal controversy.

Dispossession   The wrongful, nonconsensual ouster or removal of a person from his or her property by trick, compulsion, or misuse of the law, whereby the violator obtains actual occupation of the land.

Dispute   A conflict or controversy; a conflict of claims or rights; an assertion of a right, claim, or demand on one side, met by contrary claims or allegations on the other. The subject of litigation; the matter for which a suit is brought and upon which issue is joined, and in relation to which jurors are called and witnesses examined.

Disqualify   To deprive of eligibility or render unfit; to disable or incapacitate.

Dissent   An explicit disagreement by one or more judges with the decision of the majority on a case before them.

Dissolution   Act or process of dissolving; termination; winding up. In this sense it is frequently used in the phrase *dissolution of a partnership*.

Dissolve   To terminate; abrogate; cancel; annul; disintegrate. To release or unloose the binding force of anything.

Distinguish   To set apart as being separate or different; to point out an essential disparity.

Distrain   To seize the property of an individual and retain it until an obligation is performed. The taking of the goods and chattels of a tenant by a landlord in order to satisfy an unpaid debt.

Distress   The seizure of personal property for the satisfaction of a demand.

Distributee   An heir; a person entitled to share in the distribution of an estate. This term is used to denote one of the persons who is entitled, under the statute of distributions, to the personal estate of one who is dead intestate.

Distributor   A wholesaler; an individual, corporation, or partnership buying goods in bulk quantities from a manufacturer at a price close to the cost of manufacturing them and reselling them at a higher price to other dealers, or to various retailers, but not directly to the general public.

District   One of the territorial areas into which an entire state or country, county, municipality, or other political subdivision is divided, for judicial, political, electoral, or administrative purposes.

     The circuit or territory within which a person may be compelled to appear. Circuit of authority; province.

District and prosecuting attorneys   The elected or appointed public officers of each state, county, or other political subdivision who institute criminal proceedings on behalf of the government.

District court   A designation of an inferior state court that exercises general jurisdiction that it has been granted by the constitution or statute which created it. A U.S. judicial tribunal with original jurisdiction to try cases or controversies that fall within its limited jurisdiction.

Disturbance of the peace An offense constituting a malicious and willful intrusion upon the peace and quiet of a community or neighborhood.

Divers Several; any number more than two; different.

Diversion A turning aside or altering of the natural course or route of a thing. The term is chiefly applied to the unauthorized change or alteration of a water course to the prejudice of a lower riparian, or to the unauthorized use of funds.

A program for the disposition of a criminal charge without a criminal trial; sometimes called operation de nova, intervention, or deferred prosecution.

Diversity of citizenship A phrase used with reference to the jurisdiction of the federal courts which, under the U.S. Constitution, Art. III, § 2, extends to cases between citizens of different states designating the condition existing when the party on one side of a lawsuit is a citizen of one state and the party on the other side is a citizen of another state, or between a citizen of a state and an alien. The requisite jurisdictional amount must, in addition, be met.

Divest To deprive or take away.

Dividend The distribution of current or accumulated earnings to the shareholders of a corporation pro rata based on the number of shares owned. Dividends are usually issued in cash. However, they may be issued in the form of stock or property. The dividend on preferred shares is generally a fixed amount; however, on common shares the dividend varies depending on such things as the earnings and available cash of the corporation as well as future plans for the acquisition of property and equipment by the corporation.

Divine right of kings The authority of a monarch to rule a realm by virtue of birth.

Divorce A court decree that terminates a marriage; also known as marital dissolution.

Dock To curtail or diminish, as, for example, to dock a person's wages for lateness or poor work. The cage or enclosed space in a criminal court where prisoners stand when brought in for trial.

Docket A written list of judicial proceedings set down for trial in a court.

To enter the dates of judicial proceedings scheduled for trial in a book kept by a court.

Doctrine A legal rule, tenet, theory, or principle. A political policy.

Document A written or printed instrument that conveys information.

Documentary evidence A type of written proof that is offered at a trial to establish the existence or nonexistence of a fact that is in dispute.

Document of title Any written instrument, such as a bill of lading, a warehouse receipt, or an order for the delivery of goods, that in the usual course of business or financing is considered sufficient proof that the person who possesses it is entitled to receive, hold, and dispose of the instrument and the goods that it covers.

Doing business A qualification imposed in state long-arm statutes governing the service of process, the method by which a lawsuit is commenced, which requires nonresident corporations to engage in commercial transactions within state borders in order to be subject to the personal jurisdiction of state courts.

Domain The complete and absolute ownership of land. Also the real estate so owned. The inherent sovereign power claimed by the legislature of a state, of controlling private property for public uses, is termed the *right of eminent domain*.

National domain is sometimes applied to the aggregate of the property owned directly by a nation. Public domain embraces all lands, the title to which is in the United States, including land occupied for the purposes of federal buildings, arsenals, dock-yards, and so on, and land of an agricultural or mineral character not yet granted to private owners.

Sphere of influence. Range of control or rule; realm.

Dombec [*Saxon, Judgment book.*] The name given by the Saxons to the code of laws by which they lived.

Domesday Book An ancient record of land ownership in England.

Domestic Pertaining to the house or home. A person employed by a household to perform various servient duties. Any household servant, such as a maid or butler. Relating to a place of birth, origin, or domicile.

Domestic violence Any abusive, violent, coercive, forceful, or threatening act or word inflicted by one member of a family or household on another can constitute domestic violence.

Domiciliary administration The settlement and distribution of a decedent's estate in the state of his or her permanent residence, the place to which the decedent intended to return even though he or she might actually have resided elsewhere.

Dominant Prevalent; paramount in force or effect; of primary importance or consideration. That which is dominant possesses rights that prevail over those of others.

Dominant cause The essential or most direct source of an accident or injury, regardless of when it occurred.

Dominion Perfect control in right of ownership. The word implies both title and possession and appears to require a complete retention of control over disposition. Title to an article of property, which arises from the power of disposition and the right of claiming it. Sovereignty; as in the dominion of the seas or over a territory.

In civil law, with reference to the title to property that is transferred by a sale of it, dominion is said to be either *proximate* or *remote*, the former being the kind of title vesting in the purchaser when he or she has acquired both the ownership and the possession of the article, the latter describing the nature of the title when he or she has legitimately acquired the ownership of the property but there has been no delivery.

Donative   Relating to the gratuitous transfer of something as in the nature of a gift.

Donee   The recipient of a gift. An individual to whom a power of appointment is conveyed.

Donor   The party conferring a power. One who makes a gift. One who creates a trust.

Doom   An archaic term for a court's judgment.

Dormant   Latent; inactive; silent. That which is dormant is not used, asserted, or enforced.

Double entry   A bookkeeping system that lists each transaction twice in the ledger.

Double indemnity   A term of an insurance policy by which the insurance company promises to pay the insured or the beneficiary twice the amount of coverage if loss occurs due to a particular cause or set of circumstances.

Double insurance   Duplicate protection provided when two companies deal with the same individual and undertake to indemnify that person against the same losses.

Double jeopardy   A second prosecution for the same offense after acquittal or conviction or multiple punishments for same offense. The evil sought to be avoided by prohibiting double jeopardy is double trial and double conviction, not necessarily double punishment.

Doubt   To question or hold questionable. Uncertainty of mind; the absence of a settled opinion or conviction; the attitude of mind toward the acceptance of or belief in a proposition, theory, or statement, in which the judgment is not at rest but inclines alternately to either side.

Dower   The provision that the law makes for a widow out of the lands or tenements of her husband, for her support and the nurture of her children. A species of life estate that a woman is, by law, entitled to claim on the death of her husband, in the lands and tenements of which he was seised in fee during the marriage, and which her issue, if any, might by possibility have inherited. The life estate to which every married woman is entitled on the death of her husband, intestate, or, in case she dissents from his will, one-third in value of all lands of which her husband was beneficially seized in law or in fact, at any time during coverture.

Down payment   A percentage of the total purchase price of an item that is proffered when the item is bought on credit.

Draconian laws A code of laws prepared by Draco, the celebrated lawgiver of Athens.

Draft A written order by the first party, called the drawer, instructing a second party, called the drawee (such as a bank), to pay money to a third party, called the payee. An order to pay a sum certain in money, signed by a drawer, payable on demand or at a definite time, to order or bearer.

A tentative, provisional, or preparatory writing out of any document (as a will, contract, lease, and so on) for purposes of discussion and correction, which is afterward to be prepared in its final form.

Compulsory conscription of persons into military service.

Also, a small arbitrary deduction or allowance made to a merchant or importer, in the case of goods sold by weight or taxable by weight, to cover possible loss of weight in handling or from differences in scales.

Drafter The person who draws or frames a legal document such as a will, pleading, conveyance, or contract. One who writes an original legislative bill for the U.S. Senate or House of Representatives is called the drafter of that bill.

Drain A trench or ditch to convey water from wet land; a channel through which water may flow off. The word has no technical legal meaning. Any hollow space in the ground, natural or artificial, where water is collected and passes off, is a ditch or drain.

Also, sometimes, the easement or servitude (acquired by grant or prescription) that consists of the right to drain water through another's land.

Dramshop acts Statutes, also called civil liability acts, that impose civil liability upon one who sells intoxicating liquors when a third party has been injured as a result of the purchaser's intoxication and such sale has either caused or contributed to the state of intoxication.

Draw To aim a firearm, or deadly weapon, at a particular target.

To prepare a written bill of exchange, commercial paper, draft, or negotiable instrument and place one's signature on it, creating a legal obligation under its terms. To write a document, such as a deed, complaint, or petition, including the essential information necessary to make it legally effective upon its execution by the designated parties.

To lawfully remove money from an account held in a bank, treasury, or other depository.

Drawee A person or bank that is ordered by its depositor, a drawer, to withdraw money from an account to pay a designated sum to a person according to the terms of a check or a draft.

Drawer A person who orders a bank to withdraw money from an account to pay a designated person a specific sum according to the term of a bill, a check, or a draft. An individual who writes and signs a commercial paper, thereby becoming obligated under its terms.

Droit [*French, Justice, right, law.*] A term denoting the abstract concept of law or a right.

Druggist An individual who, as a regular course of business, mixes, compounds, dispenses, and sells medicines and similar health aids.

Drugs and narcotics *Drugs* are articles intended for use in the diagnosis, cure, mitigation, treatment, or prevention of disease in humans or animals, and any articles other than food intended to affect the mental or body function of humans or animals. *Narcotics* are any drugs that dull the senses and commonly become addictive after prolonged use.

Drunkard One who habitually overindulges in alcohol.

Drunkenness The state of an individual whose mind is affected by the consumption of alcohol.

Dual nationality An equal claim, simultaneously possessed by two nations, to the allegiance of an individual.

Duces tecum [*Latin, Bring with you.*] Commonly called a subpoena duces tecum, a type of legal writ requiring one who has been summoned to appear in court to bring some specified item with him or her for use or examination by the court.

Due Just; proper; regular; lawful; sufficient; reasonable, as in the phrases *due care, due process of law, due notice.*
  Owing; payable; justly owed. That which one contracts to pay or perform to another; that which law or justice requires to be paid or done. Owed, or owing, as distinguished from payable. A debt is often said to be due from a person where he or she is the party owing it, or primarily bound to pay, whether the time for payment has or has not arrived. The same thing is true of the phrase *due and owing.*

Due date The particular day on or before which something must be done to comply with law or contractual obligation.

Dueling The fighting of two persons, one against the other, at an appointed time and place, due to an earlier quarrel. If death results, the crime is murder. It differs from an affray in this, that the latter occurs on a sudden quarrel, while the former is always the result of design.

Due notice Information that must be given or made available to a particular person or to the public within a legally mandated period of time so that its recipient will have the opportunity to respond to a situation or to allegations that affect the individual's or public's legal rights or duties.

Due process of law A fundamental, constitutional guarantee that all legal proceedings will be fair and that one will be given notice of the proceedings and an opportunity to be heard before the government acts to take away one's life, liberty, or property. Also, a constitutional guarantee that a law shall not be unreasonable, arbitrary, or capricious.

Dummy Sham; make-believe; pretended; imitation. Person who serves in place of another, or who serves until the proper person is named or available to take his place (e.g., dummy corporate directors; dummy owners of real estate).

Duress Unlawful pressure exerted upon a person to coerce that person to perform an act that he or she ordinarily would not perform.

Durham rule A principle of criminal law used to determine the validity of the insanity defense asserted by an accused, that he or she was insane at the time of committing a crime and therefore should not be held legally responsible for the action.

Duty A legal obligation that entails mandatory conduct or performance. With respect to the laws relating to customs duties, a tax owed to the government for the import or export of goods.

Duty of tonnage A fee that encompasses all taxes and customs duties, regardless of their name or form, imposed upon a vessel as an instrument of commerce for entering, remaining in, or exiting from a port.

DWI An abbreviation for *driving while intoxicated*, which is an offense committed by an individual who operates a motor vehicle while under the influence of alcohol or drugs and narcotics.

An abbreviation for *died without issue*, which commonly appears in genealogical tables.

Dyer Act A name given to a federal law that makes it a crime to transport stolen motor vehicles across state borders in interstate or foreign commerce.

Dying declaration A statement by a person who is conscious and knows that death is imminent concerning what he or she believes to be the cause or circumstances of death that can be introduced into evidence during a trial in certain cases.

Earned income Sources of money derived from the labor, professional service, or entrepreneurship of an individual taxpayer as opposed to funds generated by investments, dividends, and interest.

Earnest money A sum of money paid by a buyer at the time of entering a contract to indicate the intention and ability of the buyer to carry out the contract. Normally such earnest money is applied against the purchase price. Often the contract provides for forfeiture of this sum if the buyer defaults. A deposit of part payment of purchase price on sale to be consummated in future.

Easement A right of use over the property of another. Traditionally the permitted kinds of uses were limited, the most important being rights of way and rights concerning flowing waters. The easement was normally for the benefit of adjoining lands, no matter who the owner was (an easement appurtenant), rather than for the benefit of a specific individual (easement in gross).

Ecclesiastical courts In England, the collective classification of particular courts that exercised jurisdiction primarily over spiritual matters. A system of courts, held by authority granted by the sovereign, that assumed jurisdiction over matters concerning the ritual and religion of the established church, and over the rights, obligations, and discipline of the clergy.

Edict A decree or law of major import promulgated by a king, queen, or other sovereign of a government.

Education law The body of state and federal constitutional provisions; local, state, and federal statutes; court opinions; and government regulations that provide the legal framework for educational institutions.

EEOC An abbreviation for Equal Employment Opportunity Commission.

Effect As a verb, to do; to produce; to make; to bring to pass; to execute; enforce; accomplish. As a noun, that which is produced by an agent or cause; result; outcome; consequence. The result that an instrument between parties will produce in their relative rights, or which a statute will produce upon the existing law, as discovered from the language used, the forms employed, or other materials for construing it. The operation of a law, of an agreement, or an act. The phrases *take effect, be in force,* and *go into operation,* are used interchangeably.

In the plural, a person's effects are the real and personal property of someone who has died or who makes a will.

Effective rate Another name for annual percentage rate that refers to the amount of yearly interest to be charged by a lender on the money borrowed by a debtor.

In federal income tax law, the actual tax rate that an individual taxpayer pays based upon his or her taxable income.

Efficient cause That which actually precipitates an accident or injury.

E.G. An abbreviation for *exempli gratia* [*Latin, For the sake of an example*].

Ejectment One of the old forms of action for recovery of the possession of real property.

Elder law A relatively new specialty devoted to the legal issues of senior citizens, including estate planning, health care, planning for incapacity or mental incompetence, the receipt of benefits, and employment discrimination.

Election of remedies The liberty of choosing (or the act of choosing) one out of several means afforded by law for the redress of an injury, or one out of several available forms of action. An *election of remedies* arises when one having two coexistent but inconsistent remedies chooses to exercise one, in which event she or he loses the right to thereafter exercise the other. Doctrine provides that if two or more remedies exist that are repugnant and inconsistent with one another, a party will be bound if he or she has chosen one of them.

Elections The processes of voting to decide a public question or to select one person from a designated group to perform certain obligations in a government, corporation, or society.

Elective share Statutory provision that a surviving spouse may choose between taking that which is provided in the will of the deceased spouse or taking a statutorily prescribed share of the estate. Such election may be presented if the will leaves the spouse less than he or she would otherwise receive by statute. This election may also be taken if the spouse seeks to set aside a will that contains a provision to the effect that an attempt to contest the will defeats the rights of one to take under the will.

Elector A voter who has fulfilled the qualifications imposed by law; a constituent; a selector of a public officer; a person who has the right to cast a ballot for the approval or rejection of a political proposal or question, such as the issuance of bonds by a state or municipality to finance public works projects.

A member of the electoral college—an association of voters elected by the populace of each state and the District of Columbia—which convenes every four years to select the president and vice president of the United States.

Electoral College Nominated persons, known as electors, from the states and the District of Columbia, who meet every four years in their home state or district and cast ballots to choose the president and vice president of the United States.

Electronic surveillance Observing or listening to persons, places, or activities—usually in a secretive or unobtrusive manner—with the aid of electronic devices such as cameras, microphones, tape recorders, or wire taps. Its objective when used in law enforcement is to gather evidence of a crime or to accumulate intelligence about suspected criminal activity. Corporations use electronic surveillance to maintain the security of their buildings and grounds or to gather information about competitors.

Element A material factor; a basic component.

Emancipation The act or process by which a person is liberated from the authority and control of another person.

Emancipation Proclamation A Civil War–era declaration, formally issued on January 1, 1863, by President Abraham Lincoln, that freed all slaves in territories still under Confederate control.

Embargo A proclamation or order of government, usually issued in time of war or threatened hostilities, prohibiting the departure of ships or goods from some or all ports until further order. Government order prohibiting commercial trade with individuals or businesses of other specified nations. Legal prohibition on commerce.

The temporary or permanent sequestration of the property of individuals for the purposes of a government, e.g., to obtain vessels for the transport of troops, the owners being reimbursed for this forced service.

Embargo Act A legislative measure enacted by Congress in 1807 at the behest of President Thomas Jefferson that banned trade between U.S. ports and foreign nations.

Embezzlement The fraudulent conversion of another's property by a person who is in a position of trust, such as an agent or employee.

Emblements Crops annually produced by the labor of a tenant. Corn, wheat, rye, potatoes, garden vegetables, and other crops that are produced annually, not spontaneously, but by labor and industry. The doctrine of emblements denotes the right of a tenant to take and carry away, after the tenancy has ended, such annual products of the land as have resulted from the tenant's care and labor.

Embracery The crime of attempting to influence a jury corruptly to one side or the other by promises, persuasions, entreaties, entertainments, and the like. The person guilty of it is called an *embraceor*. This is both a state and federal crime, and is commonly included under the offense of obstructing justice.

Emigration The act of moving from one country to another with intention not to return. It is to be distinguished from expatriation, which means the abandonment of one's country and renunciation of one's citizenship in it, while emigration denotes merely the removal of person and property to another country. Expatriation is usually the consequence of emigration. *Emigration* is also sometimes used in reference to the removal from one section to another of the same country.

Eminent domain The power to take private property for public use by a state, municipality, or private person or corporation authorized to exercise functions of public character, following the payment of just compensation to the owner of that property.

Emolument The profit arising from office, employment, or labor; that which is received as a compensation for services, or which is annexed to the possession of office as salary, fees, and perquisites. Any perquisite, advantage, profit, or gain arising from the possession of an office.

Employee Retirement Income Security Act The name of federal legislation, popularly abbreviated as ERISA (29 U.S.C.A. § 1001 et seq. [1974]), which regulates the financing, vesting, and administration of pension plans for workers in private business and industry.

Employers' liability acts State and federal laws that define or restrict the grounds under and the extent to which the owner of a business who hires workers can be held liable for damages arising from injuries to such workers that occur during the course of the work.

Employment at will	A common-law rule that an employment contract of indefinite duration can be terminated by either the employer or the employee at any time for any reason; also known as terminable at will.
Employment law	The body of law that governs the employer-employee relationship, including individual employment contracts, the application of tort and contract doctrines, and a large group of statutory regulation on issues such as the right to organize and negotiate collective bargaining agreements, protection from discrimination, wages and hours, and health and safety.
Enabling clause	The section of a constitution or statute that provides government officials with the power to put the constitution or statute into force and effect.
Enabling statute	A law that gives new or extended authority or powers, generally to a public official or to a corporation.
Enact	To establish by law; to perform or effect; to decree.
En banc	[*Latin, French. In the bench.*] Full bench. Refers to a session where the entire membership of the court will participate in the decision rather than the regular quorum. In other countries, it is common for a court to have more members than are usually necessary to hear an appeal. In the United States, the Circuit Courts of Appeal usually sit in panels of judges but for important cases may expand the bench to a larger number, when the judges are said to be sitting *en banc*. Similarly, only one of the judges of the U.S. Tax Court will typically hear and decide on a tax controversy. However, when the issues involved are unusually novel or of wide impact, the case will be heard and decided by the full court sitting *en banc*.
Encroachment	An illegal intrusion in a highway or navigable river, with or without obstruction. An encroachment upon a street or highway is a fixture, such as a wall or fence, which illegally intrudes into or invades the highway or encloses a portion of it, diminishing its width or area, but without closing it to public travel.
Encumber	To burden property by way of a charge that must be removed before ownership is free and clear.
Encumbrance	A burden, obstruction, or impediment on property that lessens its value or makes it less marketable. An encumbrance (also spelled incumbrance) is any right or interest that exists in someone other than the owner of an estate and that restricts or impairs the transfer of the estate or lowers its value. This might include an easement, a lien, a mortgage, a mechanic's lien, or accrued and unpaid taxes.
Endowment	A transfer, generally as a gift, of money or property to an institution for a particular purpose. The bestowal of money as a permanent fund, the income of which is to be used for the benefit of a charity, college, or other institution.
Enfeoffment	Complete surrender and transfer of all land ownership rights from one person to another. In old English law, an enfeoffment was a transfer of

property by which the new owner was given both the right to sell the land and the right to pass it on to heirs, evidenced by livery of seisin, a ceremony for transferring the possession of real property from one individual to another.

Enfranchisement The act of making free (as from slavery); giving a franchise or freedom to; investiture with privileges or capacities of freedom, or municipal or political liberty. Conferring the privilege of voting upon classes of persons who have not previously possessed such.

Engage To become involved with, do, or take part in something.

Engagement A binding, pledging, or coming together. A mutual pact, contract, or agreement.

English law The system of law that has developed in England from approximately 1066 to the present.

English-only laws Laws that seek to establish English as the official language of the United States.

Engross To print a final copy of a document. In archaic criminal law, engrossment was the process of forcing higher the price of a good by buying it up and creating a monopoly.

Engrossed bill A legislative proposal that has been prepared in a final form for its submission to a vote of the law-making body after it has undergone discussion and been approved by the appropriate committees.

Enhancement Increase in value; improvement.

Enjoin To direct, require, command, or admonish.

Enjoyment The exercise of a right; the possession and fruition of a right or privilege. Comfort, consolation, contentment, ease, happiness, pleasure, and satisfaction. Such includes the beneficial use, interest, and purpose to which property may be put, and implies right to profits and income therefrom.

Enoch Arden Doctrine The legal principles involved when a person leaves his or her spouse under such circumstances and for such a period of time as to make the other spouse believe that the first spouse is dead, with the result that the remaining spouse marries another, only to discover later the return of the first spouse. Generally, in most states, it is safer for the remaining spouse to secure a divorce before marrying again.

Enrolled bill The final copy of a bill or joint resolution that has passed both houses of a legislature and is ready for signature. In legislative practice, a bill that has been duly introduced, finally passed by both houses, signed by the proper officers of each, approved by the governor (or president), and filed by the secretary of state.

Entail To abridge, settle, or limit succession to real property. An estate whose succession is limited to certain people rather than being passed to all heirs.

Enter To form a constituent part; to become a part or partaker; to penetrate; share or mix with, as tin *enters* into the composition of pewter. To go or come into a place or condition; to make or effect an entrance; to cause to go into or be received into.

In the law of real property, to go upon land for the purpose of taking possession of it. In strict usage, the entering is preliminary to the taking possession but in common parlance the entry is now merged in the taking possession.

To place anything before a court, or upon or among the records, in a formal and regular manner, and usually in writing as in to *enter an appearance*, or to *enter a judgment*. In this sense the word is nearly equivalent to setting down formally in writing, in either a full or abridged form.

Entertainment law The areas of law governing professionals and businesses in the entertainment industry, particularly contracts and intellectual property; more particularly, certain legal traditions and aspects of these areas of law that are unique to the entertainment industry.

Entice To wrongfully solicit, persuade, procure, allure, attract, draw by blandishment, coax, or seduce. To lure, induce, tempt, incite, or persuade a person to do a thing. Enticement of a child is inviting, persuading, or attempting to persuade a child to enter any vehicle, building, room, or secluded place with intent to commit an unlawful sexual act upon or with the person of said child.

Entirety The whole, in contradistinction to a moiety or part only. When land is conveyed to husband and wife, they do not take by moieties, but both are seised of the entirety. Parceners, on the other hand, have not an entirety of interest, but each is properly entitled to the whole of a distinct moiety.

Entitlement An individual's right to receive a value or benefit provided by law.

Entity A real being; existence. An organization or being that possesses separate existence for tax purposes. Examples would be corporations, partnerships, estates, and trusts. The accounting entity for which accounting statements are prepared may not be the same as the entity defined by law.

Entity includes corporation and foreign corporation; not-for-profit corporation; profit and not-for-profit unincorporated association; business trust, estate, partnership, trust, and two or more persons having a joint or common economic interest; and state, U.S., and foreign governments.

An existence apart, such as a corporation in relation to its stockholders.

Entity includes person, estate, trust, governmental unit.

Entrapment The act of government agents or officials that induces a person to commit a crime he or she is not previously disposed to commit.

Entry The act of making or entering a record; a setting down in writing of particulars; or that which is entered; an item. Generally synonymous with *recording*.

Passage leading into a house or other building or to a room; a vestibule.

The act of a merchant, trader, or other businessperson in recording in his or her account books the facts and circumstances of a sale, loan, or other transaction. The books in which such memoranda are first (or originally) inscribed are called *books of original entry*, and are prima facie evidence for certain purposes.

In copyright law, depositing with the register of copyrights the printed title of a book, pamphlet, and so on, for the purpose of securing copyright on the same.

In immigration law, any coming of an alien into the United States, from a foreign part or place or from an outlying possession, whether voluntary or otherwise.

In criminal law, entry is the unlawful making of one's way into a dwelling or other house for the purpose of committing a crime therein. In cases of burglary, the least entry with the whole or any part of the body, hand, or foot, or with any instrument or weapon, introduced for the purpose of committing a felony, is sufficient to complete the offense.

In customs law, the entry of imported goods at the custom house consists in submitting them to the inspection of the revenue officers, together with a statement or description of such goods, and the original invoices of the same, for the purpose of estimating the duties to be paid thereon.

In real property law, the right or authority to assert one's possessory interest or ownership in a piece of land by going onto the land.

Entry of judgment Formally recording the result of a lawsuit that is based upon the determination by the court of the facts and applicable law, and that makes the result effective for purposes of bringing an action to enforce it or to commence an appeal.

Enumerated This term is often used in law as equivalent to *mentioned specifically, designated,* or *expressly named or granted*; as in speaking of enumerated governmental powers, items of property, or articles in a tariff schedule.

Environmental law An amalgam of state and federal statutes, regulations, and common-law principles covering air pollution, water pollution, hazardous waste, the wilderness, and endangered wildlife.

Equal protection The constitutional guarantee that no person or class of persons shall be denied the same protection of the laws that is enjoyed by other persons or other classes in like circumstances in their lives, liberty, property, and pursuit of happiness.

Equal Rights Amendment A proposed addition to the U.S. Constitution that read, "Equality of rights under the law shall not be denied or abridged by the United States or by any State on account of sex," and that failed to receive ratification by the required number of states.

Equity The pursuit of fairness. The money value of property in excess of claims, liens, or mortgages on the property. In the U.S. legal system, a body of law that seeks to achieve fairness on an individual basis.

Equity of redemption The right of a mortgagor, that is, a borrower who obtains a loan secured by a pledge of his or her real property, to prevent foreclosure proceedings by paying the amount due on the loan, a mortgage, plus interest and other expenses after having failed to pay within the time and according to the terms specified therein.

Ergo [*Latin, Therefore; hence; because.*]

Erratum [*Latin, Error.*] The term used in the Latin formula for the assignment of mistakes made in a case.

Error A mistake in a court proceeding concerning a matter of law or fact, which might provide a ground for a review of the judgment rendered in the proceeding.

Escalator clause A stipulation contained in a union contract stating that wages will be raised or lowered, based upon an external standard such as the cost of living index. A term, ordinarily in a contract or lease, that provides for an increase in the money to be paid under certain conditions.

Escape The criminal offense of fleeing legal custody without authority or consent.

Escheat The power of a state to acquire title to property for which there is no owner.

Escrow Something of value, such as a deed, stock, money, or written instrument, that is put into the custody of a third person by its owner, a grantor, an obligor, or a promisor, to be retained until the occurrence of a contingency or performance of a condition.

Espionage The act of securing information of a military or political nature that a competing nation holds secret. It can involve the analysis of diplomatic reports, publications, statistics, and broadcasts, as well as spying, a clandestine activity carried out by an individual or individuals working under a secret identity for the benefit of a nation's information gathering techniques. In the United States, the organization that heads most activities dedicated to espionage is the Central Intelligence Agency.

Esq. An abbreviation for esquire, which is a title used by attorneys in the United States. The term *esquire* has a different meaning in English law. It is used to signify a title of dignity, which ranks above *gentleman* and directly below *knight*.

Establish This word occurs frequently in the Constitution of the United States, and it is used there in different meanings: (1) to settle firmly, to fix unalterably; as in to establish justice, which is the avowed object of the Constitution; (2) to make or form; as in to establish uniform laws governing naturalization or bankruptcy; (3) to found, to create, to regulate; as in "Congress shall have power to establish post offices"; (4) to found, recognize, confirm, or admit; as in "Congress shall make no law respecting an establishment of religion"; and (5) to create, to ratify, or confirm, as in "We, the people . . . do ordain and establish this Constitution."

To settle, make, or fix firmly; place on a permanent footing; found; create; put beyond doubt or dispute; prove; convince. To enact permanently. To bring about or into existence.

Estate The degree, quantity, nature, and extent of interest that a person has in real and personal property. An estate in lands, tenements, and hereditaments signifies such interest as the tenant has therein. *Estate* is commonly used in conveyances in connection with the words *right*, *title*, and *interest*, and is, to a great degree, synonymous with all of them.

When used in connection with probate proceedings, the term encompasses the total property of whatever kind that is owned by a decedent prior to the distribution of that property in accordance with the terms of a will, or when there is no will, by the laws of inheritance in the state of domicile of the decedent. It means, ordinarily, the whole of the property owned by anyone, the realty as well as the personalty.

In its broadest sense, the social, civic, or political condition or standing of a person; or a class of persons considered as grouped for social, civic, or political purposes.

Estimated tax Federal and state tax laws require a quarterly payment of estimated taxes due from corporations, trusts, estates, non-wage employees, and wage employees with income not subject to withholding. Individuals must remit at least 100 percent of their prior year tax liability or 90 percent of their current year tax liability in order to avoid an underpayment penalty. Corporations must pay at least 90 percent of their current year tax liability in order to avoid an underpayment penalty. Additional taxes due, if any, are paid on taxpayer's annual tax return.

Estoppel A legal principle that precludes a party from denying or alleging a certain fact owing to that party's previous conduct, allegation, or denial.

Et al. An abbreviated form of *et alia*, Latin for "and others." When affixed after the name of a person, *et al.* indicates that additional persons are acting in the same manner, such as several plaintiffs or grantors.

Ethics The branch of philosophy that defines what is good for the individual and for society and establishes the nature of obligations, or duties, that people owe themselves and one another.

Et seq. An abbreviation for the Latin *et sequentes* or *et sequentia*, meaning "and the following."

Eviction The removal of a tenant from possession of premises in which he or she resides or has a property interest, done by a landlord either by reentry upon the premises or through a court action.

Evidence Any matter of fact that a party to a lawsuit offers to prove or disprove an issue in the case. A system of rules and standards used to determine which facts may be admitted, and to what extent a judge or jury may consider those facts, as proof of a particular issue in a lawsuit.

Examination A search, inspection, or interrogation.

In criminal procedure, the preliminary hearing held to decide whether a suspect arrested for a crime should be brought to trial.

In trial practice, the interrogation of a witness to elicit his or her testimony in a civil or criminal action, so that the facts he or she possesses are presented before the trial of fact for consideration.

In the law governing real property transactions, an investigation made into the history of the ownership of and conditions that exist upon land so that a purchaser can determine whether a seller is entitled to sell the land free and clear of any claims made by third persons.

In patent law, an inquiry made at the Patent and Trademark Office to determine the novelty and utility of an invention for which a patent application has been filed and whether the invention interferes with any other invention.

Examiner   An official or other person empowered by another—whether an individual, business, or government agency—to investigate and review specified documents for accuracy and truthfulness.

A court-appointed officer, such as a master or referee, who inspects evidence presented to resolve controverted matters and records statements made by witnesses in the particular proceeding pending before that court.

A government employee in the Patent and Trademark Office whose duty it is to scrutinize the application made for a patent by an inventor to determine whether the invention meets the statutory requirements of patentability.

A federal employee of the Internal Revenue Service who reviews income tax returns for accuracy and truthfulness.

Exception   The act of excepting or excluding from a number designated or from a description; that which is excepted or separated from others in a general rule or description; a person, thing, or case specified as distinct or not included; an act of excepting, omitting from mention, or leaving out of consideration. Express exclusion of something from operation of contract or deed. An *exception* operates to take something out of a thing granted that would otherwise pass or be included.

Objection to an order or ruling of a trial court. A formal objection to the action of the court, during the trial of a case, in refusing a request or overruling an objection; implying that the party excepting does not acquiesce in the decision of the court, but will seek to procure its reversal, and that he or she means to save the benefit of his or her request or objection in some future proceeding. Under rules practiced in the federal and most state courts, the need for claiming an exception to evidence or to a ruling to preserve appellate rights has been eliminated in favor of an objection.

Exchange   An association, organization, or group of persons, incorporated or unincorporated, that constitutes, maintains, or provides a marketplace or facilities for bringing together purchasers and sellers of securities or commodities futures.

Exchange of property   A transaction wherein parties trade goods, or commodities, for other goods, in contrast with a sale or trading of goods for money.

Excise　A tax imposed on the performance of an act, the engaging in an occupation, or the enjoyment of a privilege. A tax on the manufacture, sale, or use of goods or on the carrying on of an occupation or activity, or a tax on the transfer of property. In current usage the term has been extended to include various license fees and practically every internal revenue tax except the income tax (e.g., federal alcohol and tobacco excise taxes).

Exclusionary clause　A term in a sales contract that limits the remedies available to one or both parties to it in an action for breach of warranty, statements made as to the quality of the goods sold. A provision of an insurance contract that prohibits recovery pursuant to its terms if certain designated circumstances occur.

Exclusionary rule　The principle based on federal constitutional law that evidence illegally seized by law enforcement officers in violation of a suspect's right to be free from unreasonable searches and seizures cannot be used against the suspect in a criminal prosecution.

Exclusive　Pertaining to the subject alone, not including, admitting, or pertaining to any others. Sole. Shutting out; debarring from interference or participation; vested in one person alone. Apart from all others, without the admission of others to participation.

Exclusive agency　Grant to an agent of exclusive right to sell within a particular market or area. A contract to give an exclusive agency to deal with property is ordinarily interpreted as not precluding competition by the principal generally, but only as precluding him or her from appointing another agent to accomplish the result. The grant of an exclusive agency to sell, that is, the exclusive right to sell the products of a wholesaler in a specified territory, ordinarily is interpreted as precluding competition in any form within the designated area.

Exculpate　To clear or excuse from guilt.

Excuse　The explanation for the performance or nonperformance of a particular act; a reason alleged in court as a basis for exemption or relief from guilt.

Ex dividend　A phrase used by stockbrokers that denotes that a stock is sold without the purchaser receiving the right to own its recently declared dividend which has not yet been paid to the stockholders.

Execute　To complete; to make; to sign; to perform; to do; to carry out according to its terms; to fulfill the command or purpose of. To perform all necessary formalities, as to make and sign a contract, or sign and deliver a note.

Execution　The carrying out of some act or course of conduct to its completion. In criminal law, the carrying out of a death sentence (see also capital punishment).

　　The process whereby an official, usually a sheriff, is directed by an appropriate judicial writ to seize and sell as much of a debtor's nonexempt property as is necessary to satisfy a court's monetary judgment.

With respect to contracts, the performance of all acts necessary to render a contract complete as an instrument, which conveys the concept that nothing remains to be done to make a complete and effective contract.

Executive branch   The branch of the U.S. government that is composed of the president and all the individuals, agencies, and departments that report to the president, and that is responsible for administering and enforcing the laws that Congress passes.

Executive orders   Presidential policy directives that implement or interpret a federal statute, a constitutional provision, or a treaty.

Executive privilege   The right of the president of the United States to withhold information from Congress or the courts.

Executors and administrators   Those who are designated by the terms of a will or appointed by a court of probate to manage the assets and liabilities of the estate of the deceased.

Executory   That which is yet to be fully executed or performed; that which remains to be carried into operation or effect; incomplete; depending upon a future performance or event. The opposite of *executed*.

Exemplification   An official copy of a document from public records, made in a form to be used as evidence, and authenticated or certified as a true copy.

Exercise   To put into action, practice, or force; to make use of something, such as a right or option.

Exhaustion of remedies   The exhaustion-of-remedies doctrine requires that procedures established by statute, common law, contract, or custom must be initiated and followed in certain cases before an aggrieved party may seek relief from the courts. After all other available remedies have been exhausted, a lawsuit may be filed.

Exhibit   As a verb, to show or display; to offer or present for inspection. To produce anything in public, so that it may be taken into possession. To present, to offer publicly or officially. To administer; to cause to be taken, as medicines. To submit to a court or officer in the course of proceedings.

As a noun, a paper or document produced and exhibited to a court during a trial or hearing, or to a person taking depositions, or to auditors or arbitrators as a voucher, or in proof of facts, or as otherwise connected with the subject matter, and which, on being accepted, is marked for identification and annexed to the deposition, report, or other principal document, or filed of record, or otherwise made a part of the case.

A paper, document, chart, map, or the like, referred to and made a part of an affidavit, pleading, or brief. An item of physical, tangible evidence that is to be or has been offered to the court for inspection.

Ex officio   [*Latin, From office.*] By virtue of the characteristics inherent in the holding of a particular office without the need of specific authorization or appointment.

Exoneration   The removal of a burden, charge, responsibility, duty, or blame imposed by law. The right of a party who is secondarily liable for a debt, such as a surety, to be reimbursed by the party with primary liability for payment of an obligation that should have been paid by the first party.

Ex parte   [*Latin, On one side only.*] Done by, for, or on the application of one party alone.

Expatriation   The voluntary act of abandoning or renouncing one's country and becoming the citizen or subject of another.

Expectancy   A mere hope, based upon no direct provision, promise, or trust. An expectancy is the possibility of receiving a thing, rather than having a vested interest in it.

Expository statute   A law executed to explain the actual meaning and intent of a previously enacted statute.

Ex post facto laws   [*Latin, "After-the-fact" laws.*] Laws that provide for the infliction of punishment upon a person for some prior act that, at the time it was committed, was not illegal.

Express   Clear; definite; explicit; plain; direct; unmistakable; not dubious or ambiguous. Declared in terms; set forth in words. Directly and distinctly stated. Made known distinctly and explicitly, and not left to inference. Manifested by direct and appropriate language, as distinguished from that which is inferred from conduct. The word is usually contrasted with *implied*.

Expropriation   The taking of private property for public use or in the public interest. The taking of U.S. industry situated in a foreign country, by a foreign government.

Expunge   To destroy; blot out; obliterate; erase; efface designedly; strike out wholly. The act of physically destroying information—including criminal records—in files, computers, or other depositories.

Extension   An increase in the length of time specified in a contract.

A part constituting an addition or enlargement, as in an annex to a building or an extension to a house. Addition to existing facilities.

An allowance of additional time for the payment of debts. An agreement between a debtor and his or her creditors, by which they allow the debtor further time for the payment of liabilities. A creditor's indulgence by giving a debtor further time to pay an existing debt.

The word *extension*, when used in its proper and usual sense in connection with a lease, means a prolongation of the previous leasehold estate. The distinction between extension and *renewal* of lease is chiefly that, in the case of renewal, a new lease is requisite, while, in the case of extension, the same lease continues in force during an additional period upon performance of a stipulated act. An option for renewal implies giving a new lease on the same terms as those of an old lease, while an option for extension contemplates a continuance of an old lease for a further period.

Request for additional time to file an income tax return beyond the due date.

Extenuating circumstances   Facts surrounding the commission of a crime that work to mitigate or lessen it.

Extinguishment   The destruction or cancellation of a right, a power, a contract, or an estate.

Extort   To compel or coerce, as in a confession or information, by any means serving to overcome the other's power of resistance, thus making the confession or admission involuntary. To gain by wrongful methods; to obtain in an unlawful manner, as in to compel payments by means of threats of injury to person, property, or reputation. To exact something wrongfully by threatening or putting in fear. The natural meaning of the word *extort* is to obtain money or other valuable things by compulsion, by actual force, or by the force of motives applied to the will, and often more overpowering and irresistible than physical force.

Extortion   The obtaining of property from another induced by wrongful use of actual or threatened force, violence, or fear, or under color of official right.

Extra   [*Latin, Beyond, except, without, out of, outside.*] Additional.

Extradition   The transfer of an accused from one state or country to another state or country that seeks to place the accused on trial.

Extrajudicial   That which is done, given, or effected outside the course of regular judicial proceedings. Not founded upon, or unconnected with, the action of a court of law, as in extrajudicial evidence or an extrajudicial oath.

That which, though done in the course of regular judicial proceedings, is unnecessary to such proceedings, or interpolated, or beyond their scope, as in an extrajudicial opinion.

Extraordinary remedy   The designation given to such writs as habeas corpus, mandamus, and quo warranto, determined in special proceedings and granted only where absolutely necessary to protect the legal rights of a party in a particular case, as opposed to the customary relief obtained by the maintenance of an action.

Extraterritoriality   The operation of laws upon persons existing beyond the limits of the enacting state or nation but still amenable to its laws. Jurisdiction exercised by a nation in other countries by treaty, or by its own ministers or consuls in foreign lands.

Extremis   A description of the state of being ill beyond the hope of recovery, with death imminent.

Extrinsic evidence   Facts or information not embodied in a written agreement such as a will, trust, or contract.

Eyewitness   An individual who was present during an event and is called by a party in a lawsuit to testify as to what he or she observed.

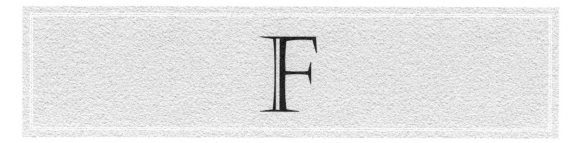

Face The external appearance or surface of anything; that which is readily observable by a spectator. The words contained in a document in their plain or obvious meaning without regard to external evidence or facts.

Face value A readily ascertainable amount of money determinable from the words of a written instrument alone without the aid of any other source.

Facsimile An exact replica of a document that is copied so as to preserve all its original marks and notations.

Fact Incident, act, event, or circumstance. A fact is something that has already been done or an action in process. It is an event that has definitely and actually taken place, and is distinguishable from a suspicion, innuendo, or supposition. A fact is a truth as opposed to fiction or mistake.

Factor An event, circumstance, influence, or element that plays a part in bringing about a result.

Factors People who are employed by others to sell or purchase goods, who are entrusted with possession of the goods, and who are compensated by either a commission or a fixed salary.

Fact situation A concise description of all the occurrences or circumstances of a particular case, without any discussion of their consequences under the law. The fact situation, sometimes referred to as a *fact pattern*, is a summary of what took place in a case for which relief is sought. The fact situation of one case is almost always distinguishable from that of another case.

Factum [*Latin, Fact, act, or deed.*] A fact in evidence, which is generally the central or primary fact upon which a controversy will be decided.

Failure of consideration As applied to contracts, this term does not necessarily mean a want of consideration, but implies that a consideration, originally existing and good, has since become worthless or has ceased to exist or been extinguished, partially or entirely. It means that sufficient consideration was contemplated by the parties at the time the contract was entered into, but either on account of some innate defect in the thing to be given, or nonperformance in whole or in part of that which the promisee agreed to do, nothing of value can be or is received by the promisee.

Failure of issue Dying without having any children or without surviving children.

Fair comment A form of qualified privilege applied to news media publications relating to discussion of matters that are of legitimate concern to the community as a whole because they materially affect the interests of all the community. A term used in the defense of libel actions, applying to statements made by a writer (e.g., in the news media) in an honest belief in their truth, relating to official acts, even though the statements are not true in fact. Fair comment must be based on facts truly stated, must not contain imputations of corrupt or dishonorable motives except as warranted by the facts, and must be an honest expression of the writer's real opinion.

Fair Credit Reporting Act Legislation embodied in title VI of the Consumer Credit Protection Act (15 U.S.C.A. § 1681 et seq. [1968]), which was enacted by Congress in 1970 to ensure that reporting activities relating to various consumer transactions are conducted in a manner that is fair to the affected individual, and to protect the consumer's right to privacy against the informational demands of a credit reporting company.

Fair hearing A judicial proceeding that is conducted in such a manner as to conform to fundamental concepts of justice and equality.

Fair Labor Standards Act Federal legislation enacted in 1938 by Congress, pursuant to its power under the Commerce Clause, that mandated a minimum wage and forty-hour work week for employees of those businesses engaged in interstate commerce.

Fair market value The amount for which real property or personal property would be sold in a voluntary transaction between a buyer and seller, neither of whom is under any obligation to buy or sell.

Fairness doctrine The doctrine that imposes affirmative responsibilities on a broadcaster to provide coverage of issues of public importance that is adequate and fairly reflects differing viewpoints. In fulfilling its fairness doctrine obligations, a broadcaster must provide free time for the presentation of opposing views if a paid sponsor is unavailable and must initiate programming on public issues if no one else seeks to do so.

Fair-trade laws State statutes enacted in the first half of the twentieth century permitting manufacturers to set minimum, maximum, or actual selling prices for their products, and thus to prevent retailers from selling products at very low prices.

False advertising "Any advertising or promotion that misrepresents the nature, characteristics, qualities or geographic origin of goods, services or commercial activities" (Lanham Act, 15 U.S.C.A. § 1125(a)).

False arrest A tort (a civil wrong) that consists of an unlawful restraint of an individual's personal liberty or freedom of movement by another purporting to act according to the law.

False demonstration An inaccurate or erroneous description of an individual or item in a written instrument.

False imprisonment	The illegal confinement of one individual against his or her will by another individual in such a manner as to violate the confined individual's right to be free from restraint of movement.
False personation	The crime of falsely assuming the identity of another to gain a benefit or avoid an expense.
False pretenses	False representations of past or present material facts, known by the wrongdoer to be false, made with the intent to defraud a victim into passing title in property to the wrongdoer.
Family car doctrine	A rule of law applied in particular cases of negligence that extends liability to the owner of an automobile for damage done by a family member while using the car.
Family law	Statutes, court decisions, and provisions of the federal and state constitutions that relate to family relationships, rights, duties, and finances.
Fatal	Deadly or mortal; destructive; devastating.
Fault	Neglect of care; an act to which blame or censure is attached. Fault implies any negligence, error, or defect of judgment.
Feasance	The performance of an act.
Federal	Relating to the general government or union of the states; based upon, or created pursuant to, the laws of the Constitution of the United States.
Federal Bank Act	A statute passed by Congress in 1791 that created the Bank of the United States as the central bank for the newly formed government.
Federal budget	An annual effort to balance federal spending on such things as forestry, education, space technology, and the national defense, with revenue, which the United States collects largely through federal taxes.
Federal courts	The U.S. judicial tribunals created by Article III of the Constitution, or by Congress, to hear and determine justiciable controversies.
Federalist Papers	A collection of eighty-five essays by Alexander Hamilton (1755–1804), James Madison (1751–1836), and John Jay (1745–1829) that explain the philosophy and defend the advantages of the U.S. Constitution.
Federal question	An issue directly involving the U.S. Constitution, federal statutes, or treaties between the United States and a foreign country.
Federal Register	A daily publication that makes available to the public the rules, regulations, and other legal notices issued by federal administrative agencies.
Federal Reporter®	A legal reference source primarily covering published decisions of federal appellate courts.

Federal Rules Decision® A reporter that reprints decisions rendered by federal district courts that interpret or apply the Federal Rules of Civil, Criminal, and Appellate Procedure and also the Federal Rules of Evidence.

Federal Supplement® A set of legal reference books containing decisions of federal courts in chronological order.

Federal Tort Claims Act A federal statute enacted in 1946 that removed the inherent immunity of the federal government from most tort actions brought against it and established the conditions for the commencement of such suits.

Federal Unemployment Compensation Act Legislation enacted by Congress to care for workers who in times of economic hardship and through no fault of their own lose their job and are unable to find new employment.

Federation A joining together of states or nations in a league or association; the league itself. An unincorporated association of persons for a common purpose.

Fee A compensation paid for particular acts, services, or labor, generally those that are performed in the line of official duties or a particular profession. An interest in land; an estate of inheritance.

Fee simple The greatest possible estate in land, wherein the owner has the right to use it, exclusively possess it, commit waste upon it, dispose of it by deed or will, and take its fruits. A fee simple represents absolute ownership of land, and therefore the owner may do whatever he or she chooses with the land. If an owner of a fee simple dies intestate, the land will descend to the heirs.

Fee tail An estate in land subject to a restriction regarding inheritance.

Fellatio A sexual act in which a male places his penis into the mouth of another person.

Fellow-servant rule A common-law rule governing job-related injuries that prevents employees from recovering damages from employers if an injury was caused by the negligence of a coworker.

Felon An individual who commits a crime of a serious nature, such as burglary or murder. A person who commits a felony.

Felonious Done with an intent to commit a serious crime or a felony; done with an evil heart or purpose; malicious; wicked; villainous.

Felony A serious crime, characterized under federal law and many state statutes as any offense punishable by death or imprisonment in excess of one year.

Felony-murder rule A rule of law that holds that if a killing occurs during the commission or attempted commission of a felony (a major crime), the person or persons responsible for the felony can be charged with murder.

Feminist jurisprudence	A philosophy of law based on the political, economic, and social equality of the sexes.
Fences	Enclosures composed of any substance that will present an adequate blockade around a field, yard, or other such expanse of land for the purpose of prohibiting intrusions from outside.
Feoffment	Total relinquishment and transfer of all rights of ownership in land from one individual to another.
Ferae naturae	[*Latin, Of a wild nature or disposition.*]
Feres doctrine	A doctrine that bars claims against the federal government by members of the armed forces and their families for injuries arising from or in the course of activity incident to military service.
Ferry	A specially constructed vessel to bring passengers and property across rivers and other bodies of water from one shoreline to another, making contact with a thoroughfare at each terminus. The landing place for a boat. A right or privilege to maintain a vessel upon a body of water in order to transport people and their vehicles across it in exchange for payment of a reasonable toll.
Fetal rights	The rights of any unborn human fetus, which is generally a developing human from roughly eight weeks after conception to birth.
Fetal tissue research	Scientific experimentation performed upon or using tissue taken from human fetuses.
Feudalism	A series of contractual relationships between the upper classes, designed to maintain control over land.
Fiat	[*Latin, Let it be done.*] In old English practice, a short order or warrant of a judge or magistrate directing some act to be done; an authority issuing from some competent source for the doing of some legal act.
	One of the proceedings in the English bankruptcy practice: a power, signed by the lord chancellor and addressed to the court of bankruptcy, authorizing the petitioning creditor to prosecute his complaint before that court. By the statute 12 & 13 Vict., c. 116, fiats were abolished.
	Arbitrary or authoritative order or decision.
F.I.C.A.	An abbreviation for the Federal Insurance Contributions Act (26 U.S.C.A. § 3101 et seq. [1954]), which established the Social Security tax on income received in the form of wages from employment.
Fiction	An assumption made by a court and embodied in various legal doctrines that a fact or concept is true when in actuality it is not true, or when it is likely to be equally false and true.
Fictitious	Based upon a fabrication or pretense.

Fidelity bond   An insurance device in the form of a personal guaranty that protects against loss resulting from disreputable or disloyal employees or other individuals who possess positions of confidence.

Fidelity insurance   An agreement whereby, for a designated sum of money, one party agrees to guarantee the loyalty and honesty of an agent, officer, or employee of an employer by promising to compensate the employer for losses incurred as a result of the disloyalty or dishonesty of such individuals.

Fiduciary   An individual in whom another has placed the utmost trust and confidence to manage and protect property or money. The relationship wherein one person has an obligation to act for another's benefit.

Field audit   A systematic investigation by the Internal Revenue Service of a taxpayer's financial records and his or her tax return that is conducted at the taxpayer's place of business or at the office of the individual who prepared the return.

Field Code of New York   The first code of civil procedure that established simplified rules for pleading an action before a court, which was proposed by David Dudley Field in 1848 for the state of New York and enacted by the state legislature.

Fieri facias   [*Latin, Cause (it) to be done.*] The name of a writ of execution that directs a sheriff to seize and sell the goods and chattels of a judgment debtor in order to satisfy the judgment against the debtor.

FIFO   An abbreviation for first-in, first-out, a method employed in accounting for the identification and valuation of the inventory of a business.

File   A record of the court. A paper is said to be filed when it is delivered to the proper officer to be kept on file as a matter of record and reference. But in general the terms *file* and *the files* are used loosely to denote the official custody of the court or the place in the offices of a court where the records and papers are kept. The file in a case includes the original complaint and all pleadings and papers belonging thereto.

Filiation proceeding   A process whereby a court determines the paternity of an illegitimate child in order to establish the father's duty to provide support for the child.

Filibuster   A tactic used by a legislative representative to hinder and delay consideration of and action to be taken on a proposed bill through prolonged, irrelevant, and procrastinating speeches on the floor of the House, Senate, or other legislative body.

Filius nullius   [*Latin, A son of nobody.*] An illegitimate child who had few legal rights under the common law.

Final decision   The resolution of a controversy by a court or series of courts from which no appeal may be taken and that precludes further action. The last act by a lower court that is required for the completion of a lawsuit, such as the handing down of a final judgment upon which an appeal to a higher court may be brought.

Finance charge
The amount owed to a lender by a purchaser-debtor to be allowed to pay for goods purchased over a series of installments, as opposed to one lump sum at the time of the sale or billing.

Financial responsibility acts
State statutes that require owners of motor vehicles to produce proof of financial accountability as a condition to acquiring a license and registration so that judgments rendered against them arising out of the operation of the vehicles may be satisfied.

Financial statement
Any report summarizing the financial condition or financial results of a person or an organization on any date or for any period. Financial statements include the balance sheet and the income statement and sometimes the statement of changes in financial position.

Finder
An intermediary who contracts to find, introduce, and bring together parties to a business opportunity, leaving ultimate negotiations and consummation of business transaction to the principals. With respect to a securities issue, refers to one who brings together an issuer and an underwriter; in connection with mergers, refers to one who brings two companies together. May also refer to one who secures mortgage financing for a borrower, locates a particular type of executive or professional for a corporation, or locates a particular type of business acquisition for a corporation.

Finding
The result of the deliberations of a jury or a court. A decision upon a question of fact reached as the result of a judicial examination or investigation by a court, jury, referee, coroner, etc. A recital of the facts as found. The word commonly applies to the result reached by a judge or jury.

Finding lost goods
The discovery of personal property that has been unintentionally removed from its owner's possession through his or her neglect or inadvertence.

Fines
Monetary charges imposed upon individuals who have been convicted of a crime or a lesser offense.

Fingerprints
Impressions or reproductions of the distinctive pattern of lines and grooves on the skin of human fingertips.

Fire
The primary result of combustion. The juridical meaning does not differ from the vernacular meaning.

Fire statute
In admiralty law, a federal law that exempts the owner of a vessel from liability to any person for loss of, or damage to, merchandise shipped, taken in, or put on board such vessel as a result of a fire, unless the fire was intentionally or negligently caused by the owner.

Firm offer
A definite and binding proposal, in writing, to enter into a contractual agreement.

First impression The initial presentation to, or examination by, a court of a particular question of law.

First instance The initial trial court where an action is brought.

Fiscal Relating to finance or financial matters, such as money, taxes, or public or private revenues.

Fishing trip Using the courts to find out information beyond the fair scope of the lawsuit. The loose, vague, unfocused questioning of a witness or the overly broad use of the discovery process. Discovery sought on general, loose, and vague allegations, or on suspicion, surmise, or vague guesses. The scope of discovery may be restricted by protective orders as provided for by the Federal Rules of Civil Procedure.

Fixed asset Property, such as machinery or buildings, utilized in a business that will not be used or liquidated during the current fiscal period.

Fixed charges Costs that do not vary with changes in output and would continue even if a firm produced no output at all, such as most management expenses, interests on bonded debt, depreciation, property taxes, and other irreducible overhead.

Fixture An article in the nature of personal property which has been so annexed to the realty that it is regarded as a part of the real property. That which is fixed or attached to something permanently as an appendage and is not removable.

A thing is deemed to be affixed to real property when it is attached to it by roots, imbedded in it, permanently resting upon it, or permanently attached to what is thus permanent, as by means of cement, plaster, nails, bolts, or screws.

Goods are fixtures when they become so related to particular real estate that an interest in them arises under real estate law, e.g., a furnace affixed to a house or other building, counters permanently affixed to the floor of a store, or a sprinkler system installed in a building.

Fixtures possess the attributes of both real and personal property.

Flag The official banner of a state or nation, often decorated with emblems or images that symbolize that state or nation.

Flagrante delicto [*Latin, In the act of perpetrating the crime.*]

Floating capital Funds retained for the purpose of paying current expenses as opposed to fixed assets.

Floating lien A security interest retained in collateral even when the collateral changes in character, classification, or location. An inventory loan in which the lender receives a security interest or general claim on all of a company's inventory. A security interest under which the borrower pledges security for present and future advances.

Flotsam   A name for the goods that float upon the sea when cast overboard for the safety of the ship or when a ship is sunk. Distinguished from jetsam (goods deliberately thrown over to lighten ship) and ligan (goods cast into the sea attached to a buoy).

F.O.B.   An abbreviation for free on board, which means that a vendor or consignor will deliver goods on a railroad car, truck, vessel, or other conveyance without any expense to the purchaser or consignee.

Follow   To conform to, comply with, or be fixed or determined by; as in the expression *costs follow the event of the suit*. To go, proceed, or come after. To seek to obtain; to accept as authority, as in adhering to precedent.

Forbearance   Refraining from doing something that one has a legal right to do. Giving of further time for repayment of an obligation or agreement; not to enforce claim at its due date. A delay in enforcing a legal right. Act by which creditor waits for payment of debt due by a debtor after it becomes due.

Within usury law, the contractual obligation of a lender or creditor to refrain, during a given period of time, from requiring the borrower or debtor to repay the loan or debt then due and payable.

Force   Power, violence, compulsion, or constraint exerted upon or against a person or thing. Power dynamically considered, that is, in motion or in action; constraining power, compulsion; strength directed to an end. Commonly the word occurs in such connections as to show that unlawful or wrongful action is meant, e.g., forcible entry.

Power statically considered, that is, at rest, or latent, but capable of being called into activity upon occasion for its exercise. Efficacy; legal validity. This is the meaning when we say that a statute or a contract is in force.

Forced sale   An involuntary transaction that occurs in the form and at the time specified by law for the purpose of applying the proceeds to satisfy debts, such as a mortgage or a tax lien, incurred by the owner of the property.

Force majeure   [*French, A superior or irresistible power.*] An event that is a result of the elements of nature, as opposed to one caused by human behavior.

Forcible detainer   A summary and expeditious statutory remedy used by a party entitled to actual possession of premises to secure its possession, where the occupant initially in lawful possession of it refuses to relinquish it when his or her right to possession ends.

Forcible entry and detainer   A summary proceeding to recover possession of land that is instituted by one who has been wrongfully ousted from, or deprived of, possession.

Foreclosure   A procedure by which the holder of a mortgage—an interest in land providing security for the performance of a duty or the payment of a debt—sells the property upon the failure of the debtor to pay the mortgage debt and, thereby, terminates his or her rights in the property.

Foreign   That which belongs to, or operates in accordance with, another nation, territory, state, or jurisdiction, as in the case of nonresident trustees, corporations, or persons.

Forensic   Belonging to courts of justice.

Forensic science   The application of scientific knowledge and methodology to legal problems and criminal investigations.

Foreseeability   The facility to perceive, know in advance, or reasonably anticipate that damage or injury will probably ensue from acts or omissions.

Forfeit   To lose to another person or to the state some privilege, right, or property due to the commission of an error, an offense, or a crime, a breach of contract, or a neglect of duty; to subject property to confiscation; or to become liable for the payment of a penalty, as the result of a particular act. To lose a franchise, estate, or other property, as provided by the applicable law, due to negligence, misfeasance, or omission.

Forfeiture   The involuntary relinquishment of money or property without compensation as a consequence of a breach or nonperformance of some legal obligation or the commission of a crime. The loss of a corporate charter or franchise as a result of illegality, malfeasance, or nonfeasance. The surrender by an owner of her or his entire interest in real property mandated by law as a punishment for illegal conduct or negligence. In old English law, the release of land by a tenant to the tenant's lord due to some breach of conduct, or the loss of goods or chattels (articles of personal property) assessed as a penalty against the perpetrator of some crime or offense and as a recompense to the injured party.

Forgery   The creation of a false written document or alteration of a genuine one, with the intent to defraud.

Form   A prototype of an instrument to be employed in a legal transaction or a judicial proceeding that includes the primary essential matters, the appropriate technical phrases or terms, and any additional material required to render it officially accurate, arranged in suitable and systematic order, and conducive to adaptation to the circumstances of the particular case.

Formal party   A person who has no interest in the dispute between the immediate litigants but has an interest in the subject matter that can be expeditiously settled in the current proceedings and thereby prevent additional litigation.

Formed design   In criminal law, and especially in regard to homicide, the killing of one human being by the instigation, act, or omission of another, who has a deliberate and fixed intention to kill, whether or not directed against a certain person.

Forms of action   The old common-law patterns for different kinds of lawsuits.

Fornication   Sexual intercourse between a man and a woman who are not married to each other.

Forswear   In criminal law, to make oath to that which the deponent knows to be untrue. This term is wider in its scope than perjury, for the latter, as a technical term, includes the idea of the oath being taken before a competent court or officer and relating to a material issue, which is not implied by the word *forswear.*

Forthwith   Immediately; promptly; without delay; directly; within a reasonable time under the circumstances of the case.

Forum   A court of justice where disputes are heard and decided; a judicial tribune that hears and decides disputes; a place of jurisdiction where remedies afforded by the law are pursued.

Forwarding fee   A payment of money made by one attorney who receives a client to another attorney who referred the client.

Foundation   A permanent fund established and maintained by contributions for charitable, educational, religious, research, or other benevolent purposes. An institution or association given to rendering financial aid to colleges, schools, hospitals, and charities and generally supported by gifts for such purposes.

The founding or building of a college or hospital. The incorporation or endowment of a college or hospital is the foundation, and those who endow it with land or other property are the founders.

Preliminary questions to a witness to establish admissibility of evidence. Laying a foundation is a prerequisite to the admission of evidence at trial. It is established by testimony that identifies the evidence sought to be admitted and connects it with the issue in question.

Four corners   The document itself; the face of a written instrument.

Franchise   A special privilege to do certain things that is conferred by government on an individual or a corporation and which does not belong to citizens generally of common right, e.g., a right granted to offer cable television service.

A privilege granted or sold, such as to use a name or to sell products or services. In its simplest terms, a franchise is a license from the owner of a trademark or trade name permitting another to sell a product or service under that name or mark. More broadly stated, a franchise has evolved into an elaborate agreement under which the franchisee undertakes to conduct a business or sell a product or service in accordance with methods and procedures prescribed by the franchisor, and the franchisor undertakes to assist the franchisee through advertising, promotion, and other advisory services.

The right of suffrage; the right or privilege of voting in public elections. Such right is guaranteed by the Fifteenth, Nineteenth, and Twenty-fourth Amendments to the U.S. Constitution.

As granted by a professional sports association, franchise is a privilege to field a team in a given geographic area under the auspices of the league that issues it. It is merely an incorporeal right.

Fraud A false representation of a matter of fact—whether by words or by conduct, by false or misleading allegations, or by concealment of what should have been disclosed—that deceives and is intended to deceive another so that the individual will act upon it to her or his legal injury.

Fraudulent The description of a willful act commenced with the specific intent to deceive or cheat, in order to cause some financial detriment to another and to engender personal financial gain.

Fraudulent conveyance A transfer of property that is made to swindle, hinder, or delay a creditor, or to put such property beyond his or her reach.

Freedom of association The right to associate with others for the purpose of engaging in constitutionally protected activities.

Freedom of Information Act A federal law (5 U.S.C.A. § 552 et seq.) providing for the disclosure of information held by administrative agencies to the public, unless the documents requested fall into one of the specific exemptions set forth in the statute.

Freedom of speech The right, guaranteed by the First Amendment to the U.S. Constitution, to express beliefs and ideas without unwarranted government restriction.

Freedom of the press The right, guaranteed by the First Amendment to the U.S. Constitution, to gather, publish, and distribute information and ideas without government restriction; this right encompasses freedom from prior restraints on publication and freedom from censorship.

Freehold A life estate, an interest in land the duration of which is restricted to the life or lives of a particular person or persons holding it, or an estate in fee, an interest in property that is unconditional and represents the broadest ownership interest recognized by law.

Freight The price or compensation paid for the transportation of goods by a carrier. *Freight* is also applied to the goods transported by such carriers.

Freight forwarder An individual who, as a regular business, assembles and combines small shipments into one lot and takes the responsibility for the transportation of such property from the place of receipt to the place of destination.

Friendly fire Fire burning in a place where it was intended to burn, although damages may result. In a military conflict, the discharge of weapons against one's own troops.

Friendly suit A lawsuit brought by an executor or administrator of the estate of a deceased person in the name of a creditor as if that creditor had initiated the action. The executor or administrator brings the suit against himself or herself in order to compel the creditors to take an equal distribution of the assets of the estate. An action brought by parties who agree to submit some doubtful question to the court in order to obtain an opinion on that issue.

Friend of the court
A person who has a strong interest in a matter that is the subject of a lawsuit in which he or she is not a party.

Frisk
A term used in criminal law to refer to the superficial running of the hands over the body of an individual by a law enforcement agent or official in order to determine whether such individual is holding an illegal object, such as a weapon or narcotics.

Frivolous
Of minimal importance; legally worthless.

Frolic
Activities performed by an employee during working hours that are not considered to be in the course of his or her employment, since they are for the employee's personal purposes only.

Fruit of the poisonous tree
The principle that proscribes the use of evidence directly derived from an illegal search and seizure.

Frustration
In the law of contracts, the destruction of the value of the performance that has been bargained for by the promisor as a result of a supervening event.

Fugitive from justice
An individual who, after having committed a criminal offense, leaves the jurisdiction of the court where such crime has taken place or hides within such jurisdiction to escape prosecution.

Fugitive Slave Act of 1850
Federal legislation enacted by Congress that mandated that states to which escaped slaves fled were obligated to return them to their masters upon their discovery and subjected persons who helped runaway slaves to criminal sanctions.

Full Faith and Credit Clause
The clause of the U.S. Constitution that provides that the various states must recognize legislative acts, public records, and judicial decisions of the other states within the United States.

Fund
A comprehensive term for any money that is set aside for a particular purpose or that is accessible for the satisfaction of debts or claims.

Fundamental law
The constitution of a state or nation; the basic law and principles contained in federal and state constitutions that direct and regulate the manner in which government is exercised.

Fungible
A description applied to items of which each unit is identical to every other unit, such as in the case of grain, oil, or flour.

Future acquired property
Property that is received or obtained by a borrower subsequent to the date that he or she executes a loan agreement which offers property currently owned as collateral.

Future earnings   Earnings that, if it had not been for an injury, could have been made in the future, but which were lost as result of the injury.

Futures   Contracts that promise to purchase or sell standard commodities at a forthcoming date and at a fixed price.

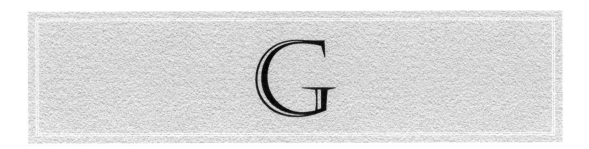

Gag order   A court order to gag or bind an unruly defendant or remove her or him from the courtroom in order to prevent further interruptions in a trial. In a trial with a great deal of notoriety, a court order directed to attorneys and witnesses not to discuss the case with the media—such order being felt necessary to assure the defendant of a fair trial. A court order, directed to the media, not to report certain aspects of a crime or criminal investigation prior to trial.

Gag rule   A rule, regulation, or law that prohibits debate or discussion of a particular issue.

Game   Wild birds and beasts. The word includes all game birds and game animals.

Gaming   The act or practice of gambling; an agreement between two or more individuals to play collectively at a game of chance for a stake or wager, which will become the property of the winner and to which all involved make a contribution.

Garnishee   An individual who holds money or property that belongs to a debtor subject to an attachment proceeding by a creditor.

Garnishment   A legal procedure by which a creditor can collect what a debtor owes by reaching the debtor's property when it is in the hands of someone other than the debtor.

Gay and lesbian rights   The goal of full legal and social equality for gay men and lesbians sought by the gay movement in the United States and other Western countries.

General appearance   The act by which a defendant completely consents to the jurisdiction of the court by appearing before it either in person or through an authorized representative thereby waiving any jurisdictional defects that might be raised except for that of the competency of the court.

General creditor   An individual to whom money is due from a debtor, but whose debt is not secured by property of the debtor. One to whom property has not been pledged to satisfy a debt in the event of nonpayment by the individual owing the money.

General execution   A court order commanding a public official, such as a sheriff, to take the personal property of a defendant to satisfy the amount of a judgment awarded against such defendant.

General intent   In criminal law and tort law, a mental plan to do that which is forbidden by the law.

General jurisdiction   The legal authority of a court to entertain whatever type of case comes up within the geographical area over which its power extends.

General legacy   A monetary gift, payable out of the collective assets of the estate of a testator—one who makes a will—and not from a designated source.

General term   A sitting of the court en banc, with the participation of the entire membership of the court rather than the regular quorum. A phrase used in some jurisdictions to signify the ordinary session of a court during which the trial determination of actions occur.

General verdict   A decision by a jury that determines which side in a particular controversy wins, and in some cases, the amount of money in damages to be awarded.

General welfare   The concern of the government for the health, peace, morality, and safety of its citizens.

Genetic engineering   The human manipulation of the genetic material of a cell.

Genetic screening   The scientific procedure of examining genetic makeup to determine if an individual possesses genetic traits that indicate a tendency toward acquiring or carrying certain diseases.

Genocide   The crime of destroying or conspiring to destroy a national, ethnic, racial, or religious group.

Gerrymander   The process of dividing a particular state or territory into election districts in such a manner as to accomplish an unlawful purpose, such as to give one party a greater advantage.

GI Bill   Federal legislation that created a comprehensive package of benefits, including financial assistance for higher education, for veterans of U.S. military service.

Gift   A present voluntary transfer of property or of a property interest from one individual to another, made gratuitously to the recipient.

Gifts to Minors Act   A law that has been enacted in every state (with only minor variations) that facilitates the management of money given to infants.

Glass-Steagall Act   Legislation passed by Congress in 1933 that prohibits commercial banks from engaging in the investment business.

Gloss An annotation, explanation, or commentary on a particular passage in a book or document, which is ordinarily placed on the same page or in the margin to elucidate or amplify the passage.

Going concern value The value inherent in an active, established company as opposed to a firm that is not yet established.

The value of the assets of a business considered as an operating whole.

Going public Altering the organization of a corporation from ownership and control by a small group of people, as in a close corporation, to ownership by the general public, as in a publicly held corporation.

Golden parachute An agreement that provides key executives with generous severance pay and other benefits in the event that their employment is terminated as a result of a change of ownership at their employer corporation; known more formally as a change-of-control agreement.

Good behavior Orderly and lawful action; conduct that is deemed proper for a peaceful and law-abiding individual.

Good cause Legally adequate or substantial grounds or reason to take a certain action.

Good faith Honesty; a sincere intention to deal fairly with others.

Goods Items; chattels; things; any personal property.

Good Samaritan Doctrine A principle of tort law that provides that a person who sees another individual in imminent and serious danger or peril cannot be charged with negligence if that first person attempts to aid or rescue the injured party, provided the attempt is not made recklessly.

Good will The favorable reputation and clientele of an established and well-run business.

Government instrumentality doctrine A rule that provides that any organization run by a branch of the government is immune from taxation.

Grab law State statutory provisions and common-law principles that govern the aggressive use of legal and equitable remedies, such as attachment and garnishment, by creditors to collect payment from debtors.

Grace period In insurance law, a period beyond the due date of a premium (usually thirty or thirty-one days) during which the insurance is continued in force and during which the payment may be made to keep the policy in good standing. The grace period for payment of the premium does not provide free insurance or operate to continue the policy in force after it expires by agreement of the parties. *Grace period* may also refer to a period of time provided for in a loan agreement during which default will not occur even though a payment is overdue.

Graduated tax Tax structured so that the rate increases as the amount of income of taxpayer increases.

Graft	A colloquial term referring to the unlawful acquisition of public money through questionable and improper transactions with public officials.
Grandfather clause	A portion of a statute that provides that the law is not applicable in certain circumstances due to preexisting facts.
Grand jury	A panel of citizens that is convened by a court to decide whether it is appropriate for the government to indict (proceed with a prosecution against) someone suspected of a crime.
Grand larceny	A category of larceny—the offense of illegally taking the property of another—in which the value of the property taken is greater than that set for petit larceny.
Grant	To confer, give, or bestow. A gift of legal rights or privileges, or a recognition of asserted rights, as in treaty.
Grantee	An individual to whom a transfer or conveyance of property is made.
Granting clause	The portion of an instrument of conveyance, such as a deed, containing the words that transfer a present interest from the grantor to the grantee.
Grantor	An individual who conveys or transfers ownership of property.
Grantor-grantee index	A master reference book, ordinarily kept in the office of official records of a particular county, which lists all recorded deeds as evidence of ownership of real property.
Gratuitous	Bestowed or granted without consideration or exchange for something of value.
Gratuitous licensee	An individual who is permitted, although not invited, to enter another individual's property and who provides no consideration in exchange for such permission.
Gravamen	The basis or essence of a grievance; the issue upon which a particular controversy turns.
Green card	The popular name for the Alien Registration Receipt Card issued to all immigrants entering the United States on a non-temporary visa who have registered with and been fingerprinted by the Immigration and Naturalization Service. The name *green card* comes from the distinctive coloration of the card.
Greenmail	A corporation's attempt to stop a takeover bid by paying a price above market value for stock held by the aggressor.
Grievance procedure	A term used in labor law to describe an orderly, established way of dealing with problems between employers and employees.
Gross	Great; culpable; general; absolute. A thing *in gross* exists in its own right, and not as an appendage to another thing. Before or without

diminution or deduction. Whole; entire; total; as in the gross sum, amount, weight—as opposed to net. Not adjusted or reduced by deductions or subtractions.

Out of all measure; beyond allowance; flagrant; shameful; as a gross dereliction of duty, a gross injustice, gross carelessness or negligence. Such conduct as is not to be excused.

Gross estate   All the real and personal property owned by a decedent at the time of his or her death.

Gross income   The financial gains received by an individual or a business during a fiscal year.

Gross negligence   An indifference to, and a blatant violation of, a legal duty with respect to the rights of others.

Ground rent   Perpetual consideration paid for the use and occupation of real property to the individual who has transferred such property, and subsequently to his or her descendants or someone to whom the interest is conveyed.

Grounds   The basis or foundation; reasons sufficient in law to justify relief.

Group legal services   Legal services provided under a plan to members, who may be employees of the same company, members of the same organization, or individual consumers.

Guarantee   One to whom a guaranty is made. This word is also used, as a noun, to denote the contract of guaranty or the obligation of a guarantor, and, as a verb, to denote the action of assuming the responsibilities of a guarantor.

Guaranty   As a verb, to agree to be responsible for the payment of another's debt or the performance of another's duty, liability, or obligation if that person does not perform as he or she is legally obligated to do; to assume the responsibility of a guarantor; to warrant.

As a noun, an undertaking or promise that is collateral to the primary or principal obligation and that binds the guarantor to performance in the event of nonperformance by the principal obligor.

Guaranty clause   A provision contained in a written document, such as a contract, deed, or mortgage, whereby one individual undertakes to pay the obligation of another individual.

The stipulation contained in Article IV, Section 4, of the U.S. Constitution, in which the federal government promises a republican form of government to every state and the defense and protection of the federal government if domestic violence occurs.

Guardian   A person lawfully invested with the power, and charged with the obligation, of taking care of and managing the property and rights of a person who, because of age, understanding, or self-control, is considered incapable of administering his or her own affairs.

Guardian ad litem   A guardian appointed by the court to represent the interests of infants, the unborn, or incompetent persons in legal actions.

Guardian and ward The legal relationship that exists between a person (the guardian) appointed by a court to take care of and manage the property of a person (the ward) who does not possess the legal capacity to do so, by reason of age, comprehension, or self-control.

Guilty Blameworthy; culpable; having committed a tort or crime; devoid of innocence.

Gun control Government regulation of the manufacture, sale, and possession of firearms.

Habeas corpus [*Latin, You have the body.*] A writ (court order) that commands an individual or a government official who has restrained another to produce the prisoner at a designated time and place so that the court can determine the legality of custody and decide whether to order the prisoner's release.

Habeas Corpus Act An English statute enacted in 1679 during the reign of King Charles II and subsequently amended and supplemented by enactments of Parliament that permitted, in certain cases, a person to challenge the legality of his or her imprisonment before a court that ordered the person to appear before it at a designated time so that it could render its decision.

Habendum clause The portion of a deed to real property that begins with the phrase *To have and to hold* and that provides a description of the ownership rights of the transferee of such property.

Habitability Fitness for occupancy. The requirement that rented premises, such as a house or apartment, be reasonably fit to occupy.

Habitual Regular or customary; usual.

Hague Tribunal An arbitration court established for the purpose of facilitating immediate recourse for the settlement of international disputes.

Harbor As a noun, a haven, or a space of deep water so sheltered by the adjacent land and surroundings as to afford a safe anchorage for ships.

As a verb, to afford lodging to, to shelter, or to give a refuge to. To clandestinely shelter, succor, and protect improperly admitted aliens. It may be aptly used to describe the furnishing of shelter, lodging, or food clandestinely or with concealment, and under certain circumstances may be equally applicable to those acts divested of any accompanying secrecy. Harboring a criminal is a crime under both federal and state statutes and a person who harbors a criminal is an accessory after the fact.

Hate crime A crime motivated by racial, religious, gender, sexual orientation, or other prejudice.

Have and hold The opening words, or habendum clause, found in a deed to real property, which describes the ownership rights of the individual to whom such property is being conveyed.

Hawkers and peddlers A *hawker* is an individual who sells wares by carrying them through the streets. The person's ordinary methods of attracting attention include addressing the public, using placards, labels, and signs, or displaying merchandise in a public place. A *peddler* is defined as a retail dealer who brings goods from place to place, exhibiting them for sale. The terms are frequently defined in state statutes or city ordinances and are often used interchangeably.

H.B. An abbreviation for a *house bill*, a proposed law brought before the House of Representatives, as opposed to the Senate.

Headnote A brief summary of a legal rule or a significant fact in a case that, among other headnotes that apply to the case, precedes the full text opinion printed in the reports or reporters. A syllabus to a reported case that summarizes the points decided in the case and is placed before the text of the opinion.

Head of household An individual in one family setting who provides actual support and maintenance to one or more individuals who are related to him or her through adoption, blood, or marriage.

Hearing A legal proceeding where an issue of law or fact is tried and evidence is presented to help determine the issue.

Hearing examiner An employee of an administrative agency who is charged with conducting adjudicative proceedings on matters within the scope of the jurisdiction of the agency.

Hearsay A statement made out of court that is offered in court as evidence to prove the truth of the matter asserted.

Heart balm acts Statutes that abrogate or restrict lawsuits brought by individuals who seek pecuniary damages to salve their broken hearts.

Heat of passion A phrase used in criminal law to describe an intensely emotional state of mind induced by a type of provocation that would cause a reasonable person to act on impulse or without reflection.

Heir An individual who receives an interest in, or ownership of, land, tenements, or hereditaments from an ancestor who has died intestate, through the laws of descent and distribution. At common law, an heir was the individual appointed by law to succeed to the estate of an ancestor who died without a will. It is commonly used today in reference to any individual who succeeds to property, either by will or law.

Held   In relation to the opinion of a court, decided.

Henceforth   From this time forward.

Hereafter   In the future.

Hereditament   Anything that can be passed by an individual to heirs.

Hierarchy   A group of people who form an ascending chain of power or authority.

High crimes and misdemeanors   The offenses for which presidents, vice presidents, and all civil officers, including federal judges, can be removed from office through a process called impeachment.

Highway   A main road or thoroughfare, such as a street, boulevard, or parkway, available to the public for use for travel or transportation.

Hijacking   The seizure of a commercial vehicle—airplane, ship, or truck—by force or threat of force.

Holder   An individual who has lawfully received possession of a commercial paper, such as a check, and who is entitled to payment on such instrument.

Holder in due course   An individual who takes a commercial paper for value, in good faith, with the belief that it is valid, with no knowledge of any defects.

Hold harmless agreement   An agreement or contract in which one party agrees to hold the other free from the responsibility for any liability or damage that might arise out of the transaction involved.

Holding   A comprehensive term applied to the property, whether real, personal, or both, owned by an individual or a business. The legal principle derived from a judicial decision. That part of the written opinion of a court in which the law is specifically applied to the facts of the instant controversy. It is relied upon when courts use the case as an established precedent in a subsequent case.

Holding company   A corporation that limits its business to the ownership of stock in and the supervision of management of other corporations.

Hold over   To continue in possession of an office and exercise the functions associated therewith following the expiration of the term thereof. To retain possession as a tenant of real property following the termination of the lease or tenancy at will.

Holiday   A day of recreation; a consecrated day; a day set apart for the suspension of business.

Holograph   A will or deed written entirely by the testator or grantor with his or her own hand and not witnessed.

Homeless person   An individual who lacks housing, including an individual whose primary residence during the night is a supervised public or private facility that provides temporary living accommodations, an individual who is a resident in transitional housing, or an individual who has as a primary residence a public or private place not designed for, or ordinarily used as, a regular sleeping accommodation for human beings.

Homeowner's warranty   An insurance protection program offered by a number of builders of residential dwellings in the United States.

Homestead   The dwelling house and its adjoining land where a family resides. Technically, and pursuant to the modern homestead exemption laws, an artificial estate in land, created to protect the possession and enjoyment of the owner against the claims of creditors by preventing the sale of the property for payment of the owner's debts so long as the land is occupied as a home.

Homicide   The killing of one human being by another human being.

Honor   As a verb, to accept a bill of exchange, or to pay a note, check, or accepted bill, at maturity. To pay or to accept and pay, or, where a credit so engages, to purchase or discount a draft complying with the terms of the draft.

As a noun, in old English law, a seigniory of several manors held under one baron or lord paramount. Also those dignities or privileges, degrees of nobility, knighthood, and other titles that flow from the crown.

In the United States, the customary title of courtesy given to judges, and occasionally to some other officers, as, *his honor*, *your honor*, *honorable*.

Honorary trust   An arrangement whereby property is placed in the hands of another to be used for specific noncharitable purposes where there is no definite ascertainable beneficiary—one who profits by the act of another—and that is unenforceable in the absence of statute.

Hornbook   A primer; a book explaining the basics, fundamentals, or rudiments of any science or branch of knowledge. The phrase *hornbook law* is a colloquial designation of the rudiments or general principles of law.

A colloquial reference to a series of textbooks that review various fields of law in summary, narrative form, as opposed to casebooks, which are designed as primary teaching tools and include many reprints of court opinions.

Hostages   Persons taken by an individual or organized group in order to force a state, government unit, or community to meet certain conditions: payment of ransom, release of prisoners, or some other act.

Hostile fire   In insurance law, a combustion that cannot be controlled, that escapes from where it was initially set and confined, or one that was not intended to exist.

Hostile witness   A witness at a trial who is so adverse to the party that called him or her that he or she can be cross-examined as though called to testify by the opposing party.

Hotchpot   The process of combining and assimilating property belonging to different individuals so that the property can be equally divided; the taking into consideration of funds or property that have already been given to children when dividing up the property of a decedent so that the respective shares of the children can be equalized.

Hot pursuit   A doctrine that provides that the police may enter the premises where they suspect a crime has been committed without a warrant when delay would endanger their lives or the lives of others and lead to the escape of the alleged perpetrator; also sometimes called fresh pursuit.

Housebreaking   The act of using physical force to gain access to, and entering, a house with an intent to commit a felony inside.

Household   Individuals who comprise a family unit and who live together under the same roof; individuals who dwell in the same place and comprise a family, sometimes encompassing domestic help; all those who are under the control of one domestic head.

House of Representatives   The lower chamber, or larger branch, of the U.S. Congress, or a similar body in the legislature of many of the states.

Human rights   Personal liberties that protect individuals and groups against individual or state conduct prohibited by international law or custom.

Hundred   A political subdivision in old England.

Hung jury   A trial jury duly selected to make a decision in a criminal case regarding a defendant's guilt or innocence, but who are unable to reach a verdict due to a complete division in opinion.

Huntley hearing   In New York state, a separate proceeding in a criminal action conducted solely for the purpose of determining the admissibility of the extrajudicial statements made by the defendant.

Husband and wife   A man and woman who are legally married to one another and are thereby given by law specific rights and duties resulting from that relationship.

Hypothecate   To pledge property as security or collateral for a debt. Generally, there is no physical transfer of the pledged property to the lender, nor is the lender given title to the property, though he or she has the right to sell the pledged property in the case of default.

Hypothesis   An assumption or theory.

Hypothetical question   A mixture of assumed or established facts and circumstances, developed in the form of a coherent and specific situation, which is presented to an expert witness at a trial to elicit his or her opinion.

Ibid.   An abbreviation of the Latin *ibidem*, meaning "in the same place; in the same book; on the same page."

Idem   [*Latin, The same.*]

I.E.   An abbreviation for the Latin *id est*, "that is to say, meaning."

Illegitimacy   The condition before the law, or the social status, of a child whose parents were not married to each other at the time of his or her birth.

Illicit   Not permitted or allowed; prohibited; unlawful; as an illicit trade; illicit intercourse.

Illusory promise   A statement that appears to assure a performance and form a contract but, when scrutinized, leaves to the speaker the choice of performance or nonperformance, which means that the speaker does not legally bind himself or herself to act.

Immaterial   Not essential or necessary; not important or pertinent; not decisive; of no substantial consequence; without weight; of no material significance.

Immediate cause   The final act in a series of provocations leading to a particular result or event, directly producing such result without the intervention of any further provocation.

Immigration   The entrance into a country of foreigners for purposes of permanent residence. The correlative term *emigration* denotes the act of such persons in leaving their former country.

Imminent   Impending; menacingly close at hand; threatening.

Immunity   Exemption from performing duties that the law generally requires other citizens to perform, or from a penalty or burden that the law generally places on other citizens.

Impanel   The act of the clerk of the court in making up a list of the jurors who have been selected for the trial of a particular case. All the steps of ascertaining who shall be the proper jurors to sit in the trial of a particular case up to the final formation.

Impartial   Favoring neither; disinterested; treating all alike; unbiased; equitable, fair, and just.

Impeach To accuse; to charge a liability upon; to sue. To dispute, disparage, deny, or contradict; as in to impeach a judgment or decree, or impeach a witness; or as used in the rule that a jury cannot *impeach its verdict*. To proceed against a public officer for crime or misfeasance, before a proper court, by the presentation of a written accusation called articles of impeachment.

Impeachment A process used to charge, try, and remove public officials for misconduct while in office.

Impediment A disability or obstruction that prevents an individual from entering into a contract.

Impersonation The crime of pretending to be another individual in order to deceive others and gain some advantage.

Impertinence Irrelevancy; the flaw of bearing no reasonable relationship to the issues or proceeding at hand.

Impleader A procedural device used in a civil action whereby a defendant brings into the lawsuit a third party who is not already a party to the action but may ultimately be liable for the plaintiff's claim against the defendant.

Implied Inferred from circumstances; known indirectly.

Implied consent Consent that is inferred from signs, actions, or facts, or by inaction or silence.

Implied warranty A promise, arising by operation of law, that something that is sold will be merchantable and fit for the purpose for which it is sold.

Impossibility A legal excuse or defense to an action for the breach of a contract; less frequently, a defense to a criminal charge of an attempted crime, such as attempted robbery or murder.

Imposts Taxes or duties; taxes levied by the government on imported goods.

Impoundment An action taken by the president in which he or she proposes not to spend all or part of a sum of money appropriated by Congress.

Impracticability Substantial difficulty or inconvenience in following a particular course of action, but not such insurmountability or hopelessness as to make performance impossible.

Imprimatur [*Latin, Let it be printed.*] A license or allowance, granted by the constituted authorities, giving permission to print and publish a book. This allowance was formerly necessary in England before any book could lawfully be printed, and in some other countries is still required.

Imprisonment Incarceration; the act of restraining the personal liberty of an individual; confinement in a prison.

Improvements Additions or alterations to real property that increase the value thereof.

Imputed   Attributed vicariously.

Imputed knowledge   The comprehension attributed or charged to a person because the facts in issue were open to discovery and it was that person's duty to apprise himself or herself of them; more accurately described as knowledge.

Imputed notice   Information regarding particular facts or circumstances that the law permits to affect the legal rights of a person who has no firsthand knowledge of them but who should have learned of them because his or her agent or representative had direct knowledge of that information and a duty to report it to him or her.

Inadmissible   That which, according to established legal principles, cannot be received into evidence at a trial for consideration by the jury or judge in reaching a determination of the action.

Inadvertence   The absence of attention or care; the failure of an individual to carefully and prudently observe the progress of a court proceeding that might have an effect upon his or her rights.

Inalienable   Not subject to sale or transfer; inseparable.

In blank   Absent limitation or restriction.

Inc.   An abbreviation for incorporated; having been formed as a legal or political entity with the advantages of perpetual existence and succession.

In camera   In chambers; in private. A judicial proceeding is said to be heard *in camera* either when the hearing is had before the judge in his or her private chambers or when all spectators are excluded from the courtroom.

Incapacity   The absence of legal ability, competence, or qualifications.

Incarceration   Confinement in a jail or prison; imprisonment.

Incest   The crime of sexual relations or marriage taking place between a male and female who are so closely linked by blood or affinity that such activity is prohibited by law.

Inchoate   Imperfect; partial; unfinished; begun, but not completed; as in a contract not executed by all the parties.

Incidental   Contingent upon or pertaining to something that is more important; that which is necessary, appertaining to, or depending upon another known as the principal.

Incident of ownership   Some aspect of the exclusive possession or control over the disposition or use of property that demonstrates that the person with such exclusive rights has not relinquished them.

Incite   To arouse; urge; provoke; encourage; spur on; goad; stir up; instigate; set in motion; as in to *incite* a riot. Also, generally, in criminal law to instigate, persuade, or move another to commit a crime; in this sense nearly synonymous with *abet*.

Income The return in money from one's business, labor, or capital invested; gains, profits, salary, wages, etc.

    The gain derived from capital, from labor or effort, or both combined, including profit or gain through sale or conversion of capital. Income is not a gain accruing to capital or a growth in the value of the investment, but is a profit, something of exchangeable value, proceeding from the property and being received or drawn by the recipient for separate use, benefit, and disposal. That which comes in or is received from any business, or investment of capital, without reference to outgoing expenditures.

Income splitting The right, created by provisions of federal tax laws, given to married couples who file joint returns to have their combined incomes subject to an income tax at a rate equal to that which would be imposed if each had filed a separate return for one-half the amount of their combined income.

Income tax A charge imposed by government on the annual gains of a person, corporation, or other taxable unit derived through work, business pursuits, investments, property dealings, and other sources determined in accordance with the Internal Revenue Code or state law.

In common Shared in respect to title, use, or enjoyment; without apportionment or division into individual parts. Held by several for the equal advantage, use, or enjoyment of all.

Incompatibility The inability of a husband and wife to cohabit in a marital relationship.

Incompetency The lack of ability, knowledge, legal qualification, or fitness to discharge a required duty or professional obligation.

Incompetent evidence Probative matter that is not admissible in a legal proceeding; evidence that is not admissible under the Federal Rules of Evidence. That which the law does not allow to be presented at all, or in connection with a particular matter, due to lack of originality, a defect in the witness or the document, or due to the nature of the evidence in and of itself.

Inconsistent Reciprocally contradictory or repugnant.

Incontestability clause A provision in a life or health insurance policy that precludes the insurer from alleging that the policy, after it has been in effect for a stated period (typically two or three years), is void because of misrepresentations made by the insured in the application for it.

Incorporate To formally create a corporation pursuant to the requirements prescribed by state statute; to confer a corporate franchise upon certain individuals.

Incorporation by reference The method of making one document of any kind become a part of another separate document by alluding to the former in the latter and declaring that the former shall be taken and considered as a part of the latter the same as if it were completely set out therein.

Incorporation doctrine   A constitutional doctrine whereby selected provisions of the Bill of Rights are made applicable to the states through the Due Process Clause of the Fourteenth Amendment.

Incorporeal   Lacking a physical or material nature but relating to or affecting a body.

Incremental   Additional or increased growth, bulk, quantity, number, or value; enlarged.

Incriminate   To charge with a crime; to expose to an accusation or a charge of crime; to involve oneself or another in a criminal prosecution or the danger thereof; as in the rule that a witness is not bound to give testimony that would tend to incriminate him or her.

Inculpate   To accuse; to involve in blame or guilt.

Incumbent   An individual who is in current possession of a particular office and who is legally authorized to discharge the duties of that office.

Incur   To become subject to and liable for; to have liabilities imposed by act or operation of law.

Indefeasible   That which cannot be defeated, revoked, or made void. This term is usually applied to an estate or right that cannot be defeated.

Indefinite term   A prison sentence for a specifically designated length of time up to a certain prescribed maximum, such as one to ten years or twenty-five years to life.

Indemnify   To compensate for loss or damage; to provide security for financial reimbursement to an individual in case of a specified loss incurred by the person.

Indemnity   Recompense for loss, damage, or injuries; restitution or reimbursement.

Independent audit   A systematic review of the accuracy and truthfulness of the accounting records of a particular individual, business, or organization by a person or firm skilled in the necessary accounting methods and not related in any way to the person or firm undergoing the audit.

Independent contractor   A person who contracts to do a piece of work according to her or his own methods and is subject to another's control only as to the end product or the final result of the work.

Independent counsel   An attorney appointed by the federal government to investigate and prosecute federal government officials.

Indeterminate   That which is uncertain or not particularly designated.

Index A book containing references, alphabetically arranged, to the contents of a series or collection of documents or volumes; or a section (normally at the end) of a single volume or set of volumes containing such references to its contents.

Statistical indexes are also used to track or measure changes in the economy (for example, the Consumer Price Index) and movement in stock markets (for example, Standard & Poor's Index). Such indexes are usually keyed to a base year, month, or other period of comparison.

In mortgage financing, the term is used to determine adjustable-rate mortgage (ARM) interest rates after the discount period ends. Common indexes for ARMs are one-year Treasury securities and the national average cost of funds to savings and loan associations.

Index to Legal Periodicals The set of volumes that lists what has appeared in print from 1926 to the present in the major law reviews and law-oriented magazines in various countries—usually organized according to author, title, and subject, and containing a table of cases.

Indicia Signs; indications. Circumstances that point to the existence of a given fact as probable, but not certain. For example, *indicia of partnership* are any circumstances which would induce the belief that a given person was in reality, though not technically, a member of a given firm.

Indictment A written accusation charging that an individual named therein has committed an act or omitted to do something that is punishable by law.

Indirect evidence Probative matter that does not proximately relate to an issue but that establishes a hypothesis by showing various consistent facts.

Indispensable party An individual who has an interest in the substantive issue of a legal action of such a nature that a final decree cannot be handed down without that interest being affected or without leaving the controversy in a condition whereby its final determination would be totally unconscionable.

Individual Retirement Account A means by which an individual can receive certain federal tax advantages while investing for retirement.

Indorse To sign a paper or document, thereby making it possible for the rights represented therein to pass to another individual.

Indorsement A signature on a commercial paper or document.

Inducement An advantage or benefit that precipitates a particular action on the part of an individual.

Industrial union A labor organization composed of members employed in a particular field, such as textiles, but who perform different individual jobs within their general type of work.

In evidence   Facts, documents, or exhibits that have been introduced before and accepted by the court for consideration as probative matter.

In extremis   [*Latin, In extremity.*] A term used in reference to the last illness prior to death.

Infamy   Notoriety; condition of being known as possessing a shameful or disgraceful reputation; loss of character or good reputation.

Infancy   Minority; the status of an individual who is below the legal age of majority.

Infants   Persons who are under the age of legal majority—at common law, twenty-one years, now generally eighteen years. According to the sense in which this term is used, it may denote the age of the person, the contractual disabilities that nonage entails, or his or her status with regard to other powers or relations.

Inference   In the law of evidence, a truth or proposition drawn from another that is supposed or admitted to be true. A process of reasoning by which a fact or proposition sought to be established is deduced as a logical consequence from other facts, or a state of facts, already proved or admitted. A logical and reasonable conclusion of a fact not presented by direct evidence but which, by process of logic and reason, a trier of fact may conclude exists from the established facts. Inferences are deductions or conclusions that with reason and common sense lead the jury to draw from facts which have been established by the evidence in the case.

Inferior court   This term may denote any court subordinate to the chief appellate tribunal in the particular judicial system (e.g., trial court); but it is also commonly used as the designation of a court of special, limited, or statutory jurisdiction, whose record must show the existence and attaching of jurisdiction in any given case.

Infirmity   Flaw, defect, or weakness.

In forma pauperis   [*Latin, In the character or manner of a pauper.*] A phrase that indicates the permission given by a court to an indigent to initiate a legal action without having to pay for court fees or costs due to his or her lack of financial resources.

Information   The formal accusation of a criminal offense made by a public official; the sworn, written accusation of a crime.

Information and belief   A standard phrase added to qualify a statement made under oath; a phrase indicating that a statement is made, not from firsthand knowledge but, nevertheless, in the firm belief that it is true.

Informed consent   Assent to permit an occurrence, such as surgery, that is based on a complete disclosure of facts needed to make the decision intelligently, such as knowledge of the risks entailed or alternatives.

  The name for a fundamental principle of law that a physician has a duty to reveal what a reasonably prudent physician in the medical community employing reasonable care would reveal to a patient as to whatever reasonably foreseeable risks of harm might result from a proposed course of treatment. This disclosure must be afforded so that a patient—exercising ordinary care for his or her own welfare and confronted with a choice of undergoing the proposed treatment, alternative treatment, or none at all—can intelligently exercise judgment by reasonably balancing the probable risks against the probable benefits.

Infra   [*Latin, Below, under, beneath, underneath.*] A term employed in legal writing to indicate that the matter designated will appear beneath or in the pages following the reference.

Infraction   Violation or infringement; breach of a statute, contract, or obligation.

Infringement   The encroachment, breach, or violation of a right, law, regulation, or contract.

Ingrossing   The act of making a perfect copy of a particular instrument, such as a deed, lease, or will, from a rough draft so that it may be properly executed to achieve its purpose.

Inherent   Derived from the essential nature of, and inseparable from, the object itself.

Inherit   To receive property according to the state laws of intestate succession from a decedent who has failed to execute a valid will, or, where the term is applied in a more general sense, to receive the property of a decedent by will.

Inheritance   Property received from a decedent, either by will or through state laws of intestate succession, where the decedent has failed to execute a valid will.

Initiative   A process of a participatory democracy that empowers the people to propose legislation and to enact or reject the laws at the polls independent of the lawmaking power of the governing body.

Injunction   A court order by which an individual is required to perform or is restrained from performing a particular act. A writ framed according to the circumstances of the individual case.

Injure   To interfere with the legally protected interest of another or to inflict harm on someone, for which an action may be brought. To damage or impair.

Injurious falsehood   A fallacious statement that causes intentional damage to an individual's commercial or economic relations.

Any type of defamatory remark, either written or spoken, that causes pecuniary loss to an individual through disparagement of a particular business dealing.

Injury   A comprehensive term for any wrong or harm done by one individual to another individual's body, rights, reputation, or property. Any interference with an individual's legally protected interest.

In kind Of the same class, category, or species.

Inland waters Canals, lakes, rivers, water courses, inlets, and bays that are nearest to the shores of a nation and subject to its complete sovereignty.

In lieu of Instead of; in place of; in substitution of. It does not mean *in addition to.*

In loco parentis [*Latin, In the place of a parent.*] The legal doctrine under which an individual assumes parental rights, duties, and obligations without going through the formalities of legal adoption.

In medias res [*Latin, Into the heart of the subject, without preface or introduction.*]

Innkeeper An individual who, as a regular business, provides accommodations for guests in exchange for reasonable compensation.

Innocent Absent guilt; acting in good faith with no knowledge of defects, objections, or inculpative circumstances.

Innocent purchaser An individual who, in good faith and by an honest agreement, buys property in the absence of sufficient knowledge to charge him or her with notice of any defect in the transaction.

Inns of Chancery Ancient preparatory colleges where qualified clerks studied the drafting of writs, which was a function of the officers of the Court of Chancery.

Inns of Court Organizations that provide preparatory education for English law students in order to teach them to practice in court.

Inoperative Void; not active; ineffectual.

In pari delicto [*Latin, In equal fault.*] A descriptive phrase that indicates that parties involved in an action are equally culpable for a wrong.

In pari materia [*Latin, Upon the same subject.*] A designation applied to statutes or general laws that were enacted at different times but pertain to the same subject or object.

In perpetuity Of endless duration; not subject to termination.

In personam [*Latin, Against the person.*] A lawsuit seeking a judgment to be enforceable specifically against an individual person.

Inquest An inquiry by a coroner or medical examiner, sometimes with the aid of a jury, into the cause of a violent death or a death occurring under suspicious circumstances. Generally an inquest may result in a finding of natural death, accidental death, suicide, or murder. Criminal prosecution may follow when culpable conduct has contributed to the death.

The body of jurors called to inquire into the circumstances of a death that occurred suddenly, by violence, or while imprisoned. Any body of jurors called to inquire into certain matters. (A grand jury is sometimes called a grand inquest, for example.)

The determination or findings of a body of persons called to make a legal inquiry or the report issued after their investigation.

Inquiry, commissions of Individuals employed, during conciliation, to investigate the facts of a particular dispute and to submit a report stating the facts and proposing terms for the resolution of the differences.

Inquisitorial system A method of legal practice in which the judge endeavors to discover facts while simultaneously representing the interests of the state in a trial.

In re [*Latin, In the matter of.*] Concerning or regarding. The usual style for the name of a judicial proceeding having some item of property at the center of the dispute rather than adverse parties.

In rem [*Latin, In the thing itself.*] A lawsuit against an item of property, not against a person (in personam).

Insanity defense A defense asserted by an accused in a criminal prosecution to avoid liability for the commission of a crime because, at the time of the crime, the person did not appreciate the nature or quality or wrongfulness of the acts.

Insecurity clause Provision in a contract that allows a creditor to make an entire debt come due if there is good reason to believe that the debtor cannot or will not pay.

Insider In the context of federal regulation of the purchase and sale of securities, anyone who has knowledge of facts not available to the general public.

Insolvency An incapacity to pay debts upon the date when they become due in the ordinary course of business; the condition of an individual whose property and assets are inadequate to discharge the person's debts.

In specie Specific; specifically. Thus, to decree performance *in specie* is to decree specific performance. In kind; in the same or like form. A thing is said to exist *in specie* when it retains its existence as a distinct individual of a particular class.

Inspection An examination or investigation; the right to see and duplicate documents, enter land, or make other such examinations for the purpose of gathering evidence.

Installment Regular, partial portion of the same debt, paid at successive periods as agreed by a debtor and creditor.

Instant Current or present.

Instigate To incite, stimulate, or induce into action; goad into an unlawful or bad action, such as a crime.

Institute To inaugurate, originate, or establish. In civil law, to direct an individual who was named as heir in a will to pass over the estate to another designated person, known as the substitute.

Institution The commencement or initiation of anything, such as an action. An establishment, particularly one that is eleemosynary or public by nature.

Instructions Directives given by a judge to a jury during a trial prescribing the manner in which the jurors should proceed in deciding the case at bar.

Instrument A formal or legal written document; a document in writing, such as a deed, lease, bond, contract, or will. A writing that serves as evidence of an individual's right to collect money, such as a check.

Instrumentality rule A principle of corporate law that permits a court to disregard the corporate existence of a subsidiary corporation when it is operated solely for the benefit of the parent corporation, which controls and directs the activities of the subsidiary while asserting the shield of limited liability.

Insurable interest A right, benefit, or advantage arising out of property that is of such nature that it may properly be indemnified.

Insurance A contract whereby, for a specified consideration, one party undertakes to compensate the other for a loss relating to a particular subject as a result of the occurrence of designated hazards.

Insured The person who obtains or is otherwise covered by insurance on his or her health, life, or property. The *insured* in a policy is not limited to the insured named in the policy but applies to anyone who is insured under the policy.

Insurer An individual or company who, through a contractual agreement, undertakes to compensate specified losses, liability, or damages incurred by another individual.

Insurrection A rising or rebellion of citizens against their government, usually manifested by acts of violence.

Intangibles Property that is a "right" such as a patent, copyright, or trademark, or one that is lacking physical existence, such as good will. A nonphysical, noncurrent asset that exists only in connection with something else, such as the good will of a business.

Integrated Completed; made whole or entire. Desegregated; converted into a nonracial, nondiscriminatory system.

Integrated agreement A contract that contains within its four corners the entire understanding of the parties and is subject to the parol evidence rule, which seeks to preserve the integrity of written agreements by refusing to allow the parties to modify their contract through the introduction of prior or contemporaneous oral declarations.

Integrated bar The process of organizing the attorneys of a state into an association, membership in which is a condition precedent to the right to practice law.

Integration   The bringing together of separate elements to create a whole unit. The bringing together of people from the different demographic and racial groups that make up U.S. society.

Intemperance   A lack of moderation. Habitual intemperance is that degree of intemperance in the use of intoxicating liquor which disqualifies the person a great portion of the time from properly attending to business. Habitual or excessive use of liquor.

Intent   A determination to perform a particular act or to act in a particular manner for a specific reason; an aim or design; a resolution to use a certain means to reach an end.

Inter alia   [*Latin, Among other things.*] A phrase used in pleading to designate that a particular statute set out therein is only a part of the statute that is relevant to the facts of the lawsuit and not the entire statute.

Interest   A comprehensive term to describe any right, claim, or privilege that an individual has toward real or personal property. Compensation for the use of borrowed money.

Interference   In the law of patents, the presence of two pending applications, or an existing patent and a pending application that encompass an identical invention or discovery.

Interim   [*Latin, In the meantime: temporary; between.*]

Interlineation   The process of writing between the lines of an instrument; that which is written between the lines of a document.

Interlocking directorate   The relationship that exists between the board of directors of one corporation with that of another due to the fact that a number of members sit on both boards and, therefore, there is a substantial likelihood that neither corporation acts independently of the other.

Interlocutory   Provisional; interim; temporary; not final; that which intervenes between the beginning and the end of a lawsuit or proceeding to either decide a particular point or matter that is not the final issue of the entire controversy or prevent irreparable harm during the pendency of the lawsuit.

Internal audit   An inspection and verification of the financial records of a company or firm by a member of its own staff to determine the accuracy and acceptability of its accounting practices.

Internal Revenue Service   The federal agency responsible for administering and enforcing all internal revenue laws in the United States, except those relating to alcohol, tobacco, firearms, and explosives, which are the responsibility of the Bureau of Alcohol, Tobacco and Firearms.

International Court of Justice   The main judicial tribunal of the United Nations, to which all member states are parties.

International law	The body of law governing the legal relations between states or nations.
International waterways	Narrow channels of marginal sea or inland waters through which international shipping has a right of passage.
Internet	A worldwide telecommunications network of business, government, and personal computers.
Interpleader	An equitable proceeding brought by a third person to have a court determine the ownership rights of rival claimants to the same money or property that is held by that third person.
Interpol	The acronym for the International Criminal Police Organization, which is a group designed to coordinate international law enforcement.
Interpolation	The process of inserting additional words in a complete document or instrument in such manner as to alter its intended meaning; the addition of words to a complete document or instrument.
Interpretation	The art or process of determining the intended meaning of a written document, such as a constitution, statute, contract, deed, or will.
Interrogatories	Written questions submitted to a party from his or her adversary to ascertain answers that are prepared in writing and signed under oath and that have relevance to the issues in a lawsuit.
In terrorem	[*Latin, In fright or terror; by way of a threat.*] A description of a legacy or gift given by will with the condition that the donee must not challenge the validity of the will or other testament.
Interstate compact	A voluntary arrangement between two or more states that is designed to solve their common problems and that becomes part of the laws of each state.
Intervening cause	A separate act or omission that breaks the direct connection between the defendant's actions and an injury or loss to another person, and may relieve the defendant of liability for the injury or loss.
Intervenor	An individual who is not already a party to an existing lawsuit but who makes himself or herself a party either by joining with the plaintiff or uniting with the defendant in resistance of the plaintiff's claims.
Intervention	A procedure used in a lawsuit by which the court allows a third person who was not originally a party to the suit to become a party, by joining with either the plaintiff or the defendant.
Inter vivos	[*Latin, Between the living.*] A phrase used to describe a gift that is made during the donor's lifetime.
Intestacy	The state or condition of dying without having made a valid will or without having disposed by will of a segment of the property of the decedent.

Intestate The description of a person who dies without making a valid will or the reference made to this condition.

Intestate succession The inheritance of an ancestor's property according to the laws of descent and distribution that are applied when the deceased has not executed a valid will.

Intoxication A state in which a person's normal capacity to act or reason is inhibited by alcohol or drugs.

Intrinsic evidence Information necessary for the determination of an issue in a lawsuit that is gleaned from the provisions of a document itself, as opposed to testimony from a witness or the terms of other writings that have not been admitted by the court for consideration by the trier of fact.

Inure To result; to take effect; to be of use, benefit, or advantage to an individual.

Invalid Null; void; without force or effect; lacking in authority.

Inventory An itemized list of property that contains a description of each specific article.

Investiture In ecclesiastical law, one of the formalities by which an archbishop confirms the election of a bishop. During the feudal ages, the rite by which an overlord granted a portion of his lands to his vassal.

Investment The placement of a particular sum of money in business ventures, real estate, or securities of a permanent nature so that it will produce an income.

Invitation The act by which an owner or occupier of particular land or premises encourages or attracts others to enter, remain in, or otherwise make use of his or her property.

Invitee An individual who enters another's premises as a result of an express or implied invitation of the owner or occupant for their mutual gain or benefit.

Invoice An itemized statement or written account of goods sent to a purchaser or consignee by a vendor that indicates the quantity and price of each piece of merchandise shipped.

Involuntary confession An admission, especially by an individual who has been accused of a crime, that is not freely offered but rather is precipitated by a threat, fear, torture, or a promise.

Involuntary manslaughter The act of unlawfully killing another human being unintentionally.

Involuntary servitude Slavery; the condition of an individual who works for another individual against his or her will as a result of force, coercion, or imprisonment, regardless of whether the individual is paid for the labor.

Ipse dixit   [*Latin, He himself said it.*] An unsupported statement that rests solely on the authority of the individual who makes it.

Ipso facto   [*Latin, By the fact itself; by the mere fact.*]

Irreconcilable differences   The existence of significant differences between a married couple that are so great and beyond resolution as to make the marriage unworkable, and for which the law permits a divorce.

Irregularity   A defect, failure, or mistake in a legal proceeding or lawsuit; a departure from a prescribed rule or regulation.

Irrelevant   Unrelated or inapplicable to the matter in issue.

Irreparable injury   Any harm or loss that is not easily repaired, restored, or compensated by monetary damages. A serious wrong, generally of a repeated and continuing nature, that has an equitable remedy of injunctive relief.

Irresistible impulse   A test applied in a criminal prosecution to determine whether a person accused of a crime was compelled by a mental disease to commit it and therefore cannot be held criminally responsible for her or his actions; in a wrongful death case, a compulsion to commit suicide created by the defendant.

Irretrievable breakdown of marriage   The situation that exists when either or both spouses no longer are able or willing to live with each other, thereby destroying their husband and wife relationship with no hope of resumption of spousal duties.

Irrevocable   Unable to cancel or recall; that which is unalterable or irreversible.

IRS   An abbreviation for the Internal Revenue Service, a federal agency charged with the responsibility of administering and enforcing internal revenue laws.

Island   A land area surrounded by water and remaining above sea level during high tide.

Issue   To promulgate or send out. In a lawsuit, a disputed point of law or question of fact, set forth in the pleadings, that is alleged by one party and denied by the other.

In the law governing the transfer or distribution of property, a child, children, and all individuals who descend from a common ancestor or descendents of any degree.

Issue preclusion   A concept that refers to the fact that a particular question of fact or law, one that has already been fully litigated by the parties in an action for which there has been a judgment on the merits, cannot be relitigated in any future action involving the same parties or their privies (persons who would be bound by the judgment rendered for the party).

Itemize   To individually state each item or article.

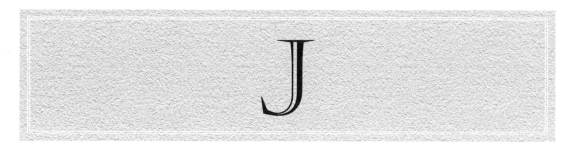

Jactitation   Deceitful boasting, a deceptive claim, or a continuing assertion prejudicial to the right of another.

Jail   A building designated or regularly used for the confinement of individuals who are sentenced for minor crimes or who are unable to gain release on bail and are in custody awaiting trial.

J.D.   An abbreviation for Juris Doctor, the degree awarded to an individual upon the successful completion of law school.

Jeopardy   Danger; hazard; peril. In a criminal action, the danger of conviction and punishment confronting the defendant.

Jetsam   Goods cast overboard from a vessel, by its owner, under exigent circumstances in order to provide for the safety of the ship by lightening its cargo load.

Jobber   A merchant, middle person, or wholesaler who purchases goods from a manufacturer in lots or bulk and resells the goods to a consumer, or to a retailer, who then sells them to a consumer. One who buys and sells on the stock exchange or who deals in stocks, shares, and securities.

John Doe or Jane Doe   Fictitious names used for centuries in the law when a specific person is not known by name.

Joinder   The union in one lawsuit of multiple parties who have the same rights or against whom rights are claimed as coplaintiffs or codefendants. The combination in one lawsuit of two or more causes of action, or grounds for relief. At common law the acceptance by opposing parties that a particular issue is in dispute.

Joint   United; coupled together in interest; shared between two or more persons; not solitary in interest or action but acting together or in unison. A combined, undivided effort or undertaking involving two or more individuals. Produced by or involving the concurring action of two or more; united in or possessing a common relation, action, or interest. To share common rights, duties, and liabilities.

Joint and several liability   A designation of liability by which members of a group are either individually or mutually responsible to a party in whose favor a judgment has been awarded.

Joint estate   Property owned by two or more people at the same time, under the same title, with the same interest, and with the same right of possession.

Joint operating agreement   Any contract, agreement, joint venture, or other arrangement entered into by two or more businesses in which the operations and the physical facilities of a failing business are merged, although each business retains its status as a separate entity in terms of profits and individual mission.

Joint resolution   A type of measure that Congress may consider and act upon, the other types being bills, concurrent resolutions, and simple resolutions, in addition to treaties in the Senate.

Joint stock company   An association engaged in a business for profit with ownership interests represented by shares of stock.

Joint tenancy   A type of ownership of real or personal property by two or more persons in which each owns an undivided interest in the whole.

Joint tortfeasor   Two or more individuals with joint and several liability in a tort action for the same injury to the same person or property.

Joint venture   An association of two or more individuals or companies engaged in a solitary business enterprise for profit without actual partnership or incorporation; also called a joint adventure.

Jones Act   Federal legislation enacted in 1920 (46 U.S.C.A. § 688) to provide a remedy to sailors for injuries or death resulting from the negligence of an owner, a master, or a fellow sailor of a vessel.

Journal   A book or log in which entries are made to record events on a daily basis. A book where transactions or events are recorded as they occur.

J.P.   An abbreviation for justice of the peace, a minor ranking judicial officer with limited statutory jurisdiction over preservation of the peace, civil cases, and lesser criminal offenses.

J.S.D.   An abbreviation for Doctor of Juridical Science, a degree awarded to highly qualified individuals who have successfully completed a prescribed course of advanced study in law after having earned J.D. and LL.M. degrees.

Judge   To make a decision or reach a conclusion after examining all the factual evidence presented. To form an opinion after evaluating the facts and applying the law.

    A public officer chosen or elected to preside over and to administer the law in a court of justice; one who controls the proceedings in a courtroom and decides questions of law or discretion.

Judge advocate   A legal adviser on the staff of a military commander. A designated officer of the Judge Advocate General's Corps of the Army, Navy, Air Force, or Marine Corps.

Judgment   A decision by a court or other tribunal that resolves a controversy and determines the rights and obligations of the parties.

Judgment creditor	A party to which a debt is owed that has proved the debt in a legal proceeding and that is entitled to use judicial process to collect the debt; the owner of an unsatisfied court decision.
Judgment debtor	A party against which an unsatisfied court decision is awarded; a person who is obligated to satisfy a court decision.
Judgment docket	A list under which judicial orders of a particular court are recorded by a clerk or other designated officer to be available for inspection by the public.
Judgment note	A promissory note authorizing an attorney, holder, or clerk of court to appear for the maker of the note and confess, or assent to, a judgment to be entered against the maker due to default in the payment of the amount owed.
Judgment notwithstanding the verdict	A judgment entered by the court in favor of one party even though the jury returned a verdict for the opposing party.
Judgment proof	A term used to describe an individual who is financially unable to pay an adverse court decision awarding a sum of money to the opposing party.
Judicare	To decide or determine in a judicial manner.
Judicature	A term used to describe the judicial branch of government; the judiciary; or those connected with the court system.
Judicature acts	English statutes that govern and revise the organization of the judiciary.
Judicial	Relating to the courts or belonging to the office of a judge; a term pertaining to the administration of justice, the courts, or a judge, as in judicial power.
Judicial action	The adjudication by the court of a controversy by hearing the cause and determining the respective rights of the parties.
Judicial administration	The practices, procedures, and offices that deal with the management of the administrative systems of the courts.
Judicial assistance	Aid offered by the judicial tribunals of one state to the judicial tribunals of a second state.
Judicial immunity	A judge's complete protection from personal liability for exercising judicial functions.
Judicial notice	A doctrine of evidence applied by a court that allows the court to recognize and accept the existence of a particular fact commonly known by persons of average intelligence without establishing its existence by admitting evidence in a civil or criminal action.
Judicial review	A court's authority to examine an executive or legislative act and to invalidate that act if it is contrary to constitutional principles.

Judicial sale	The transfer of title to and possession of a debtor's property to another in exchange for a price determined in proceedings that are conducted under a judgment or an order of court by an officer duly appointed and commissioned to do so.
Judicial writs	Orders issued by a judge in the English courts after a lawsuit had begun.
Judiciary	The branch of government that is endowed with the authority to interpret and apply the law, adjudicate legal disputes, and otherwise administer justice.
Junior	Younger; subsequently born or created; later in rank, tenure, preference, or position.
Junk bond	A security issued by a corporation that is considered to offer a high risk to bondholders.
Jural	The principles of natural and positive rights recognized by law.
Jurat	The certificate of an officer that a written instrument was sworn to by the individual who signed it.
Juridical	Pertaining to the administration of justice or to the office of a judge.
Jurimetrics	The study of law and science.
Juris	[*Latin, Of right; of law.*] A phrase that serves as the root for diverse terms and phrases dealing with the law; for example, jurisdiction, jurisprudence, or jurist.
Jurisdiction	The geographic area over which authority extends; legal authority; the authority to hear and determine causes of action.
Jurisdictional dispute	Conflicting claims made by two different labor unions to an employer regarding assignment of the work or union representation.
Juris doctor	The degree awarded to an individual upon the successful completion of law school.
Jurisprudence	From the Latin term *juris prudentia*, which means "the study, knowledge, or science of law"; in the United States, more broadly associated with the philosophy of law.
Jurist	A judge or legal scholar; an individual who is versed or skilled in law.
Juristic act	An action intended and capable of having a legal effect; any conduct by a private individual designed to originate, terminate, or alter a right.
Jury	In trials, a group of people selected and sworn to inquire into matters of fact and to reach a verdict on the basis of the evidence presented to it.

Jury commission   A group of officials charged with the responsibility of choosing the names of prospective jury members or of selecting the list of jurors for a particular term in court.

Jus   [*Latin, right; justice; law; the whole body of law; also a right.*] The term is used in two meanings:

Jus means *law*, considered in the abstract; that is, as distinguished from any specific enactment, which we call, in a general sense, *the law.* Or it means the law taken as a system, an aggregate, a whole. Or it may designate some one particular system or body of particular laws; as in the phrases *jus civile, jus gentium, jus proetorium.*

In a second sense, *jus* signifies a *right;* that is, a power, privilege, faculty, or demand inherent in one person and incident upon another; or a capacity residing in one person of controlling, with the assent and assistance of the state, the actions of another. This is its meaning in the expressions *jus in rem, jus accrescendi, jus possessionis.*

Jus cogens   That body of peremptory principles or norms from which no derogation is permitted; those norms recognized by the international community as a whole as being fundamental to the maintenance of an international legal order.

Elementary rules that concern the safeguarding of peace and notably those that prohibit recourse to force or the threat of force. Norms of a humanitarian nature are included, such as prohibitions against genocide, slavery, and racial discrimination.

Just   Legally right; conformity with that which is lawful or fair.

Just cause   A reasonable and lawful ground for action.

Just compensation   Equitable remuneration to the owner of private property that is expropriated for public use through condemnation, the implementation of the governmental power of eminent domain.

Jus tertii   The right of a third party. A tenant or bailee or another in possession of property, who pleads that the title is in some person other than that person's landlord or bailor, is said to set up a *jus tertii.*

Justice   The proper administration of the law; the fair and equitable treatment of all individuals under the law. A title given to certain judges, such as federal and state supreme court judges.

Justice Department   The Department of Justice (DOJ) is the executive-branch department responsible for handling the legal work of the federal government.

Justice of the peace   A judicial officer with limited power whose duties may include hearing cases that involve civil controversies, conserving the peace, performing judicial acts, hearing minor criminal complaints, and committing offenders.

Justiciable   Capable of being decided by a court.

Justification   A sufficient or acceptable excuse or explanation made in court for an act that is otherwise unlawful; the showing of an adequate reason, in court, why a defendant committed the offense for which he or she is accused that would serve to relieve the defendant of liability.

A legal excuse for the performance or nonperformance of a particular act that is the basis for exemption from guilt. A classic example is the excuse of self-defense offered as justification for the commission of a murder.

Juvenile law An area of the law that deals with the actions and well-being of persons who are not yet adults.

K

Kangaroo court [*Slang of U.S. origin.*] An unfair, biased, or hasty judicial proceeding that ends in a harsh punishment; an unauthorized trial conducted by individuals who have taken the law into their own hands, such as those put on by vigilantes or prison inmates; a proceeding and its leaders who are considered sham, corrupt, and without regard for the law.

Kentucky Resolutions A set of proposals formulated by Thomas Jefferson and approved by the state legislature of Kentucky during 1798 and 1799 in opposition to the enactment of the Alien and Sedition Acts (1 Stat. 566, 570, 577, 596) by Congress.

Keogh plan A retirement account that allows workers who are self-employed to set aside a percentage of their net earnings for retirement income.

Key numbers® The designation devised by West Publishing Company and given to a classification of legal subjects that are organized within their publications according to specific topics and subtopics, with one or more digits preceded by the symbol of a key assigned to each individual classification.

Kickback The seller's return of part of the purchase price of an item to a buyer or buyer's representative for the purpose of inducing a purchase or improperly influencing future purchases.

Kidnapping The crime of unlawfully seizing and carrying away a person by force or fraud, or seizing and detaining a person against his or her will with an intent to carry that person away at a later time.

Kilberg Doctrine A principle applied in lawsuits involving conflicts of law that provides that a court in the place where a wrongful death action is brought is not bound by the law of the place where the conduct causing death occurred concerning limitations on damages.

Kin Relation by blood or consanguinity; relatives by birth.

King's Bench or Queen's Bench The highest common-law court in England until its end as a separate tribunal in 1875.

Kiting The unlawful practice of drawing checks against a bank account containing insufficient funds to cover them, with the expectation that the necessary funds will be deposited before such checks are presented for payment.

Knowingly Consciously; willfully; subject to complete understanding of the facts or circumstances.

Labor law An area of the law that deals with the rights of employers, employees, and labor organizations.

Labor-Management Relations Act Federal legislation (29 U.S.C.A. § 141 et seq. [1947]), popularly known as the Taft-Hartley Act, which governs the conduct of designated union activities, such as by proscribing strikes and boycotts, and establishes the framework for the resolution of labor disputes in times of national emergencies.

Labor union An association, combination, or organization of employees who band together to secure favorable wages, improved working conditions, and better work hours, and to resolve grievances against employers.

Laches A defense to an equitable action, that bars recovery by the plaintiff because of the plaintiff's undue delay in seeking relief.

Lame duck An elected official, who is to be followed by another, during the period of time between the election and the date that the successor will fill the post.

Lame-duck amendment The popular name given to the Twentieth Amendment to the U.S. Constitution.

Land grant A conveyance of public property to a subordinate government or corporation; a muniment of title issued by a state or government for the donation of some part of the public domain.

Landlord A lessor of real property; the owner or possessor of an estate in land or a rental property, who, in an exchange for rent, leases it to another individual known as the tenant.

Landlord and tenant An association between two individuals arising from an agreement by which one individual occupies the other's real property with permission, subject to a rental fee.

Landmark A structure that has significant historical, architectural, or cultural meaning and that has been given legal protection from alteration and destruction.

Land-use control Activities such as zoning, the regulation of the development of real estate, and city planning.

Lanham Act A federal statute enacted in 1946 and subsequently amended to revise trademark law.

Lapse The termination or failure of a right or privilege because of a neglect to exercise that right or to perform some duty within a time limit, or because a specified contingency did not occur. The expiration of coverage under an insurance policy because of the insured's failure to pay the premium.

The common-law principle that a gift in a will does not take effect but passes into the estate remaining after the payment of debts and particular gifts, if the beneficiary is alive when the will is executed but subsequently predeceases the testator.

Larceny The unauthorized taking and removal of the personal property of another by a person who intends to permanently deprive the owner of it; a crime against the right of possession.

Lasciviousness Lewdness; indecency; obscenity; behavior that tends to deprave the morals in regard to sexual relations.

Last clear chance In the law of torts, the doctrine that excuses or negates the effect of the plaintiff's contributory negligence and permits him or her to recover, in particular instances, damages regardless of his or her own lack of ordinary care.

Last resort A court, such as the U.S. Supreme Court, from which there is no further appeal of a judgment rendered by it in review of a decision in a civil or criminal action by a lower court.

Latent Hidden; concealed; that which does not appear upon the face of an item.

Lateral support The right of a landowner to have his or her property naturally upheld by the adjoining land or the soil beneath.

Law A body of rules of conduct of binding legal force and effect, prescribed, recognized, and enforced by controlling authority.

Law and literature An interdisciplinary study that examines the relationship between the fields of law and literature, with each field borrowing insights and methods of analysis from the other.

Law day The date prescribed in a bond, mortgage, or deed for payment of the debt; the maturity date. May 1st, observed in schools, public assemblies, and courts, in honor of our legal system.

Law French A corrupt French dialect used by English lawyers from after the Norman Conquest in 1066 until slightly after the end of the Restoration period in 1688.

Lawful Licit; legally warranted or authorized.

Law journal A magazine or newspaper that contains articles, news items, comments on new laws and case decisions, court calendars, and suggestions for practicing law, for use by attorneys.

Law merchant The system of rules and customs and usages generally recognized and adopted by traders as the law for the regulation of their commercial transactions and the resolution of their controversies.

Law of nations The body of customary rules that determine the rights and that regulate the intercourse of independent countries in peace and war.

Law of the case The principle that if the highest appellate court has determined a legal question and returned the case to the court below for additional proceedings, the question will not be determined differently on a subsequent appeal in the same case where the facts remain the same.

Law of the land The designation of general public laws that are equally binding on all members of the community.

Law of the sea The part of public international law that deals with maritime issues.

Law review A law school publication containing case summaries written by student members and scholarly articles on current developments in the law, case decisions, and legislation written by law professors, judges, and attorneys.

Law reports Published volumes of the decisions of courts.

Lawsuit A popular designation of a legal proceeding between two parties in the courts, instituted by one party to compel another to do himself or herself justice, regardless of whether the action is based upon law or equity.

Lawyer A person, who through a regular program of study, is learned in legal matters and has been licensed to practice his or her profession. Any qualified person who prosecutes or defends causes in courts of record or other judicial tribunals of the United States, or of any of the states, or who renders legal advice or assistance in relation to any cause or matter.

Lay Nonprofessional, such as a lay witness who is not a recognized expert in the area that is the subject of the person's testimony. That which relates to persons or entities not clerical or ecclesiastical; a person not in ecclesiastical orders. To present the formal declarations by the parties of their respective claims and defenses in pleadings. A share of the profits of a fishing or whaling voyage, allotted to the officers and seamen, in the nature of wages.

Layaway An agreement between a retail seller and a consumer that provides that the seller will retain designated consumer goods for sale to the consumer at a specified price on a future date, if the consumer deposits with the seller an agreed upon sum of money.

Leading case An important judicial decision that is frequently regarded as having settled or determined the law upon all points involved in such controversies and thereby serves as a guide for subsequent decisions.

Leading question A query that suggests to the witness how it is to be answered or puts words into the mouth of the witness to be merely repeated in his or her response.

League of Nations An international confederation of countries, with headquarters in Geneva, Switzerland, that existed from 1920 to 1946, its creation following World War I and its dissolution following World War II.

Lease A contractual agreement by which one party conveys an estate in property to another party, for a limited period, subject to various conditions, in exchange for something of value, but still retains ownership.

Leaseback A transaction whereby land is sold and subsequently rented by the seller from the purchaser who is the new owner.

Leasehold An estate, interest, in real property held under a rental agreement by which the owner gives another the right to occupy or use land for a period of time.

Leave To give or dispose of by will. Willful departure with intent to remain away. See also desertion. Permission or authorization to do something.

Ledger The principal book of accounts of a business enterprise in which all the daily transactions are entered under appropriate headings to reflect the debits and credits of each account.

Legacy A disposition of personal property by will.

Legal Conforming to the law; required or permitted by law; not forbidden by law.

Legal advertising Any advertising an attorney purchases or places in publications, outdoor installations, radio, television, or any other written or recorded media.

Legal age The time of life at which a person acquires full capacity to make his or her own contracts and deeds and to transact business or to enter into some particular contract or relation, such as marriage.

Legal aid A system of nonprofit organizations that provide legal services to people who cannot afford an attorney.

Legal assistant A person, working under the supervision of a lawyer, qualified through education, training, or work experience to perform substantive legal work that requires knowledge of legal concepts and is customarily, but not exclusively, performed by a lawyer; also known as a paralegal.

Legal cap   Long stationery with a wide left-hand margin and a narrow right-hand margin, used by attorneys.

Legal cause   In the law of torts, conduct that is a substantial factor in bringing about harm, which is synonymous with proximate cause.

Legal detriment   A change in position by one to whom a promise has been made, or an assumption of duties or liabilities not previously imposed on the person, due to the person's reliance on the actions of the one who makes the promise.

Legalese   Slang; technical jargon used by attorneys that is often beyond the comprehension of the nonlawyer.

Legal fiction   An assumption that something occurred or someone or something exists which, in fact, is not the case, but that is made in the law to enable a court to equitably resolve a matter before it.

Legal history   The record of past events that deal with the law.

Legal list statutes   State laws that enumerate the investments into which certain institutions and fiduciaries—those who manage money and property for another and who must exercise a standard of care in such activity in accordance with law or contract—can venture.

Legal proceedings   All actions that are authorized or sanctioned by law and instituted in a court or a tribunal for the acquisition of rights or the enforcement of remedies.

Legal publishing   The production of texts that report laws or discuss the practice of law.

Legal realism   The school of legal philosophy that challenges the orthodox view of U.S. jurisprudence under which law is characterized as an autonomous system of rules and principles that courts can logically apply in an objective fashion to reach a determinate and apolitical judicial decision.

Legal representation   The legal work that a licensed attorney performs on behalf of a client.

Legal representative   In its broadest sense, one who stands in place of, and represents the interests of, another. A person who oversees the legal affairs of another. Examples include the executor or administrator of an estate and a court appointed guardian of a minor or incompetent person.

This term is almost always held to be synonymous with the term *personal representative*. In accident cases, the member of the family entitled to benefits under a wrongful death statute.

Legal reserve   Liquid assets that life insurance companies are required by statute to set aside and maintain to assure payment of claims and benefits. In banking, that percentage of bank deposits that must by law be maintained in cash or equally liquid assets to meet the demands of depositors.

Legal residence   The place of domicile—the permanent dwelling—to which a person intends to return despite temporary abodes elsewhere or momentary absences.

Legal right   An interest that the law protects; an enforceable claim; a privilege that is created or recognized by law, such as the constitutional right to freedom of speech.

Legal tender   All U.S. coins and currencies—regardless of when coined or issued—including (in terms of the Federal Reserve System) Federal Reserve notes and circulating notes of Federal Reserve banks and national banking associations that are used for all debts, public and private, public charges, taxes, duties, and dues.

Legal title   Ownership of property that is cognizable or enforceable in a court of law, or one that is complete and perfect in terms of the apparent right of ownership and possession, but that, unlike equitable title, carries no beneficial interest in the property.

Legatee   A person who receives personal property through a will.

Legation   The persons commissioned by one government to exercise diplomatic functions at the court of another, including the minister, secretaries, attachés, and interpreters, are collectively called the *legation* of their government. The word also denotes the official residence of a foreign minister.

Leges Henrici   [*Latin, Laws of Henry.*] A book written between 1114 and 1118 containing Anglo-Saxon and Norman law. It is an invaluable source of knowledge of the period preceding the full development of the Norman law.

Legislate   To enact laws or pass resolutions by the lawmaking process, in contrast to law that is derived from principles espoused by courts in decisions.

Legislation   Lawmaking; the preparation and enactment of laws by a legislative body.

Legislative   Pertaining to the governmental function of lawmaking or to the process of enacting laws.

Legislative acts   Statutes passed by lawmakers, as opposed to court-made laws.

Legislative facts   Matters of such general knowledge that they need not be proven to an administrative agency that is deciding a question of policy.

Legislative history   The discussions and documents, including committee reports, hearings, and floor debates, surrounding and preceding the enactment of a law.

Legislature   A representative assembly of persons that makes statutory laws for a municipality, state, or nation.

Legitimate   To make lawful, such as when a child is born prior to the parents' marriage and they subsequently wed and thereby confer upon the child the same legal status as those born in lawful wedlock. See also illegitimacy.

That which is lawful, legal, recognized by law, or in accordance with law, such as legitimate children or legitimate authority; real, valid, or genuine.

Lemon laws Laws governing the rights of purchasers of new and used motor vehicles that do not function properly and which have to be returned repeatedly to the dealer for repairs.

Lend-Lease Act Legislation enacted by Congress in 1941 that empowered the president to sell, transfer, lend, or lease war supplies—such as equipment, food, and weapons—to American allies during World War II.

Lessee One who rents real property or personal property from another.

Lesser included offense A lesser crime whose elements are encompassed by a greater crime.

Lessor One who rents real property or personal property to another.

Let To award a contract, such as for the erection of public works, to one of several bidders. See also public contract.

To lease certain property.

Letter of credit A written instrument from a bank or merchant in one location that requests that anyone or a specifically named party advance money or items on credit to the party holding or named in the document.

Letter of the law The strict and exact force of the language used in a statute, as distinguished from the spirit, general purpose, and policy of the statute.

Letter ruling In tax law a written interpretation of certain provisions of federal statutes by the Office of the Assistant Commissioner of the Internal Revenue Service.

Letters of administration A formal document issued by a court of probate appointing a manager of the assets and liabilities of the estate of the deceased in certain situations.

Letters rogatory A formal written request made by one judicial body in which an action is pending to another court in a different, independent jurisdiction that a witness who resides in that jurisdiction be examined through the use of interrogatories accompanying the request.

A device used in international law by which the courts of one country ask the courts of another to utilize their procedure to assist the country making the request in the administration of justice within its borders.

Letters testamentary The formal instrument of authority and appointment granted by the proper court to an executor (one designated in a will to manage the estate of the deceased) empowering that person to execute the functions of the office.

Levees and flood control The system constructed and maintained by government to prevent the overflow of water.

Leverage A method of financing an investment by which an investor pays only a small percentage of the purchase price in cash, with the balance supplemented by borrowed funds, in order to generate a greater rate of return than would be produced by paying primarily cash for the investment; the economic benefit gained by such financing.

Levy To assess; raise; execute; exact; tax; collect; gather; take up; seize. Thus, to levy a tax; to levy a nuisance; to levy a fine; to levy war; to levy an execution, *i.e.*, to levy or collect a sum of money on an execution.

A seizure. The obtaining of money by legal process through seizure and sale of property; the raising of the money for which an execution has been issued.

Lewdness Behavior that is deemed morally impure or unacceptable in a sexual sense; open and public indecency tending to corrupt the morals of the community; gross or wanton indecency in sexual relations.

Lex [*Latin, Law.*] In medieval jurisprudence, a body or collection of various laws peculiar to a given nation or people; not a code in the modern sense, but an aggregation or collection of laws not codified or systematized. Also, a similar collection of laws relating to a general subject, and not peculiar to any one people.

Lex fori [*Latin, The law of the forum, or court.*] The positive law of the state, nation, or jurisdiction within which a lawsuit is instituted or remedy sought.

LEXIS® An on-line legal information service that provides the full text of opinions and statutes in electronic format. Subscribers use their personal computers to search the LEXIS database for relevant cases. They may download or print the legal information they retrieve.

Lex loci [*Latin, The law of the place.*] The law of the state or the nation where the matter in litigation transpired.

Liability A comprehensive legal term that describes the condition of being actually or potentially subject to a legal obligation.

Libel and slander Two torts that involve the communication of false information about a person, a group, or an entity such as a corporation. Libel is any defamation that can be seen, such as a writing, printing, effigy, movie, or statue. Slander is any defamation that is spoken and heard.

Libelant Formerly the party who filed an initiatory pleading (a formal declaration of a claim) in an ecclesiastical or religious matter or in an admiralty case, corresponding to the plaintiff in actions at law.

Libelous In the nature of a written defamation, a communication that tends to injure reputation.

Libertarianism A political philosophy that advocates free will, individual rights, and voluntary cooperation.

License The permission granted by competent authority to exercise a certain privilege that, without such authorization, would constitute an illegal act, a trespass, or a tort. The certificate or the document itself that confers permission to engage in otherwise proscribed conduct.

Licentiousness Acting without regard to law, ethics, or the rights of others.

Lien A right given to another by the owner of property to secure a debt, or one created by law in favor of certain creditors.

Life estate An estate whose duration is limited to the life of the party holding it, or some other person.

Life in being A phrase used in the common-law and statutory rules against perpetuities, meaning the remaining duration of the life of a person who is in existence at the time when the deed or will takes effect.

Life or limb The phrase within the Fifth Amendment to the U.S. Constitution, commonly known as the Double Jeopardy Clause, that provides, "nor shall any person be subject for the same offence to be twice put in jeopardy of life or limb," pursuant to which there can be no second prosecution after a first trial for the same offense.

Lifo An abbreviation for *last in, first out*, a method used in inventory accounting to value the merchandise of a particular business.

Lift To raise; to take up.

Ligan Goods cast into the sea tied to a buoy, so that they may be found again by the owners. When goods are cast into the sea in storms or shipwrecks and remain there, without coming to land, they are distinguished by the names of jetsam, flotsam, and *ligan*.

Limitation A qualification, restriction, or circumspection.

Limitations of actions Statutes restricting the right to bring suit on certain civil causes of action or criminal prosecutions, which provide that a suit may not be commenced unless it is brought within a designated period after the time that the right to sue accrued.

Limited Restricted in duration, extent, or scope; confined.

Limited liability company A noncorporate business whose owners actively participate in the organization's management and are protected against personal liability for the organization's debts and obligations.

Limited liability partnership A form of general partnership that provides an individual partner protection against personal liability for certain partnership obligations.

Lineal That which comes in a line, particularly a direct line, as from parent to child or grandparent to grandchild.

Line of credit The maximum borrowing power granted to a person from a financial institution.

Lineup   A criminal investigation technique in which the police arrange a number of individuals in a row before a witness to a crime and ask the witness to identify which, if any, of the individuals committed the crime.

Liquid assets   Cash, or property immediately convertible to cash, such as securities, notes, life insurance policies with cash surrender values, U.S. savings bonds, or an account receivable.

Liquidate   To pay and settle the amount of a debt; to convert assets to cash; to aggregate the assets of an insolvent enterprise and calculate its liabilities in order to settle with the debtors and the creditors and apportion the remaining assets, if any, among the stockholders or owners of the corporation.

Liquidated damages   Monetary compensation for a loss, detriment, or injury to a person or a person's rights or property, awarded by a court judgment or by a contract stipulation regarding breach of contract.

Liquidation   The collection of assets belonging to a debtor to be applied to the discharge of his or her outstanding debts.

A type of proceeding pursuant to federal bankruptcy law by which certain property of a debtor is taken into custody by a trustee to be sold, the proceeds to be distributed to the debtor's creditors in satisfaction of their claims.

The settlement of the financial affairs of a business or individual through the sale of all assets and the distribution of the proceeds to creditors, heirs, or other parties with a legal claim.

Lis pendens   [*Latin, Pending lawsuit.*] A reference to the jurisdiction (or control) that courts obtain over property in a suit awaiting action.

A notice filed in the office of public records that the ownership of real property is the subject of a legal controversy and that anyone who purchases it takes it subject to any claims asserted in the action and thereby its value might be diminished.

Listing   An agreement that represents the right of a real estate agent or broker to handle the sale of real property and to receive a fee or commission for services.

Litchfield Law School   The first law school in America, founded by Tapping Reeve in 1784 in Litchfield, Connecticut. It continued operation until 1833.

Literal construction   The determination by a court of the meaning of the language of a document by an examination of only the actual words used in it, without any consideration of the intent of the parties who signed the writing except for the fact that they chose the language now in dispute.

Literary property   The interest of an author in an original and expressive composition, that entitles the author to the exclusive use and profit thereof, with no interest vested in any other individual. The corporal property in which an intellectual production is embodied.

Litigation   An action brought in court to enforce a particular right. The act or process of bringing a lawsuit in and of itself; a judicial contest; any dispute.

Littoral rights — Rights relating to the ownership of property that abuts an ocean, sea, or lake.

Litvinov Assignment of 1933 — An executive agreement made by President Franklin Delano Roosevelt as part of the arrangements by which the United States recognized the Soviet Union.

Livery of seisin — A ceremony performed in medieval England that effected the transfer of land from one party to another.

Livery stable keepers — Individuals who, as a regular course of business, provide quarters for the boarding of horses and rent them for hire.

Living trust — A property right, held by one party for the benefit of another, that becomes effective during the lifetime of the creator and is, therefore, in existence upon his or her death.

Living will — A written document that allows a patient to give explicit instructions about medical treatment to be administered when the patient is terminally ill or permanently unconscious; also called an advance directive.

LL.B. — An abbreviation denoting the degree of bachelor of laws, which was the basic degree awarded to an individual upon completion of law school until the late 1960s.

LL.M. — An abbreviation for Master of Laws, which is an advanced degree that is awarded to an individual who already holds a J.D. upon the successful completion of a prescribed course of graduate study in law.

Load lines — A marking indicating the extent to which the weight of a load may safely submerge a ship; also called *Plimsoll line*.

Loan commitment — Commitment to a borrower by a lending institution that it will loan a specific amount at a certain rate on a particular piece of real estate. Such commitment is usually limited to a specified time period (e.g., four months), which is commonly based on the estimated time that it will take the borrower to construct or purchase the home contemplated by the loan.

Loan shark — A person who lends money in exchange for its repayment at an interest rate that exceeds the percentage approved by law and who uses intimidating methods or threats of force in order to obtain repayment.

Lobbying — The process of influencing public and government policy at all levels: federal, state, and local.

Local action — A lawsuit concerning a transaction that could not occur except in some particular place. Any type of lawsuit that can be brought only in one place. A classic example is a situation where recovery of possession of a particular parcel of land is sought.

Lookout — Employer's withholding of work from employees in order to gain concession from them; it is the employers' counterpart of the employee's strike. Refusal by the employer to furnish available work to its regular employees, whether refusal is motivated by the employer's desire to protect itself against economic injury, by its desire to protect itself at the bargaining table, or by both.

Lockup A place of detention in a police station, court or other facility used for persons awaiting trial. In corporate law, a slang term that refers to the setting aside of securities for purchase by friendly interests in order to defeat or make more difficult a takeover attempt. A lockup option is a takeover defensive measure permitting a friendly suitor to purchase divisions of a corporation for a set price when any person or group acquires a certain percentage of the corporation's shares. To be legal, such agreement must advance or stimulate the bidding process, to best serve the interests of the shareholders through encouraged competition.

Loco parentis [*Latin, The place of a parent.*] A description of the relationship that an adult or an institution assumes toward an infant or minor of whom the adult is not a parent but to whom the adult or institution owes the obligation of care and supervision.

Locus [*Latin, Place; place where a thing is performed or done.*]

Lodger An occupant of a portion of a dwelling, such as a hotel or boarding-house, who has mere use of the premises without actual or exclusive possession thereof. Anyone who lives or stays in part of a building that is operated by another and who does not have control over the rooms therein.

Logging The cutting of, or commercial dealing in, tree trunks that have been cut down and stripped of all branches.

Logging in A colloquial term for the process of making the initial record of the names of individuals who have been brought to the police station upon their arrest.

Log rolling A legislative practice of embracing in one bill several distinct matters, none of which, perhaps, could singly obtain the assent of the legislature, and then procuring its passage by a combination of the minorities in favor of each of the measures into a majority that will adopt them all.

Practice of including in one statute or constitutional amendment more than one proposition, inducing voters to vote for all, notwithstanding they might not have voted for all if amendments or statutes had been submitted separately.

Long-arm statute A state law that allows the state to exercise jurisdiction over an out-of-state defendant, provided that the prospective defendant has sufficient minimum contacts with the forum state.

Loophole An omission or ambiguity in a legal document that allows the intent of the document to be evaded.

Loss Diminution, reduction, depreciation, decrease in value; that which cannot be recovered.

Loss of services A deprivation of a family member, such as a parent or spouse, of the right to benefit from the performance of various duties, coupled with the privation of love and companionship, provided by the victim of a personal injury or wrongful death.

Lost instruments Documents that cannot be located after a thorough, careful, and diligent search has been made for them.

Lot In sales, a parcel or single article that is the subject matter of a separate sale or delivery, irrespective of whether or not it is adequate to perform the contract. In the securities and commodities market, a specific number of shares or a particular quantity of a commodity specified for trading. In the law of real estate, one of several parcels into which real property is divided.

Low-tide elevation Offshore land features such as shoals, rocks, or reefs that are exposed at low tide but submerged at high tide are referred to as low-tide elevations.

Loyalty oath An oath that declares an individual's allegiance to the government and its institutions, and disclaims support of ideologies or associations that oppose or threaten the government.

L.S. An abbreviation for *locus sigilli*, Latin for "the place of the seal," signifying the place within a written contract where a seal is affixed in order to bind the agreement.

Lump-sum settlement The payment of an entire debt all at once rather than in installments; the payment of a set amount of money to satisfy a pecuniary obligation that might otherwise continue indefinitely.

Magistrate Any individual who has the power of a public civil officer or inferior judicial officer, such as a justice of the peace.

Magnuson-Moss Warranty Act The first federal statute to address the law of warranty. The act (15 U.S.C.A. § 2301 et seq.) mandates that a written warranty on any consumer product that costs more than $5 must completely and conspicuously disclose, in easily understood words, the terms and conditions of the warranty. A warranty may guarantee several things, such as that the item will perform in a certain way or that the manufacturer will repair or replace the item if it is defective.

Mail cover The process governed by the U.S. Postal Regulations (39 C.F.R. § 233.3) that allows the recording of all the information that appears on the outside cover of mail in any class, and also allows the recording of the contents of second-, third-, and fourth-class mail, international parcel post mail, and mail on which the appropriate postage has not been paid.

Mail fraud   A crime in which the perpetrator develops a scheme using the mails to defraud another of money or property. This crime specifically requires the intent to defraud, and is a federal offense governed by section 1341 of title 18 of the U.S. Code. The mail fraud statute was first enacted in 1872 to prohibit illicit mailings with the Postal Service (formerly the Post Office) for the purpose of executing a fraudulent scheme.

Maintenance   Unauthorized intervention by a nonparty in a lawsuit, in the form of financial or other support and assistance to prosecute or defend the litigation. The preservation of an asset or of a condition of property by upkeep and necessary repairs.

A periodic monetary sum paid by one spouse for the benefit of the other upon separation or the dissolution of marriage; also called alimony or spousal support.

Majority   Full age; legal age; age at which a person is no longer a minor. The age at which, by law, a person is capable of being legally responsible for all of his or her acts (e.g. contractual obligations), and is entitled to the management of his or her own affairs and to the enjoyment of civic rights (e.g. right to vote). The opposite of minority. Also the *status* of a person who is a major in age.

The greater number. The number greater than half of any total.

Maker   One who makes, frames, executes, or ordains; as a *lawmaker*, or the *maker* of a promissory note. One who signs a note to borrow and, as such, assumes the obligation to pay the note when due. The person who creates or executes a note, that is, issues it, and in signing the instrument makes the promise of payment contained therein. One who signs a check; in this context, synonymous with drawer. One who issues a promissory note or certificate of deposit.

Mala fides   [*Latin, Bad faith.*]

Mala in se   Wrongs in themselves; acts morally wrong; offenses against conscience.

Mala prohibita   [*Latin, Wrongs prohibited.*] A term used to describe conduct that is prohibited by laws, although not inherently evil.

Malfeasance   The commission of an act that is unequivocally illegal or completely wrongful.

Malice   The intentional commission of a wrongful act, absent justification, with the intent to cause harm to others; conscious violation of the law that injures another individual; a mental state indicating a disposition in disregard of social duty and a tendency toward malfeasance.

Malice aforethought   A predetermination to commit an act without legal justification or excuse. A malicious design to injure. An intent, at the time of a killing, willfully to take the life of a human being, or an intent willfully to act in callous and wanton disregard of the consequences to human life; but *malice aforethought* does not necessarily imply any ill will, spite or hatred towards the individual killed.

Malicious Involving malice; characterized by wicked or mischievous motives or intentions.

Malicious mischief Willful destruction of personal property of another, from actual ill will or resentment towards its owner or possessor. Though only a trespass at the common law, it is now a misdemeanor in most states.

Malicious prosecution An action for damages brought by one against whom a civil suit or criminal proceeding has been unsuccessfully commenced without probable cause and for a purpose other than that of bringing the alleged offender to justice.

Malpractice The breach by a member of a profession of either a standard of care or a standard of conduct.

Managed care A general term that refers to health plans that attempt to control the cost and quality of care by coordinating medical and other health-related services.

Manager One who has charge of a corporation and control of its business, or of its branch establishments, divisions, or departments, and who is vested with a certain amount of discretion and independent judgment. A person chosen or appointed to manage, direct, or administer the affairs of another person or of a business, sports team, or the like. The designation of *manager* implies general power and permits reasonable inferences that the employee so designated is invested with the general conduct and control of the employer's business.

Mandamus [*Latin, We comand.*] A writ or order that is issued from a court of superior jurisdiction that commands an inferior tribunal, corporation, municipal corporation, or individual to perform, or refrain from performing, a particular act, the performance or omission of which is required by law as an obligation.

Mandate A judicial command, order, or precept, written or oral, from a court; a direction that a court has the authority to give and an individual is bound to obey.

Mandatory Peremptory; obligatory; required; that which must be subscribed to or obeyed.

Mandatory authority Precedents, in the form of prior decisions by a higher court of the same state on point, statutes, or other sources of law that must be considered by a judge in the determination of a legal controversy.

Man-in-the-house rule A regulation that was formerly applied in certain jurisdictions that denied poor families welfare payments in the event that a man resided under the same roof with them.

Manor A house, a dwelling, or a residence.

Manslaughter The unjustifiable, inexcusable, and intentional killing of a human being without deliberation, premeditation, and malice. The unlawful killing of a human being without any deliberation, which may be involuntary, in the commission of a lawful act without due caution and circumspection.

Manufactures Items of trade that have been transformed from raw materials, either by labor, art, skill, or machine into finished articles that have new forms, qualities, or properties.

Margin The edge or border; the edge of a body of water where it meets the land. As applied to a boundary line of land, the *margin* of a river, creek, or other watercourse means the center of the stream. But in the case of a lake, bay, or natural pond, the *margin* means the line where land and water meet.

In finance, the difference between market value of loan collateral and face value of loan.

A sum of money, or its equivalent, placed in the hands of a broker by the principal or person on whose account a purchase or sale of securities is to be made, as a security to the former against losses to which he or she may be exposed by subsequent fluctuations in the market value of the stock. The amount paid by the customer when he uses a broker's credit to buy a security.

In commercial transactions the difference between the purchase price paid by an intermediary or retailer and the selling price, or difference between price received by manufacturer for its goods and costs to produce. Also called gross profit margin.

Margin call A demand by a broker that an investor who has purchased securities using credit extended by the broker (on margin) pay additional cash into his or her brokerage account to reduce the amount of debt owed.

Marital Pertaining to the relationship of husband and wife; having to do with marriage.

Marital communications privilege The right given to a husband and wife to refuse to testify in a trial as to confidential statements made to each other within and during the framework of their spousal relationship.

Maritime lien The right of a particular individual to compel the sale of a ship because he or she has not been paid a debt owed to him or her on account of such vessel.

Marketable title Ownership and possession of real property that is readily transferable since it is free from valid claims by outside parties.

Market value The highest price a willing buyer would pay and a willing seller would accept, both being fully informed, and the property being exposed for sale for a reasonable period of time. The market value may be different from the price a property can actually be sold for at a given time (market price). The market value of an article or piece of property is the price that it might be expected to bring if offered for sale in a fair market; not the price that might be obtained on a sale at public auction or a sale forced by the necessities of the owner, but such a price as would be fixed by negotiation and mutual agreement, after ample time to find a purchaser, as between a vendor who is willing (but not compelled) to sell and a purchaser who desires to buy but is not compelled to take the particular article or piece of property.

Marque and reprisal
A commission by which the head of a government authorizes a private ship to capture enemy vessels.

Marriage
The legal status, condition, or relationship that results from a contract by which one man and one woman, who have the capacity to enter into such an agreement, mutually promise to live together in the relationship of husband and wife in law for life, or until the legal termination of the relationship.

Marshal
A federal court officer whose job entails maintaining the peace, delivering legal papers, and performing duties similar to those of a state sheriff.

Marshaling assets and securities
The process of organizing, ranking, and distributing funds in a manner set forth by law as being the most effective way to discharge debts that are owed to various creditors.

Martial law
The exercise of government and control by military authorities over the civilian population of a designated territory.

Martindale-Hubbell Law Directory
A database containing information about attorneys and law firms around the world.

Massachusetts trust
A business arrangement that is used in place of a corporation or partnership in which trustees hold title to property for the advantage of beneficiaries for investment purposes.

Mass communications law
A body of primarily federal statutes, regulations, and judicial decisions that govern radio; broadcast, cable, and satellite television; and other means of electronic communication.

Master
An individual who hires employees or servants to perform services and who directs the manner in which such services are performed.

A court officer appointed by a judge to perform such jobs as examining witnesses, taking testimony, computing damages, or taking oaths, affidavits, or acknowledgments of deeds.

Master and servant
An archaic generic legal phrase that is used to describe the relationship arising between an employer and an employee.

Material
Important; affecting the merits of a case; causing a particular course of action; significant; substantial. A description of the quality of evidence that possesses such substantial probative value as to establish the truth or falsity of a point in issue in a lawsuit.

Matter of fact
That which is to be determined by the senses or by the testimony of witnesses who describe what they have perceived through the senses of sight, smell, touch, taste, and hearing.

Matter of law   That which is determined or ascertained through the use of statutes, rules, court decisions, and interpretations of legal principles.

Matter of record   Anything that has been entered in the formal written record of a court, which can be proved by the production of that record.

Maxim   A broad statement of principle, the truth and reasonableness of which are self-evident. A rule of equity, the system of justice that complements the common law.

Mayhem   Mayhem at common law required a type of injury that permanently rendered the victim less able to fight offensively or defensively; it might be accomplished either by the removal of (dismemberment), or by the disablement of, some bodily member useful in fighting. Today, by statute, permanent disfigurement has been added; and as to dismemberment and disablement, there is no longer a requirement that the member have military significance. In many states the crime of mayhem is treated as aggravated assault.

McCarran-Ferguson Act of 1945   A federal law (15 U.S.C.A. § 1011 et seq.) that gives states the authority to regulate the "business of insurance" without interference from federal regulation, unless federal law specifically provides otherwise.

McCarran Internal Security Act   Legislation proposed by Senator Patrick Anthony McCarran and enacted by Congress in 1950 that subjected alleged members of designated Communist-action organizations to regulation by the federal government.

M.C.J.   An abbreviation for master of comparative jurisprudence, a degree awarded to foreign lawyers trained in civil law countries who have successfully completed a year of full-time study of the Anglo-American legal system.

McNabb-Mallory Rule   A federal judicial doctrine that operates to exclude from evidence a confession that is obtained from a person who was not brought before a judicial officer promptly after the person's arrest.

Mechanic's lien   A charge or claim upon the property of another individual as security for a debt that is created in order to obtain priority of payment of the price or value of work that is performed and materials that are provided in the erection or repair of a building or other structure.

Mediation   A settlement of a dispute or controversy by setting up an independent person between two contending parties in order to aid them in the settlement of their disagreement.

Medicaid   A joint federal-state program that provides health care insurance to low-income persons.

Medical malpractice   Improper, unskilled, or negligent treatment of a patient by a physician, dentist, nurse, pharmacist, or other health care professional.

Medicare   A federally funded system of health and hospital insurance for persons age sixty-five and older and for disabled persons.

Meeting of creditors	One of the first steps in federal bankruptcy proceedings whereby the creditors of a debtor meet in court to present their claims against him or her and a trustee is named to handle the application of the debtor's assets to pay his or her debts.
Meeting of minds	The mutual agreement and assent of the parties to a contract to its substance and terms.
Membership corporation	A company or organization that is formed for purposes other than generating a profit.
Memorandum	An informal record, in the form of a brief written note or outline, of a particular legal transaction or document for the purpose of aiding the parties in remembering particular points or for future reference.
Memorandum decision	A court's decision that gives the ruling (what it decides and orders done), but no opinion (reasons for the decision).
Mensa et thoro	[*Latin, From bed and board.*] A type of divorce that is a partial termination of the duties of a marital relationship.
Mens rea	As an element of criminal responsibility, a guilty mind; a guilty or wrongful purpose; a criminal intent. Guilty knowledge and wilfulness.
Mental anguish	When connected with a physical injury, includes both the resultant mental sensation of pain and also the accompanying feelings of distress, fright, and anxiety. As an element of damages implies a relatively high degree of mental pain and distress; it is more than mere disappointment, anger, worry, resentment, or embarrassment, although it may include all of these, and it includes mental sensation of pain resulting from such painful emotions as grief, severe disappointment, indignation, wounded pride, shame, despair, and/or public humiliation. In other connections, and as a ground for divorce or for compensable damages or an element of damages, it includes the mental suffering resulting from the excitation of the more poignant and painful emotions, such as grief, severe disappointment, indignation, wounded pride, shame, public humiliation, despair, etc.
Mental cruelty	A course of conduct on the part of one spouse toward the other spouse that can endanger the mental and physical health and efficiency of the other spouse to such an extent as to render continuance of the marital relation intolerable. As a ground for divorce, it is conduct that causes embarrassment, humiliation, and anguish so as to render life miserable and unendurable or to cause a spouse's life, person, or health to become endangered.
Mercantile	Relating to trade or commerce; commercial; having to do with the business of buying and selling; relating to merchants.
Merchantable	Salable; of quality and type ordinarily acceptable among vendors and buyers.
Mercian law	A major body of Anglo-Saxon customs that, along with the Dane law and the West Saxon law, continued to constitute the law in England in the days immediately following the Norman Conquest.

Merger   The combination or fusion of one thing or right into another thing or right of greater or larger importance so that the lesser thing or right loses its individuality and becomes identified with the greater whole.

Mergers and acquisitions   Methods by which corporations legally unify ownership of assets formerly subject to separate controls.

Merits   The strict legal rights of the parties to a lawsuit.

Merit system   System used by federal and state governments for hiring and promoting governmental employees to civil service positions on the basis of competence.

Mesne   Intermediate; intervening; the middle between two extremes, especially of rank or time. In feudal law, an intermediate lord; a lord who stood between a tenant and the chief lord; a lord who was also a tenant.

Metes and bounds   The boundary lines of land, with their terminal points and angles. A way of describing land by listing the compass directions and distances of the boundaries. It is often used in connection with the Government Survey System.

Military government   A government that is established during or after military occupation by the victorious country in an armed conflict. According to international law, the territory that has been placed under the authority of a hostile army continues to belong to the state that has been ousted. However, it may be ruled by the occupiers under a special regime.

Military law   The body of laws, rules, and regulations developed to meet the needs of the military. It encompasses service in the military, the constitutional rights of service members, the military criminal justice system, and the international law of armed conflict.

Militia   A group of private citizens who train for military duty to be ready to defend their state or country in times of emergency. A militia is distinct from regular military forces, which are units of professional soldiers maintained both in war and peace by the federal government.

Mill   One-tenth of one cent: $0.001.

Mine and mineral law   The law governing the ownership, sale, and operation of mines, quarries, and wells, and the rights to natural resources found in the earth.

Mineral right   An interest in minerals in land, with or without ownership of the surface of the land. A right to take minerals or a right to receive a royalty.

Minimum wage   The minimum hourly rate of compensation for labor, as established by federal statute and required of employers engaged in businesses that affect interstate commerce. Most states also have similar statutes governing minimum wages.

Ministerial	Done under the direction of a supervisor; not involving discretion or policymaking.
Minor	An infant or person who is under the age of legal competence. A term derived from the civil law, which described a person under a certain age as *less than* so many years. In most states, a person is no longer a minor after reaching the age of 18 (though state laws might still prohibit certain acts until reaching a greater age; e.g., purchase of liquor). Also, less; of less consideration; lower; a person of inferior condition.
Minority	The state or condition of a minor; infancy. Opposite of majority. The smaller number of votes of a deliberative assembly; opposed to majority. In context of the Constitution's guarantee of equal protection, *minority* does not have merely numerical denotation but refers to identifiable and specially disadvantaged groups such as those based on race, religion, ethnicity, or national origin.
Minute book	An account where official proceedings are recorded.
Minutes	The written record of an official proceeding. The notes recounting the transactions occurring at a meeting or official proceeding; a record kept by courts and corporations for future reference.
Miscarriage of justice	A legal proceeding resulting in a prejudicial outcome.
Miscegenation	Mixture of races. A term formerly applied to marriage between persons of different races. Statutes prohibiting marriage between persons of different races have been held to be invalid as contrary to the equal protection Clause of the Constitution.
Misdemeanor	Offenses lower than felonies and generally those punishable by fine, penalty, forfeiture, or imprisonment other than in a penitentiary. Under federal law, and most state laws, any offense other than a felony is classified as a misdemeanor. Certain states also have various classes of misdemeanors (e.g., Class A, B, etc.).
Misfeasance	A term used in tort law to describe an act that is legal but performed improperly.
Misprision	The failure to perform a public duty.
Misrepresentation	An assertion or manifestation by words or conduct that is not in accord with the facts.
Missouri Compromise of 1820	A congressional agreement that regulated the extension of slavery in the United States for the next thirty years. Under the agreement the territory of Missouri was admitted as a slave state, the territory of Maine was admitted as a free state, and the boundaries of slavery were limited to the same latitude as the southern boundary of Missouri: 36° 30′ north latitude.
Mistake	An unintentional act, omission, or error.

Mistake of fact An error that is not caused by the neglect of a legal duty on the part of the person committing the error, but rather consists of an unconscious ignorance of a past or present material event or circumstance, or a belief in the present existence of a material event that does not exist, or a belief in the past existence of a material event that did not exist.

Mistake of law A misconception that occurs when a person with complete knowledge of the facts reaches an erroneous conclusion as to their legal effect; an incorrect opinion or inference, arising from a flawed evaluation of the facts.

Mistrial A courtroom trial that has been terminated prior to its normal conclusion. A mistrial has no legal effect and is considered an invalid or nugatory trial. It differs from a "new trial," which recognizes that a trial was completed but was set aside so that the issues could be tried again.

Mitigating circumstances Circumstances that may be considered by a court in determining culpability of a defendant or the extent of damages to be awarded to a plaintiff. Mitigating circumstances do not justify or excuse an offense but may reduce the severity of a charge. Similarly, a recognition of mitigating circumstances to reduce a damage award does not imply that the damages were not suffered but that they have been partially ameliorated.

Mitigation of damages The use of reasonable care and diligence in an effort to minimize or avoid injury.

Mittimus A court order directing a sheriff or other police officer to escort a convict to a prison.

Mixed actions Lawsuits having two purposes: to recover real property and to obtain monetary damages.

M'Naghten Rule A test applied to determine whether a person accused of a crime was sane at the time of its commission and, therefore, criminally responsible for the wrongdoing.

Model acts Statutes drafted by the National Conference of Commissioners on Uniform State Laws in cooperation with the American Law Institute. State legislatures may adopt model acts in whole or in part, or they may modify them to fit their needs. Model acts differ from uniform acts, which are adopted by the states in virtually the same form proposed by the conference and the American Law Institute.

Modification A change or alteration in existing materials.

Modus operandi [*Latin, Method of working.*] A term used by law enforcement authorities to describe the particular manner in which a crime is committed.

Moiety One-half.

Money laundering The process of taking the proceeds of criminal activity and making them appear legal.

Money paid The technical name given a declaration in assumpsit in which the plaintiff declares that the defendant had and received certain money. A common-law pleading, stating that the defendant received money that, in equity and good conscience, should be paid to the plaintiff.

Monopoly An economic advantage held by one or more persons or companies deriving from the exclusive power to carry on a particular business or trade or to manufacture and sell a particular item, thereby suppressing competition and allowing such persons or companies to raise the price of a product or service substantially above the price that would be established by a free market.

Monument Anything by which the memory of a person, thing, idea, art, science or event is preserved or perpetuated. A tomb where a dead body has been deposited.

In real-property law and surveying, visible marks or indications left on natural or other objects indicating the lines and boundaries of a survey. Any physical object on the ground that helps to establish the location of a boundary line called for; it may be either natural (e.g., trees, rivers, and other land features) or artificial (e.g., fences, stones, stakes, or the like placed by human hands).

Moot An issue presenting no real controversy.

Moot court A method of teaching law and legal skills that requires students to analyze and argue both sides of a hypothetical legal issue using procedures modeled after those employed in state and federal appellate courts.

Moral law The rules of behavior an individual or a group may follow out of personal conscience and that are not necessarily part of legislated law in the United States.

Moral turpitude A phrase used in criminal law to describe conduct that is considered contrary to community standards of justice, honesty, or good morals.

Moratorium A suspension of activity or an authorized period of delay or waiting. A moratorium is sometimes agreed upon by the interested parties, or it may be authorized or imposed by operation of law. The term also is used to denote a period of time during which the law authorizes a delay in payment of debts or performance of some other legal obligation. This type of moratorium is most often invoked during times of distress, such as war or natural disaster.

Mortality tables A means of ascertaining the probable number of years any man or woman of a given age and of ordinary health will live. A mortality table expresses on the basis of the group studied the probability that, of a number of persons of equal expectations of life who are living at the beginning of any year, a certain number of deaths will occur within that year.

Such tables are used by insurance companies to determine the premium to be charged for those in the respective age groups.

Mortgage   A legal document by which the owner (buyer) transfers to the lender an interest in real estate to secure the repayment of a debt, evidenced by a mortgage note. When the debt is repaid, the mortgage is discharged, and a satisfaction of mortgage is recorded with the register or recorder of deeds in the county where the mortgage was recorded. Because most people cannot afford to buy real estate with cash, nearly every real estate transaction involves a mortgage.

Mortmain   [*French, Dead hand.*] A term to denote the conveyance of ownership of land or tenements to any corporation, religious or secular.

Mortmain acts   Statutes designed to prevent lands from being perpetually possessed or controlled by religious corporations.

Most-favored-nation status   A method of establishing equality of trading opportunity among states by guaranteeing that if one country is given better trade terms by another, then all other states must get the same terms.

Motion   A written or oral application made to a court or judge to obtain a ruling or order directing that some act be done in favor of the applicant. The applicant is known as the moving party, or the movant.

Motive   An idea, belief, or emotion that impels a person to act in accordance with that state of mind.

Movant   One who makes a motion before a court. The applicant for a judicial rule or order.

Move   To make an application to a court for a rule or order, or to take action in any matter. The term comprehends all things necessary to be done by a litigant to obtain an order of the court directing the relief sought. To propose a resolution, or recommend action in a deliberative body. To pass over; to be transferred, as when the consideration of a contract is said to *move* from one party to the other. To occasion; to contribute to; to tend or lead to.

Movie rating   A classification given to a commercially released motion picture that indicates to consumers whether the film contains sex, profanity, violence, or other subject matter that may be inappropriate for persons in certain age-groups.

Multidistrict litigation   A procedure provided by federal statute (28 U.S.C.A. § 1407) that permits civil lawsuits with at least one common (and often intricate) question of fact that have been pending in different federal district courts to be transferred and consolidated for pretrial proceedings before one judge.

Multilevel distributorship   A type of referral sales scheme by which an individual who purchases a particular item from a company agrees to solicit and provide additional buyers for the product in exchange for a commission or rebate from the company.

Multiplicity of actions Several unnecessary attempts to litigate the same claim or issue.

Municipal In its narrower and more common sense, pertaining to a local governmental unit, commonly a city or town. In its broader sense, pertaining to the public or governmental affairs of a state, nation, or of a people. Relating to a state or nation, particularly when considered as an entity independent of other states or nations.

Municipal corporation An incorporated political subdivision of a state that is composed of the citizens of a designated geographic area and which performs certain state functions on a local level and possesses such powers as are conferred upon it by the state.

Muniments of title Documents that serve as evidence of ownership of real or personal property. Written instruments, such as stock certificates or deeds to land, by which an owner is enabled to defend his or her ownership rights.

Murder The unlawful killing of another human being without justification or excuse.

Music publishing The contractual relationship between a songwriter or music composer and a music publisher, whereby the writer assigns part or all of his or her music copyrights to the publisher in exchange for the publisher's commercial exploitation of the music.

Mutilation Cutting, tearing, erasing, or otherwise changing a document in a way that changes or destroys its legal effect. It is a federal crime to mutilate public records, coins, or passports.

In criminal law, the crime of violently, maliciously, and intentionally giving someone a serious permanent wound.

Mutiny A rising against lawful or constituted authority, particularly in the naval or armed services.

Mutual company A corporation in which members are the exclusive shareholders and the recipients of profits distributed as dividends in proportion to the business that such members did with the company.

Mutual fund A fund, in the form of an investment company, in which shareholders combine their money to invest in a variety of stocks, bonds, and money-market investments such as U.S. Treasury bills and bank certificates of deposit.

Mutuality of obligation The legal principle that provides that unless both parties to a contract are bound to perform, neither party is bound.

Mutual mistake An error of both parties to a contract, whereby each operates under the identical misconception concerning a past or existing material fact.

Naked contract   An agreement between two parties that is without any legal effect because no consideration has been exchanged between the parties.

Name   The designation of an individual person or of a firm or corporation. A word or combination of words used to distinguish a person, thing, or class from others.

Napoleonic code   The first modern organized body of law governing France, also known as the Code Napoleon or Code Civil, enacted by Napoléon I in 1804.

National Mediation Board   A three-person board created by federal statute to resolve disputes in the railroad and airline industries that could disrupt travel or imperil the economy. The board also handles railroad and airline employee representation disputes and provides administrative and financial support in adjusting minor grievances in the railroad industry.

National Security Council   The president of the United States' principal forum for considering national security and foreign policy matters; the council comprises senior national security advisors and cabinet officials.

Natural and probable consequences   Those ramifications of a particular course of conduct that are reasonably foreseeable by a person of average intelligence and generally occur in the normal course of events.

Natural law   The unwritten body of universal moral principles that underlie the ethical and legal norms by which human conduct is sometimes evaluated and governed. Natural law is often contrasted with positive law, which consists of the written rules and regulations enacted by government. The term *natural law* is derived from the Roman term *jus naturale*. Adherents to natural law philosophy are known as naturalists.

Navigable waters   Waters that provide a channel for commerce and transportation of people and goods.

Necessaries   Things indispensable, or things proper and useful, for the sustenance of human life.

Necessity   A defense asserted by a criminal or civil defendant that he or she had no choice but to break the law.

Negative covenant   A provision found in an employment agreement or a contract of sale of a business that prohibits an employee or seller from competing in the same area or market.

Neglect   An omission to do or perform some work, duty, or act.

Negligence   Conduct that falls below the standards of behavior established by law for the protection of others against unreasonable risk of harm. A person has acted negligently if he or she has departed from the conduct expected of a reasonably prudent person acting under similar circumstances.

Negligence is also the name of a cause of action in the law of torts. To establish negligence, a plaintiff must prove that the defendant had a duty to the plaintiff, the defendant breached that duty by failing to conform to the required standard of conduct, the defendant's negligent conduct was the cause of the harm to the plaintiff, and the plaintiff was, in fact, harmed or damaged.

Negotiable instrument   A commercial paper, such as a check or promissory note, that contains the signature of the maker or drawer; an unconditional promise or order to pay a certain sum in cash that is payable either upon demand or at a specifically designated time to the order of a designated person or to its bearer.

Negotiate   To conduct business transactions; to deal with another individual in regard to a purchase and sale; to bargain or trade. To conclude by way of agreement, bargain, or compact. To transfer a *negotiable instrument*, such as a promissory note, or other commercial paper.

Net   The sum that remains following all permissible deductions, including charges, expenses, discounts, commissions, or taxes.

Net worth   The difference between total assets and liabilities; the sum total of the assets of an individual or business minus the total amount owed to creditors.

Neutrality   The state of a nation that takes no part in a war between two or more other nations.

New York Constitution of 1777   The first constitution of the state of New York. It was adopted on Sunday, April 20, 1777, at Kingston, New York, by a convention of delegates empowered by the people of the colony to establish a state government.

Next friend   An individual who acts on behalf of another individual who does not have the legal capacity to act on his or her own behalf.

The individual in whose name a minor's lawsuit is brought, or who appears in court to represent such minor's interest. The French term prochein ami has been used to designate such an individual, but the term guardian ad litem is more commonly used.

Next of kin   The blood relatives entitled by law to inherit the property of a person who dies without leaving a valid will, although the term is sometimes interpreted to include a relationship existing by reason of marriage.

See also descent and distribution.

Nihil   [*Latin, Nothing.*] The abbreviated designation of a statement filed by a sheriff or constable with a court describing his or her unsuccessful attempts to serve a writ, notice, or process upon the designated person.

Ninety-day letter The name given to a written notice sent to a taxpayer by the Internal Revenue Service regarding a deficiency in the payment of tax (26 U.S.C.A. § 6212 et seq.).

Nisi prius [*Latin, Unless before.*]

No bill A term that the foreman of the grand jury writes across the face of a bill of indictment (a document drawn up by a prosecutor that states formal criminal charges against a designated individual) to indicate that the criminal charges alleged therein against a suspect have not been sufficiently supported by the evidence presented before it to warrant his or her criminal prosecution.

No contest The English translation of a nolo contendere plea used in criminal cases. Generally the terms *nolo contendere* and *no contest* are used interchangeably in the legal community. The operation of a no contest plea is similar to a plea of guilty. A defendant who enters a no contest plea concedes the charges alleged without disputing or admitting guilt and without offering a defense. No contest has a different meaning in the context of a will.

No fault A kind of automobile insurance that provides that each driver must collect the allowable amount of money from his or her own insurance carrier subsequent to an accident regardless of who was at fault.

Nolle prosequi [*Latin, Will not prosecute.*]

No-load fund A type of mutual fund that does not impose extra charges for administrative and selling expenses incurred in offering its shares for sale to the public.

Nolo contendere [*Latin, I will not contest it.*] A plea in a criminal case by which the defendant answers the charges made in the indictment by declining to dispute or admit the fact of his or her guilt.

Nominal Trifling, token, or slight; not real or substantial; in name only.

Nominal damages Minimal money damages awarded to an individual in an action where the person has not suffered any substantial injury or loss for which he or she must be compensated.

Non [*Latin, Not.*] A common prefix used to indicate negation.

Nonage Infancy or minority; lack of requisite legal age.

Noncompete agreement A contract limiting a party from competing with a business after termination of employment or completion of a business sale.

Nonconforming use Continuing use of real property, permitted by zoning ordinances, in a manner in which other similar plots of land in the same area cannot ordinarily be used.

Nonfeasance The intentional failure to perform a required duty or obligation.

Nonprofit A corporation or an association that conducts business for the benefit of the general public without shareholders and without a profit motive.

Non prosequitur [*Latin, He does not pursue, or follow up.*] The name of a judgment rendered by a court against a plaintiff because he or she fails to take any necessary steps, in legal proceedings, within the period prescribed for such proceedings by the practice of court.

Non sui juris [*Latin, Not his own master.*] A term applied to an individual who lacks the legal capacity to act on his or her own behalf, such as an infant or an insane person.

Nonsuit A broad term for any of several ways to terminate a legal action without an actual determination of the controversy on the merits.

Nonsupport The failure of one individual to provide financial maintenance for another individual in spite of a legal obligation to do so.

Non vult contendere [*Latin, He does not wish to contest it.*] A type of plea that can be entered by a defendant who is unwilling to admit guilt but is willing to submit to the court for sentencing.

Norris-LaGuardia Act One of the initial federal labor laws in favor of organized labor. It was enacted in 1932.

North American Free Trade Agreement A trade agreement between the United States, Canada, and Mexico, which took effect January 1, 1994. Its purpose is to increase the efficiency and fairness of trade between the three nations.

North Atlantic Treaty Organization A collective security group that was established by the North Atlantic Treaty (34 U.N.T.S. 243) in 1949 to block the threat of military aggression in Europe by the Soviet Union.

Northwest Ordinance An agreement adopted in 1787 by the Congress of the Confederation of States that created the Northwest Territory, organized its governing structure, and established the procedures by which territories were admitted as states to the Union.

Notary public A public official whose main powers include administering oaths and attesting to signatures, both important and effective ways to minimize fraud in legal documents.

Note To take notice of. A commercial paper that contains an express and absolute promise by the maker to pay to a specific individual, to order, or to bearer a definite sum of money on demand or at a specifically designated time.

Notes of decisions Annotations; concise summaries and references to the printed decisions of cases that are designed to explain particular rules of law or applicable sections of statutes.

Notice Information; knowledge of certain facts or of a particular state of affairs. The formal receipt of papers that provide specific information.

Novation   The substitution of a new contract for an old one. The new agreement extinguishes the rights and obligations that were in effect under the old agreement.

Nuclear power   A form of energy produced by an atomic reaction, capable of producing an alternative source of electrical power to that supplied by coal, gas, or oil.

Nuclear Regulatory Commission   An independent regulatory agency that oversees the civilian use of nuclear power in the United States.

Nudum pactum   [*Latin, Naked pact.*] A promise to pay or provide or perform something without receiving anything in return, but merely out of affection or good will.

Nugatory   Invalid; lacking legal force.

Nuisance   A legal action to redress harm arising from the use of one's property.

Null   Of no legal validity, force, or effect; nothing.

Nunc pro tunc   [*Latin, Now for then.*] When courts take some action *nunc pro tunc*, that action has retroactive legal effect, as though it had been performed at a particular, earlier date.

Nuncupative will   The oral expression of a person's wishes as to the disposition of his or her property to be performed or to take effect after the person's death, dictated by the person in his or her final illness before a sufficient number of witnesses and afterward reduced to writing.

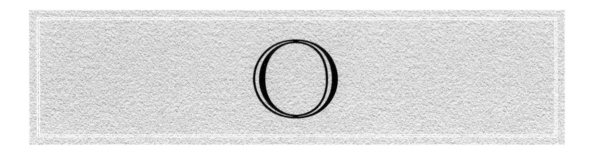

Oath   Any type of attestation by which an individual signifies that he or she is bound in conscience to perform a particular act truthfully and faithfully; a solemn declaration of truth or obligation.

　An individual's appeal to God to witness the truth of what he or she is saying or a pledge to do something enforced by the individual's responsibility to answer to God.

Obiter dictum   [*Latin, By the way.*] Words of an opinion entirely unnecessary for the decision of the case. A remark made or opinion expressed by a judge in a decision upon a cause, "by the way," that is, incidentally or collaterally, and not directly upon the question before the court or upon a point not necessarily involved in the determination of the cause, or introduced by way of illustration, or analogy or argument. Such are not binding as precedent.

Object   As a verb, to take exception to something; to declare or express the belief that something is improper or illegal.

As a noun, the thing sought to be accomplished or attained; aim; purpose; intention.

Objection   A formal attestation or declaration of disapproval concerning a specific point of law or procedure during the course of a trial; a statement indicating disagreement with a judge's ruling.

Obligation   A generic term for any type of legal duty or liability.

Obligee   The individual to whom a particular duty or obligation is owed.

Obligor   The individual who owes another person a certain debt or duty.

Obliteration   A destruction; an eradication of written words.

Obscene   Offensive to recognized standards of decency.

Obscenity   The character or quality of being obscene; an act, utterance, or item tending to corrupt the public morals by its indecency or lewdness.

Obstruction of justice   A criminal offense that involves interference, through words or actions, with the proper operations of a court or officers of the court.

Occupancy   Gaining or having physical possession of real property subject to, or in the absence of, legal right or title.

Occupational disease   A disease resulting from exposure during employment to conditions or substances that are detrimental to health (such as black lung disease contracted by miners).

Of counsel   A term commonly applied in the practice of law to an attorney who has been employed to aid in the preparation and management of a particular case but who is not the principal attorney in the action.

Of course   Any action or step that an individual might take during judicial proceedings without being required to ask the judge's permission or that will receive the judge's automatic approval if the individual does ask permission; that which is a matter of right.

Offense   A breach of law; a crime.

Offer   A promise that, according to its terms, is contingent upon a particular act, forbearance, or promise given in exchange for the original promise or the performance thereof; a demonstration of the willingness of a party to enter into a bargain, made in such a way that another individual is justified in understanding that his or her assent to the bargain is invited and that such assent will conclude the bargain.

Office audit A thorough examination and verification of the tax returns and financial records of an individual or firm by the Internal Revenue Service in the office of the agent who is conducting the review.

Office of Management and Budget An agency of the federal government that evaluates, formulates, and coordinates management procedures and program objectives within and among departments and agencies of the executive branch. It also controls the administration of the federal budget, while routinely providing the president of the United States with recommendations regarding budget proposals and relevant legislative enactments.

Officer An individual with the responsibility of performing the duties and functions of an office, that is a duty or charge, a position of trust, or a right to exercise a public or private employment.

Officers of the court An all-inclusive term for any type of court employee including judges, clerks, sheriffs, marshals, bailiffs, and constables.

Official Gazette A compilation published weekly by the Patent and Trademark Office listing all the patents and trademarks issued and registered, thereby providing notice to all interested parties.

Offset A contrary claim or demand that may cancel or reduce a given claim; a counterclaim. A kind of bookkeeping entry that counters the effect of a previous entry.

Of record Entered on the appropriate official documents maintained by a governmental body and that are usually available for inspection by the public.

Old-Age, Survivors, and Disability Insurance The system developed pursuant to the federal Social Security Act of 1935 (42 U.S.C.A. § 301 et seq. [1935]) to provide government benefits to eligible retirees, disabled individuals, and surviving spouses and their dependents.

Ombudsperson A public official who acts as an impartial intermediary between the public and government or bureaucracy, or an employee of an organization who mediates disputes between employees and management.

Omnibus [*Latin, For all; containing two or more independent matters.*] A term frequently used in reference to a legislative bill comprised of two or more general subjects that is designed to compel the executive to approve provisions that he or she would otherwise reject but that he or she signs into law to prevent the defeat of the entire bill.

On demand Payable immediately on request.

One person, one vote The principle that all citizens, regardless of where they reside in a state, are entitled to equal legislative representation.

On or about Near; approximately; without significant variance from an agreed date.

On point Directly applicable or dispositive of the matter under consideration.

Onus probandi   [*Latin, The burden of proof.*] In the strict sense, a term used to indicate that if no evidence is set forth by the party who has the burden of proof to establish the existence of facts in support of an issue, then the issue must be found against that party.

Open   To make accessible, visible, or available; to submit to review, examination, or inquiry through the elimination of restrictions or impediments.

Open account   An unpaid or unsettled account; an account with a balance that has not been ascertained, that is kept open in anticipation of future transactions. A type of credit extended by a seller to a buyer that permits the buyer to make purchases without a note or security and is based on an evaluation of the buyer's credit. A contractual obligation that may be modified by subsequent agreement of the parties, either by expressed consent or by consent implied from the conduct of the parties, provided the agreement changing the contractual obligation is based upon independent consideration.

Open bid   An offer to perform a contract, generally of a construction nature, in which the bidder reserves the right to reduce his or her bid to compete with a lower bid.

Open court   Common law requires a trial in open court; "open court" means a court to which the public has a right to be admitted. This term may mean either a court that has been formally convened and declared open for the transaction of its proper judicial business or a court that is freely open to spectators.

Open-end contract   An agreement that allows a buyer to make purchases over a period of time without a change in the price or terms by the seller.

Open-end credit   A type of revolving account that permits an individual to pay, on a monthly basis, only a portion of the total amount due.

Open-end mortgage   A mortgage that allows the borrowing of additional sums, often on the condition that a stated ratio of collateral value to the debt be maintained. A mortgage that provides for future advances on the mortgage and which so increases the amount of the mortgage.

Opening statement   An introductory statement made by the attorneys for each side at the start of a trial. The opening statement, although not mandatory, is seldom waived because it offers a valuable opportunity to provide an overview of the case to the jury and to explain the anticipated proof that will be presented during the course of the trial.

Open listing   A type of real estate listing contract whereby any agent who has a right to participate in the open listing is entitled to a commission if he or she produces the sale.

Open shop   A business in which union and nonunion workers are employed. A business in which union membership is not a condition of securing or maintaining employment.

Operation of law   The manner in which an individual acquires certain rights or liabilities through no act or cooperation of his or her own, but merely by the application of the established legal rules to the particular transaction.

Opinion evidence   Evidence of what the witness thinks, believes, or infers in regard to facts in dispute, as distinguished from personal knowledge of the facts themselves. The rules of evidence ordinarily do not permit witnesses to testify as to opinions or conclusions.

Oppression   The offense, committed by a public official, of wrongfully inflicting injury, such as bodily harm or imprisonment, upon another individual under color of office.

Option   A privilege, for which a person has paid money, that grants that person the right to purchase or sell certain commodities or certain specified securities at any time within an agreed period for a fixed price.

A right, which operates as a continuing offer, given in exchange for consideration—something of value—to purchase or lease property at an agreed price and terms within a specified time.

Oral contract   An agreement between parties that is either partly in writing and partly dependent on spoken words or that is entirely dependent on spoken words.

Ordeal   One of the most ancient forms of trial in England that required the accused person to submit to a dangerous or painful test on the theory that God would intervene and disclose his or her guilt or innocence.

Order   Direction of a court or judge normally made or entered in writing, and not included in a judgment, which determines some point or directs some step in the proceedings.

Order of the coif   An unincorporated national scholastic honor society in law. Its purpose is to foster excellence in legal scholarship and to recognize those who have attained high grades in law school or who have distinguished themselves in the teaching of law. There are more than sixty chapters located in law schools throughout the country.

Ordinance   A law, statute, or regulation enacted by a municipal corporation.

Organic law   The fundamental law or constitution of a particular state or nation, either written or unwritten, that defines and establishes the manner in which its government will be organized.

Organization   A generic term for any type of group or association of individuals who are joined together either formally or legally.

Organized crime   Criminal activity carried out by an organized enterprise.

Organ transplantation   The transfer of organs such as the kidneys, heart, or liver from one body to another.

Original intent The theory of interpretation by which judges attempt to ascertain the meaning of a particular provision of a state or federal constitution by determining how the provision was understood at the time it was drafted and ratified.

Original jurisdiction The authority of a tribunal to entertain a lawsuit, try it, and set forth a judgment on the law and facts.

Original writ A document formerly used to commence a lawsuit in English courts.

Origination fee A charge imposed by a lending institution or a bank for the service of processing a loan.

Orphan's court The designation of tribunals in a number of New England states that have probate or surrogate jurisdiction.

Ostensible Apparent; visible; exhibited.

Outlawry A declaration under Old English law by which a person found in contempt on a civil or criminal process was considered an outlaw— that is, someone who is beyond the protection or assistance of the law.

Out-of-court settlement An agreement reached between the parties in a pending lawsuit that resolves the dispute to their mutual satisfaction and occurs without judicial intervention, supervision, or approval.

Output contract In the law of sales, an agreement in which one party assents to sell his or her total production to another party, who agrees to purchase it.

Outstanding warrant An order that has not yet been carried out; an order for which the action commanded has not been taken.

Overbreadth doctrine A principle of judicial review that holds that a law is invalid if it punishes constitutionally protected speech or conduct along with speech or conduct that the government may limit to further a compelling government interest.

Overdraft A check that is drawn on an account containing less money than the amount stated on the check.

Overhead A sum total of the administrative or executive costs that relate to the management, conduct, or supervision of a business that are not attributable to any one particular product or department.

Overreaching Exploiting a situation through fraud or unconscionable conduct.

Override An arrangement whereby commissions are made by sales managers based upon the sales made by their subordinate sales representatives. A term found in an agreement between a real estate agent and a property owner whereby the agent keeps the right to receive a commission for the sale of the property for a reasonable time after the agreement expires if the sale is made to a purchaser with whom the agent negotiated prior to the expiration of the agreement.

Overrule   The refusal by a judge to sustain an objection set forth by an attorney during a trial, such as an objection to a particular question posed to a witness. To make void, annul, supersede, or reject through a subsequent decision or action.

Overt   Public; open; manifest.

Overt act   An open, manifest act from which criminality may be implied. An outward act done in pursuance and manifestation of an intent or design.

Owner   The person recognized by the law as having the ultimate control over, and right to use, property as long as the law permits and no agreement or covenant limits his or her rights.

Oyer and terminer   [*French, To hear and decide.*] The designation "court of oyer and terminer" is frequently used as the actual title, or a portion of the title, of a state court that has criminal jurisdiction over felonious offenses.

Oyez   [*French, Hear ye.*] A word used in some courts by the public crier to indicate that a proclamation is about to be made and to command attention to it.

P

Pacific Railroad Act   Legislation passed by Congress in 1862 (12 Stat. 489) that authorized the construction of the first transcontinental railway line connecting the east and west coasts.

Pacifism   A belief or policy of opposition to war or violence as a means of settling disputes.

Packing   The process of exercising unlawful, improper, or deceitful means to obtain a jury composed of individuals who are favorably disposed to the verdict sought.

Pact   A bargain, compact, or agreement. An agreement between two or more nations or states that is similar to, but less complex than, a treaty.

Pacta sunt servanda   [*Latin, Promises must be kept.*] An expression signifying that the agreements and stipulations of the parties to a contract must be observed.

Pactum   [*Latin, Pact.*] A compact, bargain, or agreement.

Pairing-off In the practice of legislative bodies, a system by which two members, who belong to opposing political parties or are on opposite sides with respect to a certain question, mutually agree that they will both be absent from voting, either for a specified period or when a vote is to be taken on the particular question.

Pais [*French, The country; the neighborhood.*] A trial *per pais* denotes a trial by the country; that is, trial by jury.

Palm off To misrepresent inferior goods of one producer as superior goods made by a reputable, well-regarded competitor in order to gain commercial advantage and promote sales.

Palpable Easily perceptible, plain, obvious, readily visible, noticeable, patent, distinct, manifest.

Pander To pimp; to cater to the gratification of the lust of another. To entice or procure a person, by promises, threats, fraud, or deception to enter any place in which prostitution is practiced for the purpose of prostitution.

Panel A list of jurors to serve in a particular court or for the trial of a designated action. A group of judges of a lesser number than the entire court convened to decide a case, such as when a nine-member appellate court divides into three, three-member groups, and each group hears and decides cases. A plan in reference to prepaid legal services.

Paper A document that is filed or introduced in evidence in a lawsuit, as in the phrases *papers in the case* and *papers on appeal*.

Any written or printed statement, including letters, memoranda, legal or business documents, and books of account, in the context of the Fourth Amendment to the U.S. Constitution, which protects the people from unreasonable searches and seizures with respect to their "papers" as well as their persons and houses.

In the context of accommodation paper and commercial paper, a written or printed evidence of debt.

Par In commercial law, equal; equality.

Parallel citation A reference to the same case or statute published in two or more sources.

Paramount title In the law of real property, ownership that is superior to the ownership with which it is compared, in the sense that the former is the source or the origin of the latter.

Parcener A joint heir.

Pardon The action of an executive official of the government that mitigates or sets aside the punishment for a crime.

Parens patriae [*Latin, Parent of the country.*] A doctrine that grants the inherent power and authority of the state to protect persons who are legally unable to act on their own behalf.

Parent and child   The legal relationship between a father or mother and his or her offspring.

Parent company   An enterprise, which is also known as a parent corporation, that owns more than 50 percent of the voting shares of its subsidiary.

Pari causa   [*Latin, With equal right.*] Upon an equal footing; having the same rights or claims.

Pari delicto   [*Latin, In equal fault.*] The doctrine, also known as *in pari delicto*, that provides that courts will not enforce an invalid contract and that no party can recover in an action where it is necessary to prove the existence of an illegal contract in order to make his or her case.

Pari materia   [*Latin, Of the same matter; on the same subject.*] The phrase used in connection with two laws relating to the same subject matter that must be analyzed with each other.

Pari passu   [*Latin, By an equal progress; equably; ratably; without preference.*] Used especially to describe creditors who, in marshalling assets, are entitled to receive out of the same fund without any precedence over each other.

Parity   Equality in amount or value. Equivalence of prices of farm products to the prices existing at some former date (the base period) or to the general cost of living; equivalence of prices of goods or services in two different markets. The relationship between two currencies such that they are exchangeable for each other at the par or official rate of exchange.

Parliamentary law   The general body of enacted rules and recognized usages governing the procedure of legislative assemblies and other deliberative sessions such as meetings of stockholders and directors of corporations, town meetings, and board meetings. Roberts Rules of Order are an example of such rules.

Parole   The conditional release of a person convicted of a crime prior to the expiration of that person's term of imprisonment, subject to both the supervision of the correctional authorities during the remainder of the term and a resumption of the imprisonment upon violation of the conditions imposed.

Parol evidence   *Parol* refers to verbal expressions or words. Verbal evidence, such as the testimony of a witness at trial.

Particular average loss   In maritime law, damage sustained by a ship, cargo, or freight that is not recompensed by contribution from all interests in the venture but must be borne by the owner of the damaged property.

Particulars   The details of a claim, or the separate items of an account.

Parties   The persons who are directly involved or interested in any act, affair, contract, transaction, or legal proceeding; opposing litigants.

Partition   Any division of real property or personal property between co-owners, resulting in individual ownership of the interests of each.

Partnership An association of two or more persons engaged in a business enterprise in which the profits and losses are shared proportionally. The legal definition of a partnership is generally stated as "an association of two or more persons to carry on as co-owners a business for profit" (Revised Uniform Partnership Act § 101 [1994]).

Party Any person involved in a transaction or proceeding. A group of voters organized for the purpose of influencing governmental policy, particularly through the nomination and election of candidates for public office.

Party of the first part A phrase used in a document to avoid repeating the name of the persons first mentioned in it.

Party wall A partition erected on a property boundary, partly on the land of one owner and partly on the land of another, to provide common support to the structures on both sides of the boundary.

Pass As a verb, to utter or pronounce, as when the court *passes* sentence upon a prisoner. Also to proceed; to be rendered or given, as when judgment is said to *pass* for the plaintiff in a suit.

In legislative parlance, a bill or resolution is said to *pass* when it is agreed to or enacted by the house, or when the body has sanctioned its adoption by the requisite majority of votes; in the same circumstances, the body is said to *pass* the bill or motion.

When an auditor appointed to examine any accounts certifies to their correctness, she is said to *pass* them; i.e., they pass through the examination without being detained or sent back for inaccuracy or imperfection.

The term also means to examine anything and then authoritatively determine the disputed questions that it involves. In this sense a jury is said to *pass upon* the rights or issues in litigation before them.

In the language of conveyancing, the term means to move from one person to another; i.e., to be transferred or conveyed from one owner to another.

To publish; utter; transfer; circulate; impose fraudulently. This is the meaning of the word when referring to the offense of *passing* counterfeit money or a forged paper.

As a noun, permission to pass; a license to go or come; a certificate, emanating from authority, wherein it is declared that a designated person is permitted to go beyond certain boundaries that, without such authority, he could not lawfully pass. Also a ticket issued by a railroad or other transportation company, authorizing a designated person to travel free on its lines, between certain points or for a limited time.

Passim [*Latin, Everywhere.*] A term frequently used to indicate a general reference to a book or legal authority.

Passport A document that indicates permission granted by a sovereign to its citizen to travel to foreign countries and return and requests foreign governments to allow that citizen to pass freely and safely.

With respect to international law, a passport is a license of safe conduct, issued during a war, that authorizes an individual to leave a warring nation or to remove his or her effects from that nation to another country; it also authorizes a person to travel from country to country without being subject to arrest or detention because of the war.

In maritime law, a passport is a document issued to a neutral vessel by its own government during a war that is carried on the voyage as evidence of the nationality of the vessel and as protection against the vessels of the warring nations. This paper is also labeled a *pass*, *sea-pass*, *sea-letter*, or *sea-brief*. It usually contains the captain's or master's name and residence; the name, property, description, tonnage, and destination of the ship; the nature and quantity of the cargo; and the government under which it sails.

Patent   Open; manifest; evident.

Patents   Rights, granted to inventors by the federal government, pursuant to its power under Article I, Section 8, Clause 8, of the U.S. Constitution, that permit them to exclude others from making, using, or selling an invention for a definite, or restricted, period of time.

Patent writ   An open court order in earlier times; a writ that was not folded and sealed up as a close writ would be.

Paternity   The state or condition of a father; the relationship of a father.

Paternity suit   A civil action brought against an unwed father by an unmarried mother to obtain support for an illegitimate child and for payment of bills incident to the pregnancy and the birth.

Patients' rights   The legal interests of persons who submit to medical treatment.

Pat. pend.   An abbreviation displayed prominently on an invention for which an application for a patent has been made but has not yet been issued.

Patronage   The practice or custom observed by a political official of filling government positions with qualified employees of his or her own choosing.

Pauper   An impoverished person who is supported at public expense; an indigent litigant who is permitted to sue or defend without paying costs; an impoverished criminal defendant who has a right to receive legal services without charge.

Pawn   To deliver personal property to another as a pledge or as security for a debt. A deposit of goods with a creditor as security for a sum of money borrowed.

Pawnbroker   A person who engages in the business of lending money, usually in small sums, in exchange for personal property deposited with him or her that can be kept or sold if the borrower fails or refuses to repay the loan.

Payable   Justly due; legally enforceable.

Payee   The person who is to receive the stated amount of money on a check, bill, or note.

Payment   The fulfillment of a promise; the performance of an agreement. A delivery of money, or its equivalent in either specific property or services, by a debtor to a creditor.

P.C.   An abbreviation for professional corporation, which is a special corporation established by professionals, such as physicians, accountants, or, in some states, attorneys, who practice together.

Peace bond   The posting of money in court, as required by a judge or magistrate, by a person who has threatened to commit a breach of the peace.

Peace officers   Sheriffs, constables, marshals, city police officers, and other public officials whose duty it is to enforce and preserve the public order.

Peculation   The unlawful appropriation, by a depositary of public funds, of the government property entrusted to the care of the depository; the fraudulent diversion to an individual's personal use of money or goods entrusted to that person's care.

Pecuniary   Monetary; relating to money; financial; consisting of money or that which can be valued in money.

Pederasty   The criminal offense of unnatural copulation between men.

Peers   Equals; those who are an individual's equals in rank and station.

Penal   Punishable; inflicting a punishment.

Penalty   A punitive measure that the law imposes for the performance of an act that is proscribed, or for the failure to perform a required act.

Pendente lite   [*Latin, Pending the litigation.*] During the actual progress of a lawsuit.

Pendent jurisdiction   The discretionary power of a federal court to permit the assertion of a related state law claim, along with a federal claim between the same parties, properly before the court, provided that the federal claim and the state law claim derive from the same set of facts.

Pending   Begun, but not yet completed; during; before the conclusion of; prior to the completion of; unsettled; in the process of adjustment.

Penitentiary   A prison or place of confinement where persons convicted of felonies serve their term of imprisonment.

Penny stocks   Inexpensive issues of stock, typically selling at less than $1 a share, in companies that often are newly formed or involved in highly speculative ventures.

Penology   The science of prison administration and rehabilitation of criminals.

Pen register A device that decodes or records electronic impulses, allowing outgoing numbers from a telephone to be identified.

Pension A benefit, usually money, paid regularly to retired employees or their survivors by private businesses and federal, state, and local governments. Employers are not required to establish pension benefits but do so to attract qualified employees.

Pent road A street that is closed at its terminal points.

Penumbra The rights guaranteed by implication in a constitution or the implied powers of a rule.

Peonage A condition of enforced servitude by which a person is restrained of his or her liberty and compelled to labor in payment of some debt or obligation.

People The aggregate of the individuals who comprise a state or a nation.

Per [*Latin, By, through, or by means of.*]

Per capita [*Latin, By the heads or polls.*] A term used in the descent and distribution of the estate of one who dies without a will. It means to share and share alike according to the number of individuals.

Percentage lease A rental agreement, usually with respect to a retail business property, whereby a portion of the gross sales or net sales of the tenant is used to determine the rent.

Per curiam [*Latin, By the court.*] A phrase used to distinguish an opinion of the whole court from an opinion written by any one judge.

Peremptory challenge The right to challenge a juror without assigning, or being required to assign, a reason for the challenge.

Peremptory ruling An immediate and absolute decision by the court on some point of law that is rendered without consideration of alternatives.

Perfect Complete; finished; executed; enforceable; without defect; merchantable; marketable.

Performance The fulfillment or accomplishment of a promise, contract, or other obligation according to its terms.

Peril The designated contingency, risk, or hazard against which an insured seeks to protect himself or herself when purchasing a policy of insurance.

Perjury A crime that occurs when an individual willfully makes a false statement during a judicial proceeding, after he or she has taken an oath to speak the truth.

Permissive counterclaim A claim by a defendant opposing the claim of the plaintiff and seeking some relief from the plaintiff for the defendant.

Perpetrator	A term commonly used by law enforcement officers to designate a person who actually commits a crime.
Perpetuating testimony	The procedure permitted by federal and state discovery rules for preserving the attestation of a witness that might otherwise be lost prior to the trial in which it is intended to be used.
Perpetuation of evidence	The procedure employed to assure that proof will be available for possible use at a later trial.
Perquisites	Fringe benefits or other incidental profits or benefits accompanying an office or position.
Per quod	[*Latin, Whereby.*] With respect to a complaint in a civil action, a phrase that prefaces the recital of the consequences of certain acts as a ground of special harm to the plaintiff.
Per se	[*Latin, In itself.*] Simply as such; in its own nature without reference to its relation.
Person	In general usage, a human being; by statute, however, the term can include firms, labor organizations, partnerships, associations, corporations, legal representatives, trustees, trustees in bankruptcy, or receivers.
Personal actions	Lawsuits initiated in order, among other things, to recover damages for some injury to a plaintiff's personal right or property, for breach of contract, for money owed on a debt, or for the recovery of a specific item of personal property.
Personal injury	Any violation of an individual's right, other than his or her rights in property.
Personal jurisdiction	The power of a court to hear and determine a lawsuit involving a defendant by virtue of the defendant's having some contact with the place where the court is located.
Personal property	Everything that is the subject of ownership that does not come under the denomination of real property; any right or interest that an individual has in movable things.
Personal representative	A person who manages the financial affairs of another person who is unable to do so.
Personal service	The actual delivery of process to the individual to whom it is directed or to someone authorized to receive it on his or her behalf.
Personalty	Goods; chattels; articles; movable property, whether animate or inanimate.
Per stirpes	[*Latin, By roots or stocks; by representation.*] A term used to denote a method used in dividing the estate of a person. A person who takes per stirpes, sometimes called by right of representation, does not inherit in an individual capacity but as a member of a group.

Persuasive authority Sources of law, such as related cases or legal encyclopedias, that the court consults in deciding a case, but which, unlike binding authority, the court need not apply in reaching its conclusion.

Petition A written application from a person or persons to some governing body or public official asking that some authority be exercised to grant relief, favors, or privileges.

A formal application made to a court in writing that requests action on a certain matter.

Petitioner One who presents a formal, written application to a court, officer, or legislative body that requests action on a certain matter.

Petition in bankruptcy A document filed in a specialized federal court to commence a proceeding to provide a means by which a debtor who is unwilling or financially unable to pay personal debts will satisfy the claims of his or her creditors as they come due.

Petit jury The ordinary panel of twelve persons called to issue a verdict in a civil action or a criminal prosecution.

Petit larceny A form of larceny—the stealing of another's personal property—in which the value of the property taken is generally less than $50.

Petitory action A legal proceeding by which the plaintiff seeks to establish and enforce his or her title to property, as distinguished from a possessory proceeding, where the plaintiff's right to possession is the issue. Such petitory actions must be based on a claim of legal title to the property, as opposed to a mere equitable interest in it.

In admiralty, suits to try title to property independent of questions concerning possession. See also admiralty and maritime law.

In the civil-law jurisdiction of Louisiana, a proceeding instituted by an alleged owner who does not have possession to determine ownership against one in possession.

Petty offense A minor crime, the maximum punishment for which is generally a fine or a short term in a prison or a house of correction.

Philadelphia lawyer A colloquial term that was initially a compliment to the legal expertise and competence of an attorney due to the outstanding reputation of the Philadelphia bar during colonial times. More recently the term has become a disparaging label for an attorney who is skillful in the manipulation of the technicalities and intricacies of the law to the advantage of his or her client, although the spirit of the law might be violated.

Photo lineup A presentation of photographs to a victim or witness of a crime.

Physical fact In the law of evidence, an event having a corporeal existence, as distinguished from a mere conception of the mind; one that is visible, audible, or tangible, such as the sound of footsteps or impressions made by human feet on the ground.

Picketing The presence at an employer's business of one or more employees and/or other persons who are publicizing a labor dispute, influencing employees or customers to withhold their work or business, respectively, or showing a union's desire to represent employees; picketing is usually accompanied by patrolling with signs.

Pilot   In maritime law, a person who assumes responsibility for a vessel at a particular place for the purpose of navigating it through a river or channel, or from or into a port.

Pimp   In feudal England, a type of tenure by which a tenant was permitted to use real property that belonged to a lord in exchange for the performance of some service, such as providing young women for the use and pleasure of the lord.

An individual who, for a fee, supplies another individual with a prostitute for sexual purposes. To pander, or cater to the sexual desires of others in exchange for money.

Piracy   The act of violence or depredation on the high seas; also, the theft of intellectual property, especially in electronic media.

P.J.   An abbreviation for presiding judge, the individual who directs, controls, or governs a particular tribunal as its chief officer.

Plagiarism   The act of appropriating the literary composition of another author, or excerpts, ideas, or passages therefrom, and passing the material off as one's own creation.

Plain-error rule   The principle that an appeals court can reverse a judgment and order a new trial because of a serious mistake in the proceedings, even though no objection was made at the time the mistake occurred.

Plain-meaning rule   A principle used by courts in interpreting contracts that provides that the objective definitions of contractual terms are controlling, irrespective of whether the language comports with the actual intention of either party.

Plaintiff   The party who sues in a civil action; a complainant; the prosecution—that is, a state or the United States representing the people—in a criminal case.

Plaintiff in error   The unsuccessful party in a lawsuit who commences proceedings for appellate review of the action because a mistake or "error" has been made resulting in a judgment against him or her; an appellant.

Plain view doctrine   In the context of searches and seizures, the principle that provides that objects perceptible by an officer who is rightfully in a position to observe them can be seized without a search warrant and are admissible as evidence.

Plat   A map of a town or a section of land that has been subdivided into lots showing the location and boundaries of individual parcels with the streets, alleys, easements, and rights of use over the land of another.

Plea   A formal response by the defendant to the affirmative assertions of the plaintiff in a civil case or to the charges of the prosecutor in a criminal case.

Plea bargaining   The process whereby a criminal defendant and prosecutor reach a mutually satisfactory disposition of a criminal case, subject to court approval.

Pleading   Asking a court to grant relief. The formal presentation of claims and defenses by parties to a lawsuit. The specific papers by which the allegations of parties to a lawsuit are presented in proper form; specifically the complaint of a plaintiff and the answer of a defendant plus any additional responses to those papers that are authorized by law.

Plea in abatement   In common-law pleading, a response by the defendant that does not dispute the plaintiff's claim but objects to its form or the time or place where it is asserted.

Plea in bar   An answer to a plaintiff's claim that absolutely and entirely defeats it.

Pledge   A bailment or delivery of personal property to a creditor as security for a debt or for the performance of an act.

Plurality   The opinion of an appellate court in which more justices join than in any concurring opinion.

    The excess of votes cast for one candidate over those votes cast for any other candidate.

Poaching   The illegal shooting, trapping, or taking of game or fish from private or public property.

Pocket part   An addition to many lawbooks that updates them until a new edition is published.

Point   A distinct proposition or question of law arising or propounded in a case. In the case of shares of stock, a point means $1. In the case of bonds a point means $10, since a bond is quoted as a percentage of $1,000. In the case of market averages, the word point means merely that and no more. If, for example, the Dow-Jones Industrial Average rises from 8,349.25 to 8,350.25, it has risen a point. A point in this average, however, is not equivalent to $1.

    With respect to the home mortgage finance industry, a fee or charge of one percent of the principal of the loan that is collected by the lender at the time the loan is made and is in addition to the constant long-term stated interest rate on the face of the loan.

Poison   Any substance dangerous to living organisms that if applied internally or externally, destroy the action of vital functions or prevent the continuance of life.

    Economic poisons are those substances that are used to control insects, weeds, fungi, bacteria, rodents, predatory animals, or other pests. Economic poisons are useful to society but are still dangerous.

Poison pill   A defensive strategy based on issuing special stock that is used to deter aggressors in corporate takeover attempts.

Police power   The authority conferred upon the states by the Tenth Amendment to the U.S. Constitution and which the states delegate to their political subdivisions to enact measures to preserve and protect the safety, health, welfare, and morals of the community.

Policy The general principles by which a government is guided in its management of public affairs, or the legislature in its measures. A general term used to describe all contracts of insurance.

As applied to a law, ordinance, or rule of law, the general purpose or tendency considered as directed to the welfare or prosperity of the state or community.

Political crime A serious violation of law that threatens the security or existence of the government, such as treason or sedition.

Political question An issue that the federal courts refuse to decide because it properly belongs to the decision-making authority of elected officials.

Political trial A trial that addresses political questions, involves political officials, or serves political agendas. In certain circumstances the term is used in a pejorative sense to criticize a particular trial or proceeding as unfair or unjust.

Polling the jury A practice whereby the jurors are asked individually whether they assented, and still assent, to the verdict; it consists of calling the name of each juror and requiring a declaration of his or her verdict before it is recorded.

Polls The place where voters cast their ballots. Heads; individuals; persons singly considered.

Poll tax A specified sum of money levied upon each person who votes.

Pollution The contamination of the air, water, or earth by harmful or potentially harmful substances.

Polygamy The offense of having more than one wife or husband at the same time.

Polygraph An instrument used to measure physiological responses in humans when they are questioned in order to determine if their answers are truthful.

Ponzi scheme A fraudulent investment plan in which the investments of later investors are used to pay earlier investors, giving the appearance that the investments of the initial participants dramatically increase in value in a short amount of time.

Popular name tables Reference charts that aid in locating statutes, if the names by which they are commonly referred to are known.

Pornography The representation in books, magazines, photographs, films, and other media of scenes of sexual behavior that are erotic or lewd and are designed to arouse sexual interest.

Positive evidence Direct proof of the fact or point in issue, as distinguished from circumstantial proof; proof that if believed, establishes the truth or falsity of a fact in issue and does not arise from a presumption.

Positive law   Those laws that have been duly enacted by a properly instituted and popularly recognized branch of government.

Positivism   A school of jurisprudence whose advocates believe that the only legitimate sources of law are those written rules, regulations, and principles that have been expressly enacted, adopted, or recognized by a government body, including administrative, executive, legislative, and judicial bodies.

Posse comitatus   [*Latin, Power of the county.*] Referred at common law to all males over the age of fifteen on whom a sheriff could call for assistance in preventing any type of civil disorder.

Possession   The ownership, control, or occupancy of a thing, most frequently land or personal property, by a person.

Possessory action   A proceeding instituted to obtain or recover the actual possession of property, as distinguished from a proceeding that merely seeks to establish the plaintiff's title or ownership of property.

In admiralty law, a possessory action is one that is brought to recover the possession of a vessel that is had under a claim of title.

Possessory warrant   A rare statutory remedy for the recovery of personal property that has been taken by fraud, violence, enticement, or seduction, or that has disappeared and is believed to be in the detention and control of the party complained against.

Postconviction remedies   A variety of relief sought by a convicted criminal to have his or her sentence vacated, set aside, or corrected because such a sentence was based upon some violation of the U.S. Constitution.

Postdate   To designate a written instrument, such as a check, with a time or date later than that at which it is really made.

Posthumous child   An infant who is born subsequent to the death of the father or, in certain cases, the mother.

Posting   In accounting, the act of transferring an original entry to a ledger. The act of mailing a document. A form of substituted service of process consisting of displaying the process in a prominent place when other forms of service are unavailing.

In connection with trespass statutes, the act of placing or affixing signs on private property in a manner to give notice of the trespass.

Postmarital agreement   An agreement made between spouses after marriage concerning the rights and responsibilities of the parties upon divorce or the death of one of the spouses.

Post mortem   [*Latin, After death.*] Pertaining to matters occurring after death. A term generally applied to an autopsy or examination of a corpse in order to ascertain the cause of death or to the inquisition for that purpose by the coroner.

Pour-over A clause in a will or trust that provides that, upon the death of the creator of the trust, his or her money or property will be transferred into some other existing trust.

Power The right, ability, or authority to perform an act. An ability to generate a change in a particular legal relationship by doing or not doing a certain act.

In a restricted sense, a liberty or authority that is reserved by, or limited to, a person to dispose of real or personal property, for his or her own benefit or for the benefit of others, or that enables one person to dispose of an interest that is vested in another.

Power of attorney A written document in which one person (the principal) appoints another person to act as an agent on his or her behalf, thus conferring authority on the agent to perform certain acts or functions on behalf of the principal.

Power of sale A clause commonly inserted in a mortgage and deed of trust that grants the creditor or trustee the right and authority, upon default in the payment of the debt, to advertise and sell the property at public auction, without resorting to a court for authorization to do so.

Power of termination A future interest in real property whereby the grantor conveys an estate to another, called the grantee, subject to a particular condition, the breach of which forfeits the grantee's interest in the property.

Practice Repeated or customary action; habitual performance; a succession of acts of similar kind; custom; usage. The exercise of any profession.

The form or mode or proceeding in courts of justice for the enforcement of rights or the redress of wrongs, as distinguished from the substantive law that gives the right or denounces the wrong. The form, manner, or order of instituting and conducting an action or other judicial proceeding, through its successive stages to its end, in accordance with the rules and principles laid down by law or by the regulations and precedents of the courts.

Praecipe [*Latin, Give an order.*] An original writ, one of the forms of legal process used to commence an action. A praecipe was drawn up in the alternative and commanded the defendant to do what was ordered or to appear and show why he or she had not done it. An order that commands the clerk of a court to issue a formal writ of execution directing the enforcement of a judgment already rendered and commanding a public officer to seize the defendant's property in order to satisfy the debt.

Prayer The request contained in a bill in equity that the court will grant the process, aid, or relief that the complainant desires.

Preamble A clause at the beginning of a constitution or statute explaining the reasons for its enactment and the objectives it seeks to attain.

Precatory language Words in a will or a trust used by the testator (the person making the will) or settlor (the person making a trust) to express a wish or desire to have his or her property disposed of in a certain way or to have some other task undertaken, which do not necessarily impose a mandatory obligation upon anyone to carry out the wish.

Precedent   A court decision that is cited as an example or analogy to resolve similar questions of law in later cases.

Precept   An order, writ, warrant, or process. An order or direction, emanating from authority, to an officer or body of officers, commanding that officer or those officers to do some act within the scope of their powers. Rule imposing a standard of conduct or action.

In English law, the direction issued by a sheriff to the proper returning officers of cities and boroughs within his jurisdiction for the election of members to serve in parliament.

In old French law, a kind of letters issued by the king in subversion of the laws, being orders to the judges to do or tolerate things contrary to law.

Precinct   A constable's or police district. A small geographical unit of government. An election district created for convenient localization of polling places. A county or municipal subdivision for casting and counting votes in elections.

Preclusion order   A court sanction that prevents a party who has not complied with a direction to supply information in the discovery stage of a lawsuit from later supporting or challenging designated claims or defenses related to the facts that he or she withheld.

Preemption   A doctrine based on the Supremacy Clause of the U.S. Constitution that holds that certain matters are of such a national, as opposed to local, character that federal laws preempt or take precedence over state laws. As such, a state may not pass a law inconsistent with the federal law.

A doctrine of state law that holds that a state law displaces a local law or regulation that is in the same field and is in conflict or inconsistent with the state law.

Preemptive right   The privilege of a stockholder to maintain a proportionate share of the ownership of a corporation by purchasing a proportionate share of any new stock issues.

Preference   The act of an insolvent debtor who pays one or more creditors the full amount of their claims or a larger amount than they would be entitled to receive on a pro rata distribution.

Preferred stock   Stock shares that have preferential rights to dividends or to amounts distributable on liquidation, or to both, ahead of common shareholders.

Prejudice   A forejudgment; bias; partiality; preconceived opinion. A leaning toward one side of a cause for some reason other than a conviction of its justice.

Prelaw education   A preparatory curriculum comprising introductory law courses and interdisciplinary subjects, offered to undergraduate students to instruct them in and acquaint them with the subject matter of law, thereby assisting them in deciding whether to seek admission to law school and facilitating the process of law study in law school.

Preliminary hearing   A proceeding before a judicial officer in which the officer must decide whether a crime was committed, whether the crime occurred within the territorial jurisdiction of the court, and whether there is probable cause to believe that the defendant committed the crime.

Preliminary injunction   A temporary order made by a court at the request of one party that prevents the other party from pursuing a particular course of conduct until the conclusion of a trial on the merits.

Premarital agreement   A contract made in anticipation of marriage that specifies the rights and obligations of the parties. Such an agreement typically includes terms for property distribution in the event the marriage terminates.

Premeditate   To think of an act beforehand; to contrive and design; to plot or lay plans for the execution of a purpose.

Premium   A reward for an act done.

Preponderance of evidence   A standard of proof that must be met by a plaintiff if he or she is to win a civil action.

Prerogative   An exclusive privilege. The special power or peculiar right possessed by an official by virtue of his or her office. In English law, a discretionary power that exceeds and is unaffected by any other power; the special preeminence that the monarch has over and above all others, as a consequence of his or her sovereignty.

Prerogative writ   Formerly a court order issued under certain circumstances on the authority of the extraordinary powers of the monarch.

Prescription   A method of acquiring a nonpossessory interest in land through the long, continuous use of the land.

Present   To submit for consideration or action. Immediate, not in the future.

Presentence investigation   Research that is conducted by court services or a probation officer relating to the prior criminal record, education, employment, and other information about a person convicted of a crime, for the purpose of assisting the court in passing sentence.

Presentment   A grand jury statement that a crime was committed; a written notice, initiated by a grand jury, that states that a crime occurred and that an indictment should be drawn.

 In relation to commercial paper, presentment is a demand for the payment or acceptance of a negotiable instrument, such as a check. The holder of a negotiable instrument generally makes a presentment to the maker, acceptor, drawer, or drawee.

Presents   The present instrument. The phrase *these presents* is used in any legal document to designate the instrument in which the phrase itself occurs.

Presidential powers	The executive authority given to the president of the United States by Article II of the Constitution to carry out the duties of the office.
President of the United States	The head of the executive branch, one of the three branches of the federal government.
Presumption	A conclusion made as to the existence or nonexistence of a fact that must be drawn from other evidence that is admitted and proven to be true. A rule of law.
Presumption of innocence	A principle that requires the government to prove the guilt of a criminal defendant and relieves the defendant of any burden to prove his or her innocence.
Pretermitted heir	A child or other descendent omitted from the will of a testator.
Pretrial conference	A meeting of the parties to an action and their attorneys held before the court prior to the commencement of actual courtroom proceedings.
Prevailing party	The litigant who successfully brings or defends an action and, as a result, receives a favorable judgment or verdict.
Preventive detention	The confinement in a secure facility of a person who has not been found guilty of a crime.
Price-fixing	The organized setting of what the public will be charged for certain products or services agreed to by competitors in the marketplace in violation of the Sherman Anti-Trust Act (15 U.S.C.A. § 1 et seq.).
Prima facie	[*Latin, On the first appearance.*] A fact presumed to be true unless it is disproved.
Primary authority	Law, in various forms, that a court must follow in deciding a case.
Primary evidence	An authentic document or item that is offered as proof in a lawsuit, as contrasted with a copy of, or substitute for, the original.
Prime lending rate	The lowest rate of interest that a financial institution, such as a bank, charges its best customers, usually large corporations, for short-term unsecured loans.
Primogeniture	The status of being the firstborn child among several children of the same parents. A rule of inheritance at common law through which the oldest male child has the right to succeed to the estate of an ancestor to the exclusion of younger siblings, both male and female, as well as other relatives.
Principal	A source of authority; a sum of a debt or obligation producing interest; the head of a school. In an agency relationship, the principal is the person who gives authority to another, called an agent, to act on his or her behalf. In criminal law, the principal is the chief actor or

perpetrator of a crime; those who aid, abet, counsel, command, or induce the commission of a crime may also be principals. In investments and banking, the principal refers to the person for whom a broker executes an order; it may also mean the capital invested or the face amount of a loan.

Principal and surety A contractual relationship whereby one party—the surety—agrees to pay the principal's debt or perform his or her obligation in case of the principal's default.

Principle A fundamental, well-settled rule of law. A basic truth or undisputed legal doctrine; a given legal proposition that is clear and does not need to be proved.

Printers ink statute Statutes enacted in a number of states making it a misdemeanor to use representations that are untrue, deceptive, or misleading in advertisements.

Prior inconsistent statements Communications made by a witness before the time he or she takes the stand to testify in an action that contradict subsequent testimony given on the same exact facts.

Prior restraint Government prohibition of speech in advance of publication.

Prison A public building used for the confinement of people convicted of serious crimes.

Prisoners' rights The nature and extent of the privileges afforded to individuals kept in custody or confinement against their will because they were convicted of performing an unlawful act.

Privacy In constitutional law, the right of people to make personal decisions regarding intimate matters; under the common law, the right of people to lead their lives in a manner that is reasonably secluded from public scrutiny, whether such scrutiny comes from a neighbor's prying eyes, an investigator's eavesdropping ears, or a news photographer's intrusive camera; and in statutory law, the right of people to be free from unwarranted drug testing and electronic surveillance.

Private That which affects, characterizes, or belongs to an individual person, as opposed to the general public.

Private attorney general A private citizen who commences a lawsuit to enforce a legal right that benefits the community as a whole.

Private bill Legislation that benefits an individual or a locality. Also called special legislation or a private act.

Privateer A vessel that is owned, equipped, and armed by one or more private parties, that is commissioned by a hostile power to cruise the high seas to perform acts of war upon the enemy, ordinarily by attacking ships involved in commerce with the enemy. Also, the commander or a crew member of the vessel.

Private international law A branch of jurisprudence arising from the diverse laws of various nations that applies when private citizens of different countries interact or transact business with one another.

Private law That portion of the law that defines, regulates, enforces, and administers relationships among individuals, associations, and corporations. As used in distinction to public law, the term means that part of the law that is administered between citizen and citizen, or that is concerned with the definition, regulation, and enforcement of rights in cases where both the person in whom the right inheres and the person upon whom the obligation rests are private individuals.

Private roads A street or route that is designated by a public authority to accommodate a person or a group of people.

Privilege A particular benefit, advantage, or immunity enjoyed by a person or class of people that is not shared with others. A power of exemption against or beyond the law. It is not a right but, rather, exempts one from the performance of a duty, obligation, or liability.

Privilege against self-incrimination The right, under the Fifth Amendment to the U.S. Constitution, not to be a witness against oneself in a criminal proceeding.

Privileged communication An exchange of information between two individuals in a confidential relationship.

Privileges and immunities Concepts contained in the U.S. Constitution that place the citizens of each state on an equal basis with citizens of other states in respect to advantages resulting from citizenship in those states and citizenship in the United States.

Privity A close, direct, or successive relationship; having a mutual interest or right.

Privy One who has a direct, successive relationship to another individual; a coparticipant; one who has an interest in a matter; private.

Prize Anything offered as a reward for a contest. It is distinguished from a *bet* or *wager* in that it is known before the event who is to give either the premium or the prize, and there is but one operation until the accomplishment of the act, thing, or purpose for which it is offered. In time of war, an enemy vessel or a ship captured at sea by a belligerent power.

Prize courts Tribunals with jurisdiction to decide disputes involving captures made upon the high seas during times of war and to declare the captured property as a prize if it is lawfully subject to that sentence.

Prize law During times of war, belligerent states may attempt to interfere with maritime commerce to prevent ships from carrying goods that will aid the war effort of an opponent. After ships are captured and brought to a friendly port, a local tribunal called a prize court will determine the legality of the seizure, or the destruction of the vessel and cargo if the vessel cannot be sailed to a friendly port. The body of customary international law and treaties that determines the appropriateness of such actions is referred to as prize law.

Pro [*Latin, For; in respect of; on account of; in behalf of.*]

Probable cause Apparent facts discovered through logical inquiry that would lead a reasonably intelligent and prudent person to believe that an accused person has committed a crime, thereby warranting his or her prosecution, or that a cause of action has accrued, justifying a civil lawsuit.

Probate The court process by which a will is proved valid or invalid. The legal process wherein the estate of a decedent is administered.

Probation A sentence whereby a convict is released from confinement but is still under court supervision; a testing or a trial period. It can be given in lieu of a prison term or can suspend a prison sentence if the convict has consistently demonstrated good behavior.

The status of a convicted person who is given some freedom on the condition that for a specified period she act in a manner approved by a special officer to whom she must report.

An initial period of employment during which a new, transferred, or promoted employee must show the ability to perform the required duties.

Probationer A convict who is released from prison provided he maintains good behavior. One who is on probation whereby she is given some freedom to reenter society subject to the condition that for a specified period the individual conduct herself in a manner approved by a special officer to whom the probationer must report.

Probative Having the effect of proof, tending to prove, or actually proving.

Pro bono Short for *pro bono publico* [*Latin, For the public good*]. The designation given to the free legal work done by an attorney for indigent clients and religious, charitable, and other nonprofit entities.

Procedural law The body of law that prescribes formal steps to be taken in enforcing legal rights.

Procedure The methods by which legal rights are enforced; the specific machinery for carrying on a lawsuit, including process, the pleadings, rules of evidence, and rules of civil procedure or criminal procedure.

Proceeding A lawsuit; all or some part of a cause heard and determined by a court, an administrative agency, or other judicial authority. Any legal step or action taken at the direction of, or by the authority of, a court or agency; any measures necessary to prosecute or defend an action.

Proceeds The yield, income, money, or anything of value produced from a sale of property or a particular transaction.

Process A series of actions, motions, or occurrences; a method, mode, or operation, whereby a result or effect is produced; normal or actual course of procedure; regular proceeding, as, the process of vegetation or decomposition; a chemical process; processes of nature.

In patent law, an art or method by which any particular result is produced. A definite combination of new or old elements, ingredients, operations, ways, or means to produce a new, improved, or old result, and any substantial change therein by omission, to the same or better result, or by modification or substitution, with different function, to the same or better result, is a new and patentable process.

In civil and criminal proceedings, any means used by a court to acquire or exercise its jurisdiction over a person or over specific property. A summons or summons and complaint; sometimes, a writ.

Process server A person authorized by law to deliver papers, typically the complaint, to the defendant.

Proclamation An act that formally declares to the general public that the government has acted in a particular way. A written or printed document issued by a superior government executive, such as the president or governor, which sets out such a declaration by the government.

Proctor A person appointed to manage the affairs of another or to represent another in a judgment.

In English law, the name formerly given to practitioners in ecclesiastical and admiralty courts who performed duties similar to those of solicitors in ordinary courts.

Procure To cause something to happen; to find and obtain something or someone.

Produce As a noun, the product of natural growth, labor, or capital. Articles produced or grown from or on the soil, or found in the soil.

As a verb, to bring forward; to show or exhibit; to bring into view or notice; as, to present a play, including its presentation in motion pictures. To produce witnesses or documents at trial in obedience to a subpoena or to be compelled to produce materials subject to discovery rules.

To make, originate, or yield, as gasoline. To bring to the surface, as oil. To yield, as revenue. Thus, funds are *produced* by taxation, not when the tax is levied, but when the sums are collected.

Product liability The responsibility of a manufacturer or vendor of goods to compensate for injury caused by a defective good that it has provided for sale.

Profanity Irreverence towards sacred things; particularly, an irreverent or blasphemous use of the name of God. Vulgar, irreverent, or coarse language.

Professio juris The right of contracting parties to stipulate in the document the law that will govern their agreement.

Professional responsibility The obligation of lawyers to adhere to rules of professional conduct.

Proffer   To offer or tender, as, the production of a document and offer of the same in evidence.

Profit   Most commonly, the gross proceeds of a business transaction less the costs of the transaction; i.e., net proceeds. Excess of revenues over expenses for a transaction; sometimes used synonymously with net income for the period. Gain realized from business or investment over and above expenditures.

Accession of good, valuable results, useful consequences, avail, or gain. The benefit, advantage, or pecuniary gain accruing to the owner or occupant of land from its actual use; as in the familiar phrase *rents, issues and profits*, or in the expression *mesne profits*.

Profit a prendre   [*French, Right of taking.*] The right of persons to share in the land owned by another.

Pro forma   As a matter of form or for the sake of form. Used to describe accounting, financial, and other statements or conclusions based upon assumed or anticipated facts.

Progressive tax   A type of graduated tax that applies higher tax rates as the income of the taxpayer increases.

Pro hac vice   For this turn; for this one particular occasion. For example, an out-of-state lawyer may be admitted to practice in a local jurisdiction for a particular case only.

Prohibition   The popular name for the period in U.S. history from 1920 to 1933 when the manufacture and sale of alcoholic beverages were illegal.

Prohibition, writ of   An order from a superior court to a lower court or tribunal directing the judge and the parties to cease the litigation because the lower court does not have proper jurisdiction to hear or determine the matters before it.

Promise   A written or oral declaration given in exchange for something of value that binds the maker to do, or forbear from, a certain specific act and gives to the person to whom the declaration is made the right to expect and enforce performance or forbearance. An undertaking that something will or will not occur. It is a manifestation of intent to act, or refrain from acting, in a certain manner.

In the law of commercial paper, an undertaking to pay. It must be more than an acknowledgment of an obligation.

Promissory estoppel   In the law of contracts, the doctrine that provides that if a party changes his or her position substantially either by acting or forbearing from acting in reliance upon a gratuitous promise, then that party can enforce the promise although the essential elements of a contract are not present.

Promissory note   A written, signed, unconditional promise to pay a certain amount of money on demand at a specified time. A written promise to pay money that is often used as a means to borrow funds or take out a loan.

Promoter
A person who devises a plan for a business venture; one who takes the preliminary steps necessary for the formation of a corporation.

Promulgate
To officially announce, to publish, to make known to the public; to formally announce a statute or a decision by a court.

Proof
The establishment of a fact by the use of evidence. Anything that can make a person believe that a fact or proposition is true or false. It is distinguishable from evidence in that proof is a broad term comprehending everything that may be adduced at a trial, whereas evidence is a narrow term describing certain types of proof that can be admitted at trial.

Proper
Fit; correct; reasonably sufficient. That which is well adapted or appropriate.

Property right
A generic term that refers to any type of right to specific property whether it is personal or real property, tangible or intangible; e.g., a professional athlete has a valuable property right in his or her name, photograph, and image, and such right may be saleable by the athlete.

Property settlement
An agreement entered into by a husband and wife in connection with a divorce that provides for the division of their assets between them.

Proponent
One who offers or proposes.

Propound
To offer or propose. To form or put forward an item, plan, or idea for discussion and ultimate acceptance or rejection.

Proprietary
As a noun, a proprietor or owner; one who has the exclusive title to a thing; one who possesses or holds the title to a thing in his or her own right; one who possesses the dominion or ownership of a thing in his or her own right.

As an adjective, belonging to ownership; owned by a particular person; belonging or pertaining to a proprietor; relating to a certain owner or proprietor.

Pro rata
[*Latin, Proportionately.*] A phrase that describes a division made according to a certain rate, percentage, or share.

Prorate
To divide proportionately. To adjust, share, or distribute something or some amount on a pro rata basis.

Prorogation
Prolonging or putting off to another day. The discontinuation or termination of a session of the legislature, parliament, or the like. In English law, a prorogation is the continuance of the parliament from one session to another, as an adjournment is a continuation of the session from day to day. In civil law, giving time to do a thing beyond the term previously fixed.

Pro se For one's own behalf; in person. Appearing for oneself, as in the case of one who does not retain a lawyer and appears for himself or herself in court.

Prosecute To follow through; to commence and continue an action or judicial proceeding to its ultimate conclusion. To proceed against a defendant by charging that person with a crime and bringing him or her to trial.

Prosecutor One who prosecutes another for a crime in the name of the government.

Prospectus A document, notice, circular, advertisement, letter, or communication in written form or by radio or television that offers any security for sale, or confirms the sale of any security.

Prostitution The act of offering one's self for hire to engage in sexual relations.

Pro tanto [*Latin, For so much; for as much as one is able; as far as it can go.*] A term that refers to a partial payment made on a claim.

Protective custody An arrangement whereby a person is safeguarded by law enforcement authorities in a location other than the person's home because his or her safety is seriously threatened.

Protective order A court order, direction, decree, or command to protect a person from further harassment, service of process, or discovery.

Protectorate A form of international guardianship that arises under international law when a weaker state surrenders by treaty the management of some or all of its international affairs to a stronger state.

Pro tem [*Latin, For the time being.*] An abbreviation used for *pro tempore*, Latin for "temporary or provisional."

Protest A formal declaration whereby a person expresses a personal objection or disapproval of an act. A written statement, made by a notary, at the request of a holder of a bill or a note that describes the bill or note and declares that on a certain day the instrument was presented for, and refused, payment.

Prothonotary A title given to the principal clerk of a court.

Protocol A brief summary; the minutes of a meeting; the etiquette of diplomacy.

Province The district into which a country has been divided; as, the province of Ontario in Canada. More loosely, a sphere of activity or a profession such as medicine or law.

Provisional Temporary; not permanent. Tentative, contingent, preliminary.

Proviso A condition, stipulation, or limitation inserted in a document.

Provocation Conduct by which one induces another to do a particular deed; the act of inducing rage, anger, or resentment in another person that may cause that person to engage in an illegal act.

Proximate cause   An act from which an injury results as a natural, direct, uninterrupted consequence and without which the injury would not have occurred.

Proxy   A representative; an agent; a document appointing a representative.

Prudent person rule   A standard that requires that a fiduciary entrusted with funds for investment may invest such funds only in securities that any reasonable individual interested in receiving a good return of income while preserving his or her capital would purchase.

Public   As a noun, the whole body politic, or the aggregate of the citizens of a state, nation, or municipality. The community at large, without reference to the geographical limits of any corporation like a city, town, or county; the people.

As an adjective, open to all; notorious. Open to common use. Belonging to the people at large; relating to or affecting the whole people of a state, nation, or community; not limited or restricted to any particular class of the community.

Public administrative bodies   Agencies endowed with governmental functions.

Publication   Making something known to the community at large, exhibiting, displaying, disclosing, or revealing.

Public contract   An agreement to perform a particular task to benefit the community at large that is financed by government funds.

Public defender   An attorney appointed by a court or employed by the government to represent indigent defendants in criminal actions.

Public domain   Land that is owned by the United States. In copyright law, literary or creative works over which the creator no longer has an exclusive right to restrict, or receive a royalty for, their reproduction or use but which can be freely copied by the public.

Public figure   A description applied in libel and slander actions, as well as in those alleging invasion of privacy, to anyone who has gained prominence in the community as a result of his or her name or exploits, whether willingly or unwillingly.

Public interest   Anything affecting the rights, health, or finances of the public at large.

Public lands   Land that is owned by the United States government.

Public law   A general classification of law concerned with the political and sovereign capacity of a state.

Public offering   An issue of securities offered for sale to the public.

Public policy   A principle that no person or government official can legally perform an act that tends to injure the public.

Public utilities Businesses that provide the public with necessities, such as water, electricity, natural gas, and telephone and telegraph communication.

Publish To circulate, distribute, or print information for the public at large.

In libel and slander law, to utter to a third person or to make public a defamatory statement; in commercial paper law, to present an instrument for payment or declare or assert that a forged instrument is genuine.

Publishing law The body of law relating to the publication of books, magazines, newspapers, electronic materials, and other artistic works.

Puffing An opinion or judgment that is not made as a representation of fact.

Punishment The imposition of hardship in response to misconduct.

Punitive damages Monetary compensation awarded to an injured party that goes beyond that which is necessary to compensate the individual for losses and that is intended to punish the wrongdoer.

Purchase To buy; the transfer of property from one person to another by an agreement. Under the Uniform Commercial Code (UCC), taking by sale, discount, negotiation, mortgage, pledge, lien, issue, reissue, gift, or any voluntary transaction.

Purchase money mortgage A security device entered into when the seller of property, as opposed to a bank or financial institution, advances a sum of money or credit to the purchaser in return for holding the mortgage on the property.

Purchase order A document authorizing a seller to deliver goods, with payment to be made at a later date.

Pure Food and Drug Act of 1906 The first federal law (34 Stat. 768) prohibiting the interstate transportation and sale of adulterated food enacted by Congress pursuant to its power under the Commerce Clause.

Pure speech Written and spoken words that fall within the scope of protection provided by the First Amendment to the Constitution.

Purge To exonerate someone; to clear someone of guilt, charges, or accusations.

Purport To convey, imply, or profess; to have an appearance or effect.

Pursuant According to a prescribed method or some authority. To follow after or follow out; to execute or carry out by reason of something.

Purview The part of a statute or a law that delineates its purpose and scope.

Put An option—a right that operates as a continuing proposal—given in exchange for consideration—something of value—permitting its holder to sell a particular stock or commodity at a fixed price for a stated quantity and within a limited time period.

Putative Alleged; supposed; reputed.

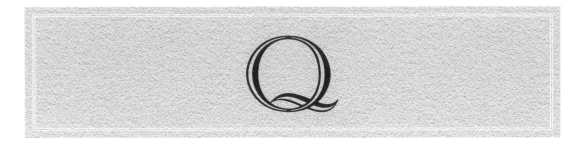

Qua   [*Latin, Considered as; in the character or capacity of.*] For example, "the trustee *qua* trustee [that is, in his or her role as trustee] is not liable."

Qualification   A particular attribute, quality, property, or possession that an individual must have in order to be eligible to fill an office or perform a public duty or function.

Qualified acceptance   In contract law, an assent to an offer that is either conditional or partial and alters the offer by changing the time, amount, mode, or place of payment.

Quantum meruit   [*Latin, As much as is deserved.*] In the law of contracts, a doctrine by which the law infers a promise to pay a reasonable amount for labor and materials furnished, even in the absence of a specific legally enforceable agreement between the parties.

Quantum valebant   [*Latin, As much as they were worth.*] An archaic form of pleading a lawsuit to recover payment for goods that have been sold and delivered.

Quare   [*Latin, Wherefore; for what reason; on what account.*] The introductory term used in the Latin form of a number of common-law writs at the beginning of the statement of the reason for the dispute.

Quash   To overthrow; to annul; to make void or declare invalid; e.g., "quash a subpoena."

Quasi   [*Latin, Almost as it were; as if; analogous to.*] In the legal sense, the term denotes that one subject has certain characteristics in common with another subject but that intrinsic and material differences exist between them.

Quasi contract   An obligation that the law creates in the absence of an agreement between the parties. It is invoked by the courts where unjust enrichment, which occurs when a person retains money or benefits that in all fairness belong to another, would exist without judicial relief.

Quasi in rem jurisdiction   The power of a court to hear a case and enforce a judgment against a party, even if the party is not personally before the court, solely because the party has an interest in real property or personal property within the geographical limits of the court.

Quasi-judicial The action taken and discretion exercised by public administrative agencies or bodies that are obliged to investigate or ascertain facts and draw conclusions from them as the foundation for official actions.

Quasi-legislative The capacity in which a public administrative agency or body acts when it makes rules and regulations.

Question of fact An issue that involves the resolution of a factual dispute or controversy and is within the sphere of the decisions to be made by a jury.

Question of law An issue that is within the province of the judge, as opposed to the jury, because it involves the application or interpretation of legal principles or statutes.

Quick assets Personal property that is readily marketable.

Quid pro quo [*Latin, What for what or Something for something.*] The mutual consideration that passes between two parties to a contractual agreement, thereby rendering the agreement valid and binding.

Quiet enjoyment A covenant that promises that the grantee or tenant of an estate in real property will be able to possess the premises in peace, without disturbance by hostile claimants.

Quiet title action A proceeding to establish an individual's right to ownership of real property against one or more adverse claimants.

Quit To vacate; remove from; surrender possession.

Qui tam actions Civil actions maintained by private persons on behalf of both themselves and the government to recover damages or to enforce penalties available under a statute prohibiting specified conduct. The term *qui tam* is short for the Latin *qui tam pro domino rege quam pro se ipso in hac parte sequitur*, which means "who brings the action for the king as well as for himself."

Quitclaim deed An instrument of conveyance of real property that passes any title, claim, or interest that the grantor has in the premises but does not make any representations as to the validity of such title.

Quo animo [*Latin, With what intention or motive.*] A term sometimes used instead of the word *animus*, which means design or motive.

Quorum A majority of an entire body; e.g., a quorum of a legislative assembly.

Quo warranto A legal proceeding during which an individual's right to hold an office or governmental privilege is challenged.

Racketeer Influenced and Corrupt Organizations Act	A set of federal laws (18 U.S.C.A. § 1961 et seq. [1970]) specifically designed to punish criminal activity by business enterprises.
Rape	A criminal offense defined in most states as forcible sexual relations with a person against that person's will.
Ratable	That which can be appraised, assessed, or adjusted through the application of a formula or percentage.
Rate	Value, measure, or degree; a charge, payment, or price determined through the application of a mathematical formula or based upon a scale or standard.
Ratification	The confirmation or adoption of an act that has already been performed.
Ratio decidendi	[*Latin, The ground or reason of decision.*] The legal principle upon which the decision in a specific case is founded.
Rational basis test	A judicial standard of review that examines whether a legislature had a reasonable and not an arbitrary basis for enacting a particular statute.
Ravishment	Unlawful carnal knowledge of a female by a male by force, against her will and without her consent.
Re	[*Latin, In the matter of; in the case of.*]
Real	In civil law, relating to a *thing* (whether movable or immovable), as distinguished from a person. Relating to *land*, as distinguished from personal property. This term is applied to lands, tenements, and hereditaments.
Real actions	Lawsuits concerning real property, or land. Under the common law, one of three categories of forms of actions, the procedures by which a lawsuit was begun.
Real estate	Land, buildings, and things permanently attached to land and buildings. Also called realty and real property.
Real evidence	Probative matter furnished by items that are actually on view, as opposed to a verbal description of them by a witness.

Realized   Actual; converted into cash.

Reasonable   Suitable; just; proper; ordinary; fair; usual.

Reasonable doubt   A standard of proof that must be surpassed to convict an accused in a criminal proceeding.

Reasonable person   A phrase frequently used in tort and criminal law to denote a hypothetical person in society who exercises average care, skill, and judgment in conduct and who serves as a comparative standard for determining liability.

Reasonable woman   A standard used by fact finders in sexual harassment litigation to determine whether sexual harassment has occurred.

Rebate   Discount; diminution of interest on capital lent in consideration of prompt repayment thereof; reduction of a stipulated charge that is not credited in advance but is returned subsequent to payment in full.

Rebus sic stantibus   [*Latin, At this point of affairs; in these circumstances.*] A tacit condition attached to all treaties to the effect that they will no longer be binding as soon as the state of facts and conditions upon which they were based changes to a substantial degree.

Rebut   To defeat, dispute, or remove the effect of the other side's facts or arguments in a particular case or controversy.

Rebuttable presumption   A conclusion as to the existence or nonexistence of a fact that a judge or jury must draw when certain evidence has been introduced and admitted as true in a lawsuit but that can be contradicted by evidence to the contrary.

Rebutter   In common-law pleading, the response made by a defendant to a plaintiff's surrejoinder, which rebuts earlier denials made by the defendant.

Recall   The right or procedure by which a public official may be removed from a position by a vote of the people prior to the end of the term of office.

Recaption   Regaining possession of; taking back.

Receipt   Acknowledgment in writing that something of value, or cash, has been placed into an individual's possession; written confirmation of payment rendered. *Receipt of goods* refers to the act of taking physical possession of them.

Receiver   An archaic term, used in common law and civil law countries, to designate an individual who holds and conceals stolen goods for thieves. Currently an independent individual appointed by a court to handle money or property during a lawsuit.

Receivership   A court order whereby all the property subject to dispute in a legal action is placed under the dominion and control of an independent person known as a receiver.

Receiving stolen property
The offense of acquiring goods with the knowledge that they have been stolen, extorted, embezzled, or unlawfully taken in any manner.

Recess
In the practice of courts, a brief interval during which all business is suspended without an adjournment.

Recidivism
The behavior of a repeat or habitual criminal. A measurement of the rate at which offenders commit other crimes, either by arrest or conviction baselines, after being released from incarceration.

Reciprocal
Bilateral; two-sided; mutual; interchanged.

Recital
A formal statement appearing in a legal document such as a deed that is preliminary in nature and provides an explanation of the reasons for the transaction.

Recklessness
Rashness; heedlessness; wanton conduct. The state of mind accompanying an act that either pays no regard to its probably or possibly injurious consequences, or which, though foreseeing such consequences, persists in spite of such knowledge.

Recognition
The confirmation or acknowledgment of the existence of an act performed, of an event that transpired, or of a person who is authorized by another to act in a particular manner.

Recognizance
A recorded obligation, entered into before a tribunal, in which an individual pledges to perform a specific act or to subscribe to a certain course of conduct.

Reconciliation
The restoration of peaceful or amicable relations between two individuals who were previously in conflict with one another.

Reconveyance
The transfer of real property that takes place when a mortgage is fully paid off and the land is returned to the owner free from the former debt.

Recording of land titles
A process by which proof of ownership of real property is filed in the appropriate county office or court to allow purchasers, creditors, and other interested parties to determine the status of the property interests therein.

Records
Written accounts of acts, transactions, or instruments that are drawn up pursuant to legal authority by an appropriate officer and appointed to be retained as memorials or permanent evidence of matters to which they are related.

Recoupment
To recover a loss by a subsequent gain. In pleading, to set forth a claim against the plaintiff when an action is brought against one as a defendant. Keeping back of something that is due, because there is an equitable reason to withhold it. A right of the defendant to have a deduction from the amount of the plaintiff's damages, for the reason that the plaintiff has not complied with the cross-obligations or independent covenants arising under the same contract.

Recourse The right of an individual who is holding a commercial paper, such as a check or promissory note, to receive payment on it from anyone who has signed it if the individual who originally made it is unable, or refuses, to tender payment.

Recovered memory The remembrance of traumatic childhood events, usually involving sexual abuse, many years after the events occurred.

Recovery The acquisition of something of value through the judgment of a court, as the result of a lawsuit initiated for that purpose.

Recrimination A charge made by an individual who is being accused of some act against the accuser.

Recuse To disqualify or remove oneself as a judge over a particular proceeding because of one's conflict of interest. Recusal, or the judge's act of disqualifying himself or herself from presiding over a proceeding, is based on the maxim that judges are charged with a duty of impartiality in administering justice.

Redemption The liberation of an estate in real property from a mortgage.

Redlining A discriminatory practice whereby lending institutions refuse to make mortgage loans, regardless of an applicant's credit history, on properties in particular areas in which conditions are allegedly deteriorating.

Redress Compensation for injuries sustained; recovery or restitution for harm or injury; damages or equitable relief. Access to the courts to gain reparation for a wrong.

Reductio ad absurdum [*Latin, Reduction to absurdity.*] In logic, a method employed to disprove an argument by illustrating how it leads to an absurd consequence.

Referee A judicial officer who presides over civil hearings but usually does not have the authority or power to render judgment.

Reference The process by which a tribunal sends a civil action, or a particular issue in the action, to an individual who has been appointed by the tribunal to hear and decide upon it, or to obtain evidence, and make a report to the court.

Referendum The right reserved to the people to approve or reject an act of the legislature, or the right of the people to approve or reject legislation that has been referred to them by the legislature.

Reformation A remedy utilized by the courts to correct a written instrument so that it conforms to the original intent of the parties to such an instrument.

Reformatories State institutions for the confinement of juvenile delinquents.

Refreshing memory The process of aiding a witness's recollection of certain details during a trial by allowing him or her to consult documents, memoranda, or books in order to better remember past transactions or events about which he or she is testifying.

Refugees   Individuals who leave their native country for social, political, or religious reasons, or who are forced to leave, as a result of any type of disaster, including war, political upheaval, and famine.

Refunding   Reimbursing funds in restitution or repayment. The process of refinancing or borrowing money, ordinarily through the sale of bonds, to pay off an existing debt with the proceeds derived therefrom.

Register   To record, or enter precisely in a designated place, certain information in the public records as is mandated by statute. A book of public records.

Register of deeds   The designation, in certain jurisdictions, of the public officers who record documents that establish ownership of property, mortgages, and other instruments that relate to real property in official record books provided and maintained for such purpose.

Registrar   The public official charged with the duty of making and maintaining public records.

Registration   Enrollment; the process of recording entries in an official book.

Registration of land titles   A system by which ownership of real property is established through the issuance of an official certificate indicating the name of the individual in whom such ownership is vested.

Regressive tax   A tax with a rate that decreases as the taxpayer's income increases.

Regular   Customary; usual; with no unexpected or unusual variations; in conformity with ordinary practice.

Regulation   A rule of order having the force of law, prescribed by a superior or competent authority, relating to the actions of those under the authority's control.

Rehabilitation   The restoration of former rights, authority, or abilities.

Reinstate   To restore to a condition that has terminated or been lost; to reestablish.

Reinsurance   The contract made between an insurance company and a third party to protect the insurance company from losses. The contract provides for the third party to pay for the loss sustained by the insurance company when the company makes a payment on the original contract.

Rejoinder   The answer made by a defendant in the second stage of common-law pleading that rebuts or denies the assertions made in the plaintiff's replication.

Relation   Kin; relative. The connection of two individuals, or their situation with respect to each other, who are associated, either by law, agreement, or kinship in a social status or union for purposes of domestic life, such as parent and child or husband and wife.

Relator | The individual in whose name a legal action is brought by a state; the individual who relates the facts on which an action is based.

Release | A contractual agreement by which one individual assents to relinquish a claim or right under the law to another individual against whom such claim or right is enforceable.

Release time program | The name of the arrangement by which local public school boards permit students to be dismissed from classes prior to the completion of the regular school day for purposes of religious instruction.

Relevancy | The tendency of a fact offered as evidence in a lawsuit to prove or disprove the truth of a point in issue.

Relief | Financial assistance provided to the indigent by the government. The redress, or benefit, given by a court to an individual who brings a legal action.

Remainder | A future interest held by one person in the real property of another that will take effect upon the expiration of the other property interests created at the same time as the future interest.

Remand | To send back.

Remedial statute | A law enacted for the purpose of correcting a defect in a prior law, or in order to provide a remedy where none previously existed.

Remedy | The manner in which a right is enforced or satisfied by a court when some harm or injury, recognized by society as a wrongful act, is inflicted upon an individual.

Remission | Extinguishment or release of a debt.

Remit | To transmit or send. To relinquish or surrender, such as in the case of a fine, punishment, or sentence.

Remittance | Money sent from one individual to another in the form of cash, check, or some other manner.

Remittitur | The procedural process by which an excessive verdict of the jury is reduced. If money damages awarded by a jury are grossly excessive as a matter of law, the judge may order the plaintiff to remit a portion of the award.

Removal | The transfer of a person or thing from one place to another. The transfer of a case from one court to another. In this sense, removal generally refers to a transfer from a court in one jurisdiction to a court in another, whereas a change of venue may be granted simply to move a case to another location within the same jurisdiction.

Render | Return; yield; pay or perform, as in charges or services.

Renewal | Rehabilitation; reestablishment; substitution of a new right or obligation for another of the same or similar nature.

Rent strike   An organized protest on the part of tenants in which they withhold the payment of consideration for the use or occupation of property from their landlord until their grievances are settled.

Renunciation   The abandonment of a right; repudiation; rejection.

Renvoi   The process by which a court adopts the rules of a foreign jurisdiction with respect to any conflict of laws that arises.

Reorganization   The process of carrying out, through agreements and legal proceedings, a business plan for winding up the affairs of, or foreclosing a mortgage upon, the property of a corporation that has become insolvent.

Reorganization plan   A scheme authorized by federal law and promulgated by the president whereby he or she alters the structure of federal agencies to promote government efficiency and economy through a transfer, consolidation, coordination, authorization, or abolition of functions.

Reparable injury   A tort, or civil wrong, that can be compensated through the payment of pecuniary damages, as distinguished from irreparable injury or harm that is not compensable through the payment of money.

Reparation   Compensation for an injury; redress for a wrong inflicted.

Repeal   The annulment or abrogation of a previously existing statute by the enactment of a later law that revokes the former law.

Replevin   A legal action to recover the possession of items of personal property.

Replication   In common-law pleading, the response of a plaintiff to the defendant's plea in an action at law, or to the defendant's answer in a suit in equity.

Reply   The pleading in which a plaintiff responds to the defendant's demand for relief asserted in a set-off or counterclaim.

Report   An official or formal statement of facts or proceedings. To give an account of; to relate; to tell or convey information; the written statement of such an account.

Reporter   One who prepares a summary or gives an account. A court reporter is a person who records court proceedings as they take place and then later transcribes the account. A published volume of the decisions of a court or a group of courts.

Repossession   The taking back of an item that has been sold on credit and delivered to the purchaser because the payments have not been made on it.

Represent   To exhibit or expose; to appear in the character of.

Representation   Any action or conduct that can be turned into a statement of fact.

Representative   An individual who stands in the place of another.

Representative action	A legal action in which one or a few members of a class sue on behalf of themselves and other members of the same class; a lawsuit brought by the stockholders of a corporation, on its behalf, for the enforcement of a corporate right.
Reprieve	The suspension of the execution of the death penalty for a period of time.
Republic	That form of government in which the administration of affairs is open to all the citizens. A political unit or "state," independent of its form of government.
Republication	The reexecution or reestablishment by a testator of a will that he or she had once revoked.
Repudiation	The rejection or refusal of a duty, relation, right, or privilege.
Repugnancy	An inconsistency or opposition between two or more clauses of the same deed, contract, or statute, between two or more material allegations of the same pleading or between any two writings.
Requirements contract	A written agreement whereby a buyer assents to purchase for a sufficient consideration (the inducement to enter into an agreement) all the merchandise of a designated type that he or she might require for use in his or her own established business.
Requisition	A written demand; a formal request or requirement. The formal demand by one government upon another, or by the governor of one state upon the governor of another state, of the surrender of a fugitive from justice. The taking or seizure of property by government.
Res	[*Latin, A thing.*] An object, a subject matter, or a status against which legal proceedings have been instituted.
Rescind	To declare a contract void—of no legal force or binding effect—from its inception and thereby restore the parties to the positions they would have occupied had no contract ever been made.
Rescission	The cancellation of a prison inmate's tentative parole date. The abrogation of a contract, effective from its inception, thereby restoring the parties to the positions they would have occupied if no contract had ever been formed.
Rescue	The crime of forcibly and knowingly freeing another from arrest, imprisonment, or legal custody. In admiralty and maritime law, the taking back of property seized as prize from the possession of the captors by the party who originally lost it.
Rescue doctrine	The principle that one who has, through her negligence, endangered the safety of another can be held liable for injuries sustained by a third person who attempts to save the imperiled person from injury.

Reservation A clause in a deed of real property whereby the grantor, one who transfers property, creates and retains for the grantor some right or interest in the estate granted, such as rent or an easement, a right of use over the land of another. A large tract of land that is withdrawn by public authority from sale or settlement and appropriated to specific public uses, such as parks or military posts. A tract of land under the control of the Bureau of Indian Affairs to which an American Indian tribe retains its original title to ownership, or that has been set aside from the public domain for use by a tribe.

Reserve Funds set aside to cover future expenses, losses, or claims. To retain; to keep in store for future or special use; to postpone to a future time.

Res gestae [*Latin, Things done.*] Secondhand statements considered trustworthy for the purpose of admission as evidence in a lawsuit when repeated by a witness because they were made spontaneously and concurrently with an event.

Residence Personal presence at some place of abode.

Residency A duration of stay required by state and local laws that entitles a person to the legal protection and benefits provided by applicable statutes.

Residuary clause A provision in a will that disposes of property not expressly disposed of by other provisions of the will.

Residuum That which remains after any process of separation or deduction; a balance; that which remains of a decedent's estate after debts have been paid and gifts deducted.

Res ipsa loquitur [*Latin, The thing speaks for itself.*] A rebuttable presumption or inference that the defendant was negligent, which arises upon proof that the instrumentality or condition causing the injury was in the defendant's exclusive control and that the accident was one that ordinarily does not occur in the absence of negligence.

Res judicata [*Latin, A thing adjudged.*] A rule that a final judgment on the merits by a court having jurisdiction is conclusive between the parties to a suit as to all matters that were litigated or that could have been litigated in that suit.

Resolution The official expression of the opinion or will of a legislative body.

Respondeat superior [*Latin, Let the master answer.*] A common-law doctrine that makes an employer liable for the actions of an employee when the actions take place within the scope of employment.

Respondent In equity practice, the party who answers a bill or other proceeding in equity. The party against whom an appeal or motion, an application for a court order, is instituted and who is required to answer in order to protect his or her interests.

Responsive pleading A formal declaration by a party in reply to a prior declaration by an opponent.

Rest　To cease motion, exertion, or labor.

Restatement of law　A series of volumes regarded as an authoritative work of legal scholarship prepared by the authors, scholars, and members of the judiciary who comprise the American Law Institute (ALI), which presents a survey of a general area of the law and the changes that have occurred therein.

Restitution　In the context of criminal law, state programs under which an offender is required, as a condition of his or her sentence, to repay money or donate services to the victim or society; with respect to maritime law, the restoration of articles lost by jettison, done when the remainder of the cargo has been saved, at the general charge of the owners of the cargo; in the law of torts, or civil wrongs, a measure of damages; in regard to contract law, the restoration of a party injured by a breach of contract to the position that party occupied before she or he entered the contract.

Restorative justice　A philosophical framework and a series of programs for the criminal justice system that emphasize the need to repair the harm done to crime victims through a process of negotiation, mediation, victim empowerment, and reparation.

Restraining order　A command of the court issued upon the filing of an application for an injunction, prohibiting the defendant from performing a threatened act until a hearing on the application can be held.

Restraint of trade　Contracts or combinations that tend, or are designed, to eliminate or stifle competition, create a monopoly, artificially maintain prices, or otherwise hamper or obstruct the course of trade as it would be carried on if it were left to the control of natural economic forces.

Restrictive covenant　A provision in a deed limiting the use of the property and prohibiting certain uses. A clause in contracts of partnership and employment prohibiting a contracting party from engaging in similar employment for a specified period of time within a certain geographical area.

Restrictive indorsement　The act of a payee or other holder of an instrument, such as a check, that consists of signing his or her name upon the back of the instrument in order to transfer it to another and wording the signature in such a manner as to bar the further negotiability of the instrument.

Resulting trust　An arrangement whereby one person holds property for the benefit of another, which is implied by a court in certain cases where a person transfers property to another and gives him or her legal title to it but does not intend him or her to have an equitable or beneficial interest in the property.

Retainer　A contract between attorney and client specifying the nature of the services to be rendered and the cost of the services.

Retaliatory eviction　The act of a landlord in ejecting or attempting to eject a tenant from the rented premises, or in refusing to renew a lease, because of the tenant's complaints or participation in a tenant's union or in similar activities with which the landlord is not in accord.

Retorsion   A phrase used in international law to describe retaliatory action taken by one foreign government against another for the stringent or harsh regulation or treatment of its citizens who are within the geographical boundaries of the foreign country.

Retraction   In the law of defamation, a formal recanting of the libelous or slanderous material.

Retro   [*Latin, Back; backward; behind.*] A prefix used to designate a prior condition or time.

Retroactive   Having reference to things that happened in the past, prior to the occurrence of the act in question.

Return   To bring, carry, or send back; to restore, redeliver, or replace in the custody of someone. Merchandise brought back to a seller for credit or a refund. The profit made on a sale; the income from an investment. A schedule of information required by some governmental agencies, such as the tax return that must be submitted to the Internal Revenue Service.

The official report made by a court, body of magistrates, or other official board charged with counting votes cast in an election. The redelivery of a writ, notice, or other form of legal process to the court after its proper service on the defendant or after it cannot be served.

Return day   The day on which votes are counted and the election results announced. The day named in a writ or other form of legal process as the date when the response to that paper must be made.

The day on which an officer, such as a U.S. marshal, must file proof with the court that he or she has served legal process on a defendant or that he or she cannot serve the papers. The statement is made under oath and is called the return or return of process.

Revenue   Return or profit such as the annual or periodic rents, profits, interest, or income from any type of real or personal property, received by an individual, a corporation, or a government.

Reverse   To overthrow, invalidate, repeal, or revoke.

Reversion   Any future interest kept by a person who transfers property to another.

Reverter, possibility of   A contingent future interest in real property that a grantor of a determinable fee possesses after he or she has conveyed property.

Review   To reexamine judicially or administratively; a judicial reconsideration for purposes of correction, for example, the examination of a case by an appellate court.

Revised statutes   A body of statutes that have been revised, collected, arranged in order, and reenacted as a whole. The legal title of the collection of compiled laws of the United States, as well as some of the individual states.

Revival of an action   A mechanism of legal procedure that operates at the pleading stage of litigation to subsequently renew an action that has been abated, terminated, or suspended for reasons other than the merits of the claim.

Revive To renew.

Revocation The recall of some power or authority that has been granted.

Revoke To annul or make void by recalling or taking back; to cancel, rescind, repeal, or reverse.

Revolution A sudden, tumultuous, and radical transformation of an entire system of government, including its legal and political components.

Revolving charge A type of credit arrangement that permits a buyer or a borrower to purchase merchandise or obtain loans on a continuing basis as long as the outstanding balance of the account does not exceed a certain limit.

Reward A sum of money or other compensation offered to the public in general, or to a class of persons, for the performance of a special service.

Rex [*Latin, The king.*] The phrase used to designate the king as the party prosecuting an accused in a criminal action, such as an action entitled *Rex v. Doe.*

Rider A schedule or writing annexed to a document such as a legislative bill or insurance policy.

Right In an abstract sense, justice, ethical correctness, or harmony with the rules of law or the principles of morals. In a concrete legal sense, a power, privilege, demand, or claim possessed by a particular person by virtue of law.

Right of action The privilege of instituting a lawsuit arising from a particular transaction or state of facts, such as a suit that is based on a contract or a tort, a civil wrong.

Right of election The prerogative of a surviving spouse to accept the provision the dead spouse made in the will or to disregard the will and claim the share specified by statute.

Right of reentry A right, retained by the grantor at the time land is conveyed, to reenter and take possession of the land if a certain condition occurs or fails to occur.

Right of survivorship The power of the successor or successors of a deceased individual to acquire the property of that individual upon his or her death; a distinguishing feature of joint tenancy.

Right of way An easement, a privilege to pass over the land of another, whereby the holder of the easement acquires only a reasonable and usual enjoyment of the property, and the owner of the land retains the benefits and privileges of ownership consistent with the easement.

Right-to-work laws	State laws permitted by section 14(b) of the Taft-Hartley Act that provide in general that employees are not required to join a union as a condition of getting or retaining a job.
Riot	A disturbance of the peace by several persons, assembled and acting with a common intent in executing a lawful or unlawful enterprise in a violent and turbulent manner.
Riparian rights	The rights, which belong to landowners through whose property a natural watercourse runs, to the benefit of such stream for all purposes to which it can be applied.
Ripeness	The mandate contained in Article III of the Constitution that requires an appellate court to consider whether a case has matured into a controversy worthy of adjudication before it can hear the case.
Risk	The potential danger that threatens to harm or destroy an object, event, or person.
Risk arbitrage	The purchase of stock in a corporation that appears to be the target of an imminent takeover in the hope of making large profits if the takeover occurs.
Robbery	The taking of money or goods in the possession of another, from his or her person or immediate presence, by force or intimidation.
Roe	A fictitious surname used for an unknown or anonymous person or for a hypothetical person in an illustration.
Rogatory letters	A commission from one judge to another judge requesting the latter to examine a witness.
Roll	To commit a robbery by force. A record of the proceedings of a court or public office.
Royalty	Compensation for the use of property, usually copyrighted works, patented inventions, or natural resources, expressed as a percentage of receipts from using the property or as a payment for each unit produced.
Rubric of a statute	The title of a statute indicating the objective of the legislation and providing a means of interpreting the body of the act.

Rule	To command or require pursuant to a principle of the court, as to rule the sheriff to serve the summons.
	    To settle or decide a point of law at a trial or hearing.
	    An established standard, guide, or regulation governing conduct, procedure, or action.

Rule against accumulations	A principle that prohibits adding income or interest earned by a trust back into the principal of the fund beyond the time allowed by the rule against perpetuities.
Rule against perpetuities	Under the common law, the principle that no interest in property is valid unless it vests not later than twenty-one years, plus the period of

gestation, after some life or lives in being which exist at the time of the creation of the interest.

Rule in Shelley's case　An English common-law doctrine that provided that a conveyance that attempts to give a person a life estate, with a remainder to that person's heirs, will instead give both the life estate and the remainder to the person, thus giving that person the land in fee simple absolute (full ownership without restriction).

Rule of law　Rule according to law; rule under law; or rule according to a higher law.

Rule of 78　A method of computing refunds of unearned finance charges on early payment of a loan so that the refund is proportional to the monthly unpaid balance.

Rules of decision act　A federal statute (28 U.S.C.A. § 1652 [1948]) that provides that where the Constitution, treaties, or acts of Congress are inapplicable, the law of the state in which the federal court is sitting should apply to civil actions.

Rules of war　A body of customs, practices, usages, conventions, protocols, treaties, laws, and other norms that govern the commencement, conduct, and termination of hostilities between belligerent states or parties.

Ruling　A judicial or administrative interpretation of a provision of a statute, order, regulation, or ordinance. The judicial determination of matters before the court such as the admissibility of evidence or the granting of a motion, which is an application for an order.

Run　To have legal validity in a prescribed territory; as in, the writ (a court order) *runs* throughout the county. To have applicability or legal effect during a prescribed period of time; as in, the statute of limitations has *run* against the claim. To follow or accompany; to be attached to another thing in pursuing a prescribed course or direction; as in, the covenant (a written promise or restriction) *runs* with the land.

Running with the land　Passing with a transfer of the property. A provision in a deed by which the person to whom the land is transferred agrees to maintain a fence is an example of a covenant that runs with the land.

Sabotage　The willful destruction or impairment of, or defective production of, war material or national defense material, or harm to war premises or war utilities. During a labor dispute, the willful and malicious destruction of an employer's property or interference with his normal operations.

Said Mentioned earlier.

Sailors Persons who navigate ships or assist in the conduct, maintenance, or service of ships.

Sales law The law relating to the transfer of ownership of property from one person to another for value, which is codified in article 2 of the Uniform Commercial Code (UCC), a body of law governing mercantile transactions adopted in whole or in part by the states.

Sales tax A state or local-level tax on the retail sale of specified property or services. It is a percentage of the cost of such. Generally, the purchaser pays the tax but the seller collects it as an agent for the government. Various taxing jurisdictions allow exemptions for purchases of specified items, including certain foods, services, and manufacturing equipment. If the purchaser and seller are in different states, a use tax usually applies.

Salvage The portion of goods or property that has been saved or remains after some type of casualty, such as a fire.

Sanction To assent, concur, confirm, approve, or ratify. The part of a law that is designed to secure enforcement by imposing a penalty for violation of the law or offering a reward for its observance. A punitive act taken by one nation against another nation that has violated a treaty or international law.

San Francisco Vigilance Committees of 1851 and 1856 Self-appointed law enforcement committees that were organized to maintain order in San Francisco, California, during the mid-nineteenth century.

Sanity Reasonable understanding; sound mind; possessing mental faculties that are capable of distinguishing right from wrong so as to bear legal responsibility for one's actions.

Satisfaction The discharge of an obligation by paying a party what is due—as on a mortgage, lien, or contract—or by paying what is awarded to a person by the judgment of a court or otherwise. An entry made on the record, by which a party in whose favor a judgment was rendered declares that she has been satisfied and paid.

    The fulfillment of a gift by will, whereby the testator—one who dies leaving a will—makes an inter vivos gift, one which is made while the testator is alive to take effect while the testator is living, to the beneficiary with the intent that it be in lieu of the gift by will. In equity, something given either in whole or in part as a substitute or equivalent for something else.

Save To except, reserve, or exempt; as where a statute *saves* vested—fixed—rights. To toll, or suspend the running or operation of; as, to *save* the statute of limitations.

Saving clause In a statute, an exception of a special item out of the general things mentioned in the statute. A restriction in a repealing act, which is intended to save rights, while proceedings are pending, from the obliteration that would result from an unrestricted repeal. The provision in a statute, sometimes referred to as the severability clause, that rescues the balance of the statute from a declaration of unconstitutionality if one or more parts are invalidated.

Savings and loan association A financial institution owned by and operated for the benefit of those using its services. The savings and loan association's primary purpose is making loans to its members, usually for the purchase of real estate or homes.

Scab A pejorative term used colloquially in reference to a nonunion worker who takes the place of a union employee on strike or who works for wages and other conditions that are inferior to those guaranteed to a union member by virtue of the union contract.

School desegregation The attempt to end the practice of separating children of different races into distinct public schools.

Scienter [*Latin, Knowingly.*] Guilty knowledge that is sufficient to charge a person with the consequences of his or her acts.

Scientific evidence Evidence presented in court that is produced from scientific tests or studies.

Scintilla A glimmer; a spark; the slightest particle or trace.

Scire facias [*Latin, Made known.*] A judicial writ requiring a defendant to appear in court and prove why an existing judgment should not be executed against him or her.

Scope of employment Activities of an employee that are in furtherance of duties that are owed to an employer and where the employer is, or could be, exercising some control, directly or indirectly, over the activities of the employee.

Scorched-earth plan A slang expression for a defensive tactic used by an unwilling corporate takeover target to make itself less attractive to a buyer.

S corporation A type of corporation that is taxed under subchapter S of the Internal Revenue Code (26 U.S.C.A. § 1 et seq.).

Seabed Arms Control Treaty of 1971 An agreement for the denuclearization of the seabed, the ocean floor, and the subsoil of the seabed.

Seal To close records by any type of fastening that must be broken before access can be obtained. An impression upon wax, wafer, or some other substance capable of being impressed.

Sealed verdict A decision reached by the jury when the court is not in session, which is placed in a closed envelope by the jurors, who then separate.

Seal of the United States   The official die or signet, which has a raised emblem and is used by federal officials on documents of importance.

Search and seizure   In international law, the right of ships of war, as regulated by treaties, to examine a merchant vessel during war in order to determine whether the ship or its cargo is liable to seizure.

A hunt by law enforcement officials for property or communications believed to be evidence of crime, and the act of taking possession of this property.

Search warrant   A court order authorizing the examination of a place for the purpose of discovering contraband, stolen property, or evidence of guilt to be used in the prosecution of a criminal action.

Seasonable   Within a reasonable time; timely.

Seat belts   A restraining device used to secure passengers in motorized vehicles.

SEC   An abbreviation for the Securities and Exchange Commission.

Secession   The act of withdrawing from membership in a group.

Secondary authority   Sources of information that describe or interpret the law, such as legal treatises, law review articles, and other scholarly legal writings, cited by lawyers to persuade a court to reach a particular decision in a case, but which the court is not obligated to follow.

Secondary boycott   A group's refusal to work for, purchase from, or handle the products of a business with which the group has no dispute.

Secondary evidence   A reproduction of, or substitute for, an original document or item of proof that is offered to establish a particular issue in a legal action.

Secondary meaning   A doctrine of trademark law that provides that protection is afforded to the user of an otherwise unprotectable mark when the mark, through advertising or other exposure, has come to signify that an item is produced or sponsored by that user.

Second look doctrine   In the law of future interests, a rule that provides that even though the validity of interests created by the exercise of a power of appointment is ordinarily measured from the date the power is created, not from its exercise, the facts existing on the date of its exercise can be considered in order to determine if the rule against perpetuities has been violated.

Section   The distinct and numbered subdivisions in legal codes, statutes, and textbooks. In the law of real property, a parcel of land equal in area to one square mile, or 640 acres.

Secure   To assure the payment of a debt or the performance of an obligation; to provide security.

Secured creditor   One who holds some special monetary assurance of payment of a debt owed to him or her, such as a mortgage, collateral, or lien.

Secured transactions	Business dealings that grant a creditor a right in property owned or held by a debtor to assure the payment of a debt or the performance of some obligation.
Securities	Evidence of a corporation's debts or property.
Security	Protection; assurance; indemnification.
Security deposit	Money aside from the payment of rent that a landlord requires a tenant to pay to be kept separately in a fund for use should the tenant cause damage to the premises or otherwise violate terms of the lease.
Sedition	A revolt or an incitement to revolt against established authority, usually in the form of treason or defamation against government.
Seduction	The act by which a man entices a woman to have unlawful sexual relations with him by means of persuasions, solicitations, promises, or bribes without the use of physical force or violence.
Segregation	The act or process of separating a race, class, or ethnic group from a society's general population.
Seizure	Forcible possession; a grasping, snatching, or putting in possession.
Selden Society	An association of legal historians that publishes scholarly works on the legal history of England.
Selective prosecution	Criminal prosecution based on an unjustifiable standard such as race, religion, or other arbitrary classification.
Selectman or selectwoman	A municipal officer elected by a town in the New England states.
Self-dealing	The conduct of a trustee, an attorney, or other fiduciary that consists of taking advantage of his or her position in a transaction and acting for his or her own interests rather than for the interests of the beneficiaries of the trust or the interests of his or her clients.
Self-defense	The protection of one's person or property against some injury attempted by another.
Self-determination	The political right of the majority to the exercise of power within the boundaries of a generally accepted political unit, area, or territory.
Self-executing	Anything (e.g., a document or legislation) that is effective immediately without the need of intervening court action, ancillary legislation, or other type of implementing action.
Self-executing treaty	A compact between two nations that is effective immediately without the need for ancillary legislation.
Self-help	Redressing or preventing wrongs by one's own action without recourse to legal proceedings.

Self-incrimination Giving testimony in a trial or other legal proceeding that could subject one to criminal prosecution.

Senate The upper chamber, or smaller branch, of the U.S. Congress. The upper chamber of the legislature of most of the states.

Senior citizens Elderly persons, usually more than sixty or sixty-five years of age.

Senior interest A right that takes effect prior to others or has preference over others.

Seniority Precedence or preference in position over others similarly situated. As used, for example, with reference to job seniority, the worker with the most years of service is first promoted within a range of jobs subject to seniority, and is the last laid off, proceeding so on down the line to the youngest in point of service. The term may also refer to the priority of a lien or encumbrance.

Sentencing The postconviction stage of the criminal justice process, in which the defendant is brought before the court for the imposition of a penalty.

Separate but equal The doctrine first enunciated by the U.S. Supreme Court in *Plessy v. Ferguson*, 163 U.S. 537, 16 S. Ct. 1138, 41 L. Ed. 256 (1896), to the effect that establishing different facilities for blacks and whites was valid under the Equal Protection Clause of the Fourteenth Amendment as long as they were equal.

Separate maintenance Money paid by one married person to the other for support if they are no longer living as husband and wife. Commonly it is referred to as separate support and follows from a court order.

Separation A termination of cohabitation of husband and wife either by mutual agreement or, in the case of *judicial separation*, under the decree of a court.

Separation of powers The division of state and federal government into three independent branches.

Sequestration In the context of trials, the isolation of a jury from the public, or the separation of witnesses to ensure the integrity of testimony. In other legal contexts the seizure of property or the freezing of assets by court order.

Seriatim [*Latin, Severally; separately; individually; one by one.*]

Serjeant at law In English legal history, an elite order of attorneys who had the exclusive privilege of arguing before the Court of Common Pleas and also supplied the judges for both Common Pleas and the Court of the King's Bench.

Service Any duty or labor performed for another person.
　　The delivery of a legal document that notifies the recipient of the commencement of a legal action or proceeding in which he or she is involved.

Service mark A trademark that is used in connection with services.

Service of process	Delivery of a writ, summons, or other legal papers to the person required to respond to them.
Servitude	The state of a person who is subjected, voluntarily or involuntarily, to another person as a servant. A charge or burden resting upon one estate for the benefit or advantage of another.
Session	The sitting of a court, legislature, council, or commission for the transaction of its proper business.
Set aside	To cancel, annul, or revoke a judgment or order.
Setback	A distance from a curb, property line, or structure within which building is prohibited.
Set down	To list a case in a court calendar or docket for trial or hearing during a particular term.
Set-off	A demand made by the defendant against the plaintiff that is based on some transaction or occurrence other than the one that gave the plaintiff grounds to sue.
Settle	To agree, to approve, to arrange, to ascertain, to liquidate, or to reach an agreement.
Settlement	The act of adjusting or determining the dealings or disputes between persons without pursuing the matter through a trial.
Settlement statement	A breakdown of costs involved in a real estate sale.
Settlor	One who establishes a trust—a right of property, real or personal—held and administered by a trustee for the benefit of another.
Severable	That which is capable of being separated from other things to which it is joined and maintaining nonetheless a complete and independent existence.
Several	Separate; individual; independent.
Severalty ownership	Sole proprietorship of property; individual dominion.
Severance	The act of dividing, or the state of being divided.
Sex discrimination	Discrimination on the basis of gender.
Sex offenses	A class of sexual conduct prohibited by the law.
Sexual abuse	Illegal sex acts performed against a minor by a parent, guardian, relative, or acquaintance.
Sexual harassment	Unwelcome sexual advances, requests for sexual favors, and other verbal or physical conduct of a sexual nature that tends to create a hostile or offensive work environment.

Sham   False; without substance.

Share   A portion or part of something that may be divided into components, such as a sum of money. A unit of stock that represents ownership in a corporation.

Shelter   A general term used in statutes that relates to the provision of food, clothing, and housing for specified individuals; a home with a proper environment that affords protection from the weather.

Shepardizing   A term used in the legal profession to describe the process of using a citator to discover the history of a case or statute to determine whether it is still good law.

Shepard's® Citations   A set of volumes published primarily for use by judges when they are in the process of writing judicial decisions and by lawyers when they are preparing briefs, or memoranda of law, that contain a record of the status of cases or statutes.

Sheriff   Usually the chief peace officer of a county.

Sheriff's deed   A document giving ownership rights in property to a buyer at a sheriff's sale (a sale held by a sheriff to pay a court judgment against the owner of the property). A deed given at a sheriff's sale in foreclosure of a mortgage. The giving of said deed begins a statutory redemption period.

Shield laws   Statutes affording a privilege to journalists not to disclose in legal proceedings confidential information or sources of information obtained in their professional capacities.
   Statutes that restrict or prohibit the use of certain evidence in sexual offense cases, such as evidence regarding the lack of chastity of the victim.

Shifting the burden of proof   The process of transferring the obligation to affirmatively prove a fact in controversy or an issue brought during a lawsuit from one party in a legal controversy to the other party.

Shipping law   The area of maritime law that is concerned with ships and the individuals employed in or around them, as well as the shipment of goods by merchant vessels.

Shock-the-conscience test   A determination of whether a state agent's actions fall outside the standards of civilized decency.

Shop-book rule   A doctrine that allows the admission into evidence of books that consist of original entries made in the normal course of a business, which are introduced to the court from proper custody upon general authentication.

Shoplifting   Theft of merchandise from a store or business establishment.

Shop steward   A labor union official elected to represent members in a plant or particular department. The shop steward's duties include collection of dues, recruitment of new members, and initial negotiations for settlement of grievances.

Short cause A legal matter that will not take up a significant amount of the time of the court and may be entered on the list of short causes upon application of one of the parties, where it will be dealt with more expediently than it would be in its regular order.

Short sale A method of gaining profit from an anticipated decline in the price of a stock.

Show cause An order by a court that requires a party to appear and to provide reasons why a particular thing should not be performed or allowed and mandates such party to meet the prima facie case set forth in the complaint or affidavit of the applicant.

Show cause order A court order, made upon the motion of an applicant, that requires a party to appear and provide reasons why the court should not perform or not allow a particular action and mandates this party to meet the prima facie case set forth in the complaint or affidavit of the applicant.

Show-up The live presentation of a criminal suspect to a victim or witness of a crime.

Sic *Latin, In such manner; so; thus.*

Sight draft A commercial paper that is payable upon presentment.

Signature A mark or sign made by an individual on an instrument or document to signify knowledge, approval, acceptance, or obligation.

Simple Unmixed; not aggravated or compounded.

Simultaneous death Loss of life by two or more individuals concurrently or pursuant to circumstances that render it impossible to ascertain who predeceased whom.

Sine die [*Latin, Without day.*] Without day; without assigning a day for a further meeting or hearing.

Sine qua non [*Latin, Without which not.*] A description of a requisite or condition that is indispensable.

Single name paper A type of commercial paper, such as a check or promissory note that has only one original signer or more than one maker signing for the exact same purpose.

Single name partnership A business arrangement whereby two or more individuals, the partners, unite their skill, capital, and work in exchange for a proportional alloca

Sit To hold court or perform an act that is judicial in nature; to hold a session, such as of a court, grand jury, or legislative body.

Situs [*Latin, Situation; location.*] The place where a particular event occurs.

S.J.D. An abbreviation for doctor of judicial science, a degree awarded to highly qualified individuals who have successfully completed a prescribed course of legal doctorate study after having earned J.D. and LL.M. degrees.

Slating The procedure by which law enforcement officials record on the blotter information about an individual's arrest and charges, together with identification and facts about his or her background.

Slavery A civil relationship in which one person has absolute power over the life, fortune, and liberty of another.

Slip decision A copy of a judgment by the U.S. Supreme Court or other tribunal that is printed and distributed almost immediately subsequent to the time that it is handed down by the court.

Slip law A copy of a bill that is passed by a state legislature and endorsed by the governor, or passed by Congress and signed by the president, and is printed and distributed almost immediately.

Small business A type of enterprise that is independently owned and operated, has few employees, does a small amount of business, and is not predominant in its area of operation.

Small claims court A special court, sometimes called conciliation court, that provides expeditious, informal, and inexpensive adjudication of small claims.

Smart money Vindictive, punitive, or exemplary damages given by way of punishment and example, in cases of gross misconduct of a defendant.

Smith Act An antisedition enactment (54 Stat. 670) by Congress in 1940 that proscribed, among other things, the advocacy of the forcible or violent overthrow of the government.

Smuggling The criminal offense of bringing into, or removing from, a country items that are prohibited or upon which customs or excise duties have not been paid.

Socialism An economic and social theory that seeks to maximize wealth and opportunity for all people through public ownership and control of industries and social services.

Social Security Act of 1935 Legislation (42 U.S.C.A. § 301 et seq.) designed to assist in the maintenance of the financial well-being of eligible persons, enacted in 1935 as part of President Franklin D. Roosevelt's New Deal.

Sodomy Anal or oral intercourse between human beings, or any sexual relations between a human being and an animal, the act of which may be punishable as a criminal offense.

Soldiers' and Sailors' Civil Relief Act A federal statute (50 App. U.S.C.A. § 501 et seq.) created to ensure that individuals in the armed services are totally informed of legal proceedings against them and have sufficient time and opportunity to appear and defend their rights.

Sole proprietorship
A form of business in which one person owns all the assets of the business, in contrast to a partnership or a corporation.

Solicitation
Urgent request, plea, or entreaty; enticing, asking. The criminal offense of urging someone to commit an unlawful act.

Solicitor
A type of practicing lawyer in England who handles primarily office work.

The title of the chief law officer of a government body or department, such as a city, town, or municipal corporation.

Solicitor general
An officer of the U.S. Department of Justice who represents the U.S. government in cases before the U.S. Supreme Court.

Solomon Amendment
Federal legislation, 50 U.S.C.A. App. § 462(f), that denies male college students between the ages of 18 and 26 who fail to register for the military draft (under the Selective Service Act, 50 U.S.C.A. App. § 451 et seq.) eligibility to receive financial aid provided by the Basic Educational Opportunity Grant Program.

Solvency
The ability of an individual to pay his or her debts as they mature in the normal and ordinary course of business, or the financial condition of owning property of sufficient value to discharge all of one's debts.

Son of Sam laws
Laws that enable a state to use the proceeds a criminal earns from recounting his or her crime in a book, movie, television show, or other depiction. The laws are named after David Berkowitz, a New York serial killer who left a note signed "Son of Sam" at the scene of one of his crimes.

Sovereign immunity
The legal protection that prevents a sovereign state or person from being sued without consent.

Sovereignty
The supreme, absolute, and uncontrollable power by which an independent state is governed and from which all specific political powers are derived; the intentional independence of a state, combined with the right and power of regulating its internal affairs without foreign interference.

Special appearance
The act of presenting oneself in a court and thereby submitting to the court's jurisdiction, but only for a specific purpose and not for all the purposes for which a lawsuit is brought.

Special assessment
A real property tax proportionately levied on homeowners and landowners to cover the costs of improvements that will be for the benefit of all upon whom it is imposed.

Special courts
Bodies within the judicial branch of government that are organized to administer justice and generally address only one area of law or have specifically defined powers.

Specialization
A career option pursued by some attorneys that entails the acquisition of detailed knowledge of, and proficiency in, a particular area of law.

Special term	In court practice in some jurisdictions, a branch of the court system held by a single judge for hearing and deciding motions and equitable actions in the first instance.
Specialty	A contract under seal.
Special warranty deed	A written instrument that conveys real property in which the grantor (original owner) only covenants to warrant and defend the title against claims and demands by him or her and all persons claiming by, through, and under him or her.
Specific intent	The mental purpose, aim, or design to accomplish a specific harm or result by acting in a manner prohibited by law.
Specific legacy	A gift by will of designated personal property.
Specific performance	An extraordinary equitable remedy that compels a party to execute a contract according to the precise terms agreed upon or to execute it substantially so that, under the circumstances, justice will be done between the parties.
Speculative damages	Alleged injuries or losses that are uncertain or contingent and cannot be used as a basis of recovery for tort or contract actions.
Speech plus	A form of expression in which behavior is used by itself or in coordination with written or spoken words to convey an idea or message.
Spending power	The power of legislatures to tax and spend.
Spendthrift	One who spends money profusely and improvidently, thereby wasting his or her estate.
Spendthrift trust	An arrangement whereby one person sets aside property for the benefit of another in which, either because of a direction of the settlor (one who creates a trust) or because of statute, the beneficiary (one who profits from the act of another) is unable to transfer his or her right to future payments of income or capital, and his or her creditors are unable to subject the beneficiary's interest to the payment of his or her debts.
Spin-off	The situation that arises when a parent corporation organizes a subsidiary corporation, to which it transfers a portion of its assets in exchange for all of the subsidiary's capital stock, which is subsequently transferred to the parent corporation's shareholders.
Split decision	A decision by an appellate court that is not unanimous.
Split-off	The process whereby a parent corporation organizes a subsidiary corporation to which it transfers part of its assets in exchange for all of the subsidiary's capital stock, which is subsequently transferred to the shareholders of the parent corporation in exchange for a portion of their parent stock.
Split-up	An arrangement whereby a parent corporation transfers all of its assets to two or more corporations and then winds up its affairs.

Spoliation Any erasure, interlineation, or other alteration made to commercial paper, such as a check or promissory note, by an individual who is not acting pursuant to the consent of the parties who have an interest in such instrument.

Sports law The laws, regulations, and judicial decisions that govern sports and athletes.

Spot zoning The granting to a particular parcel of land a classification concerning its use that differs from the classification of other land in the immediate area.

Squatter An individual who settles on the land of another person without any legal authority to do so, or without acquiring a legal title.

SS An abbreviation used in the portion of an affidavit, pleading, or record known as the statement of venue.

Stale check A document that is a promise to pay money that is held for too long a period of time before being presented for payment.

Stalking Criminal activity consisting of the repeated following and harassing of another person.

Stamp Act English act of 1765 requiring that revenue stamps be affixed to all official documents in the American colonies.

Stamp tax A pecuniary charge imposed upon certain transactions.

Stand The location in a courtroom where the parties and witnesses offer their testimony. To appear in court; to submit to the jurisdiction of the court.

Standard deduction The name given to a fixed amount of money that may be subtracted from the adjusted gross income of a taxpayer who does not itemize certain living expenses for income tax purposes.

Standing The legally protectible stake or interest that an individual has in a dispute that entitles him to bring the controversy before the court to obtain judicial relief.

Stand mute The state of affairs that arises when a defendant in a criminal action refuses to plead either guilty or not guilty.

Star Chamber An ancient high court of England, controlled by the monarch, which was abolished in 1641 by Parliament for abuses of power.

Stare decisis [*Latin, Let the decision stand.*] The policy of courts to abide by or adhere to principles established by decisions in earlier cases.

State As a noun, a people permanently occupying a fixed territory bound together by common habits and custom into one body politic exercising, through the medium of an organized government, independent sovereignty and control over all persons and things within its boundaries, capable of making war and peace and of entering into international relations with other states. The section of territory occupied by one of the United States. The people of a state, in their collective capacity, considered as the party wronged by a criminal deed; the public; as in the title of a case, "The State v. A. B." The circumstances or condition of a being or thing at a given time.

As a verb, to express the particulars of a thing in writing or in words; to set down or set forth in detail; to aver, allege, or declare. To set down in gross; to mention in general terms, or by way of reference; to refer.

State action   A requirement for claims that arise under the Due Process Clause of the Fourteenth Amendment and civil rights legislation, for which a private citizen seeks relief in the form of damages or redress based on an improper intrusion by the government into his or her private life.

State courts   Judicial tribunals established by each of the fifty states.

State interest   A broad term for any matter of public concern that is addressed by a government in law or policy.

State lottery   A game of chance operated by a state government.

Statement of affairs   A document that must be filed in bankruptcy, which sets forth answers to questions concerning the debtor's past and present financial situation.

State's evidence   A colloquial term for testimony given by an accomplice or joint participant in the commission of a crime, subject to an agreement that the person will be granted immunity from prosecution if she voluntarily, completely, and fairly discloses her own guilt as well as that of the other participants.

States' rights   A doctrine and strategy in which the rights of the individual states are protected by the U.S. Constitution from interference by the federal government.

Status   The standing, state, or condition of an individual; the rights, obligations, capacities, and incapacities that assign an individual to a given class.

Status offense   A type of crime that is not based upon prohibited action or inaction but rests on the fact that the offender has a certain personal condition or is of a specified character.

Status quo   [*Latin, The existing state of things at any given date.*] *Status quo ante bellum* means the state of things before the war. The *status quo* to be preserved by a preliminary injunction is the last actual, peaceable, uncontested status which preceded the pending controversy.

Statute   An act of a legislature that declares, proscribes, or commands something; a specific law, expressed in writing.

Statute of frauds   A type of state law, modeled after an old English law, that requires certain types of contracts to be in writing.

Statute of limitations	A type of federal or state law that restricts the time within which legal proceedings may be brought.
Statute of uses	An English law enacted in 1535 to end the practice of creating uses in real property by changing the purely equitable title of those entitled to a use into absolute ownership with the right of possession.
Statute of wills	An early English law that provided that all individuals who owned land were permitted to leave or devise two-thirds of their property to anyone by written will and testament, effective upon their death.
Statute of York	An English law enacted in 1318 that required the consent of Parliament in all legislative matters.
Statutes at large	An official compilation of the acts and resolutions of each session of Congress published by the Office of the Federal Register in the National Archives and Record Service.
Statutory	Created, defined, or relating to a statute; required by statute; conforming to a statute.
Statutory rape	Sexual intercourse by an adult with a person below a statutorily designated age.
Statutory redemption	The right granted by legislation to a mortgagor, one who pledges property as security for a debt, as well as to certain others, to recover the mortgaged property after a foreclosure sale.
Stay	The act of temporarily stopping a judicial proceeding through the order of a court.
Steering	The process whereby builders, brokers, and rental property managers induce purchasers or lessees of real property to buy land or rent premises in neighborhoods composed of persons of the same race.
Stenographer	An individual who records court proceedings either in shorthand or through the use of a paper-punching device.
Stipulation	An agreement between attorneys that concerns business before a court and is designed to simplify or shorten litigation and save costs.
Stock	A security issued by a corporation that represents an ownership right in the assets of the corporation and a right to a proportionate share of profits after payment of corporate liabilities and obligations.
Stock dividend	A corporate distribution to shareholders declared out of profits, at the discretion of the directors of the corporation, which is paid in the form of shares of stock, as opposed to money, and increases the number of shares.
Stockholder's derivative suit	A legal action in which a shareholder of a corporation sues in the name of the corporation to enforce or defend a legal right because the corporation itself refuses to sue.

Stock market   The various organized stock exchanges and over-the-counter markets.

Stock warrant   A certificate issued by a corporation that entitles the person holding it to buy a certain amount of stock in the corporation, usually at a specified time and price.

Stop and frisk   The situation where a police officer who is suspicious of an individual detains the person and runs his hands lightly over the suspect's outer garments to determine if the person is carrying a concealed weapon.

Stop order   A direction by a customer to a stock broker, directing the broker to wait until a stock reaches a particular price and then to complete the transaction by purchasing or selling shares of that stock.

Stoppage in transit   The right of a seller to prevent the delivery of goods to a buyer after such goods have been delivered to a common carrier for shipment.

Stop payment order   Revocation of a check; a notice made by a depositor to his or her bank directing the bank to refuse payment on a specific check drawn by the depositor.

Straddle   In the stock and commodity markets, a strategy in options contracts consisting of an equal number of put options and call options on the same underlying share, index, or commodity future.

Straight-line depreciation   A method employed to calculate the decline in the value of income-producing property for the purposes of federal taxation.

Stranger   A third person; anyone who is not a party to a particular legal action or agreement.

Strategic Lawsuits Against Public Participation (SLAPPs)   Retaliatory lawsuits intended to silence, intimidate, or punish those who have used public forums to speak, petition, or otherwise move for government action on an issue.

Straw man   An individual who acts as a front for others who actually incur the expense and obtain the profit of a transaction.

Street railroad   A railway that is constructed upon a thoroughfare or highway to aid in the transportation of people or property along the roadway.

Strict construction   A close or narrow reading and interpretation of a statute or written document.

Strict foreclosure   A decree that orders the payment of a mortgage of real property.

Strict liability   Absolute legal responsibility for an injury that can be imposed on the wrongdoer without proof of carelessness or fault.

Strict scrutiny   A standard of judicial review for a challenged policy in which the court presumes the policy to be invalid unless the government can demonstrate a compelling interest to justify the policy.

Strike	A work stoppage; the concerted refusal of employees to perform work that their employer has assigned to them in order to force the employer to grant certain demanded concessions, such as increased wages or improved employment conditions.
String citation	A series of references to cases that establish legal precedents and to other authorities that appear one after another and are printed following a legal assertion or conclusion as supportive authority.
Strong-arm provision	The segment of the federal bankruptcy law that grants the trustee the rights of the most secured creditor, so that he or she is able to seize all of the debtor's property for proper distribution.
Struck jury	A special jury chosen in a manner whereby an appropriate official prepares a panel containing the names of forty-eight potential jurors and the parties strike off names until the number of jurors is reduced to twelve.
Sua sponte	[*Latin, Of his or her or its own will; voluntarily.*]
Subcontractor	One who takes a portion of a contract from the principal contractor or from another subcontractor.
Subject matter jurisdiction	The power of a court to hear and determine cases of the general class to which the proceedings in question belong.
Subletting	The leasing of part or all of the property held by a tenant, as opposed to a landlord, during a portion of his or her unexpired balance of the term of occupancy.
Submerged lands	Soil lying beneath water or on the oceanside of the tideland.
Submission of controversy	A procedure by which the parties to a particular dispute place any matter of real controversy existing between them before a court for a final determination.
Submit	To offer for determination; commit to the judgment or discretion of another individual or authority.
Sub nomine	[*Latin, Under the name; in the name of; under the title of.*]
Subordination	To put in an inferior class or order; to make subject to, or subservient. A legal status that refers to the establishment of priority between various existing liens or encumbrances on the same parcel of property.
Subornation of perjury	The criminal offense of procuring another to commit perjury, which is the crime of lying, in a material matter, while under oath.
Subpoena	[*Latin, Under penalty.*] A formal document that orders a named individual to appear before a duly authorized body at a fixed time to give testimony.
Subpoena duces tecum	The judicial process used to command the production before a court of papers, documents, or other tangible items of evidence.

Subrogation The substitution of one person in the place of another with reference to a lawful claim, demand, or right, so that he or she who is substituted succeeds to the rights of the other in relation to the debt or claim, and its rights, remedies, or securities.

Subscribe To write underneath; to put a signature at the end of a printed or written instrument.

Subscription The act of writing one's name under a written instrument; the affixing of one's signature to any document, whether for the purpose of authenticating or attesting it, of adopting its terms as one's own expressions, or of binding one's self by an engagement which it contains. A written contract by which one engages to take and pay for capital stock of a corporation, or to contribute a sum of money for a designated purpose, either gratuitously, as in the case of subscribing to a charity, or in consideration of an equivalent to be rendered, as a subscription to a periodical, a forthcoming book, a series of entertainments, or the like.

Subsidiary Auxiliary; aiding or supporting in an inferior capacity or position. In the law of corporations, a corporation or company owned by another corporation that controls at least a majority of the shares.

Sub silentio [*Latin, Under silence; without any notice being taken.*]

Substance Essence; the material or necessary component of something.

Substantial Of real worth and importance; of considerable value; valuable. Belonging to substance; actually existing; real; not seeming or imaginary; not illusive; solid; true; veritable.

Substantiate To establish the existence or truth of a particular fact through the use of competent evidence; to verify.

Substantive due process The substantive limitations placed on the content or subject matter of state and federal laws by the Due Process Clauses of the Fifth and Fourteenth Amendments to the U.S. Constitution.

Substantive law The part of the law that creates, defines, and regulates rights, including, for example, the law of contracts, torts, wills, and real property; the essential substance of rights under law.

Substituted service Service of process upon a defendant in any manner, authorized by statute or rule, other than personal service within the jurisdiction; as by publication, by mailing a copy to his or her last known address, or by personal service in another state.

Succession The transfer of title to property under the law of descent and distribution. The transfer of legal or official powers from an individual who formerly held them to another who undertakes current responsibilities to execute those powers.

Sue To initiate a lawsuit or continue a legal proceeding for the recovery of a right; to prosecute, assert a legal claim, or bring action against a particular party.

Suffer	To admit, allow, or permit.
Suffrage	The right to vote at public elections.
Suicide	The deliberate taking of one's own life.
Sui generis	[*Latin, Of its own kind or class.*] That which is the only one of its kind.
Sui juris	[*Latin, Of his or her own right.*] Po ssessing full social and civil rights; not under any legal disability, or the power of another, or guardianship. Having the capacity to manage one's own affairs; not under legal disability to act for one's self.
Suit	A generic term, of comprehensive signification, referring to any proceeding by one person or persons against another or others in a court of law in which the plaintiff pursues the remedy that the law affords for the redress of an injury or the enforcement of a right, whether at law or in equity.
Summary	As a noun, an abridgment; brief; compendium; digest; also a short application to a court or judge, without the formality of a full proceeding. As an adjective, short; concise; immediate; peremptory; off-hand; without a jury; provisional; statutory. The term as used in connection with legal proceedings means a short, concise, and immediate proceeding.
Summary judgment	A procedural device used during civil litigation to promptly and expeditiously dispose of a case without a trial. It is used when there is no dispute as to the material facts of the case and a party is entitled to judgment as a matter of law.
Summary proceedings	An alternative form of litigation for the prompt disposition of legal actions.
Summary process	A legal procedure used for enforcing a right that takes effect faster and more efficiently than ordinary methods. The legal papers—a court order, for example—used to achieve an expeditious resolution of the controversy.
Summons	The paper that tells a defendant that he or she is being sued and asserts the power of the court to hear and determine the case. A form of legal process that commands the defendant to appear before the court on a specific day and to answer the complaint made by the plaintiff.
Sumptuary laws	Rules made for the purpose of restraining luxury or extravagance.
Sunday closing laws	Laws that prohibit the conduct of business on Sundays.
Sunset provision	A statutory provision providing that a particular agency, benefit, or law will expire on a particular date, unless it is reauthorized by the legislature.

Sunshine laws   Statutes that mandate that meetings of governmental agencies and departments be open to the public at large.

Superior   One who has a right to give orders; belonging to a higher grade.

Supersede   To obliterate, replace, make void, or useless.

Supersedeas   The name given to a writ, a court order, from a higher court commanding a lower court to suspend a particular proceeding.

Supervening   Unforeseen, intervening, an additional event or cause.

Supplementary proceedings   A proceeding in which a judgment debtor is summoned into court for questioning by a judgment creditor who has not received payment.

Support   As a verb, furnishing funds or means for maintenance; to maintain; to provide for; to enable to continue; to carry on. To provide a means of livelihood. To vindicate, to maintain, to defend, to uphold with aid or countenance.

   As a noun, that which furnishes a livelihood; a source or means of living; subsistence, sustenance, maintenance, or living.

Suppress   To stop something or someone; to prevent, prohibit, or subdue.

Supra   [*Latin, Above; beyond.*] A term used in legal research to indicate that the matter under current consideration has appeared in the preceding pages of the text in which the reference is made.

Supremacy clause   The clause of Article VI of the U.S. Constitution that declares that all laws and treaties made by the federal government shall be the "supreme law of the land."

Supreme court   An appellate tribunal with high powers and broad authority within its jurisdiction.

Surcharge   An overcharge or additional cost.

Surety   An individual who undertakes an obligation to pay a sum of money or to perform some duty or promise for another in the event that person fails to act.

Surplusage   Extraneous matter; impertinent, superfluous, or unnecessary.

Surprise   An unexpected action, sudden confusion, or an unanticipated event.

Surrebutter   In common-law pleading, the plaintiff's factual reply to the defendant's rebutter or answer.

Surrejoinder   In the second stage of common-law pleading, the plaintiff's answer to the defendant's rejoinder.

Surrender   To give up, return, or yield.

Surrogate court   A tribunal in some states with subject matter jurisdiction over actions and proceedings involving, among other things, the probate of wills, affairs of decedents, and the guardianship of the property of infants.

Surrogate motherhood
A relationship in which one woman bears and gives birth to a child for a person or a couple who then adopts or takes legal custody of the child; also called mothering by proxy.

Surtax
An additional charge on an item that is already taxed.

Suspect classification
A presumptively unconstitutional distinction made between individuals on the basis of race, national origin, alienage, or religious affiliation, in a statute, ordinance, regulation, or policy.

Suspended sentence
A sentence given after the formal conviction of a crime that the convicted person is not required to serve.

Suspicion
The apprehension of something without proof to verify the belief.

Sustain
To carry on; to maintain. To affirm, uphold or approve, as when an appellate court sustains the decision of a lower court. To grant, as when a judge sustains an objection to testimony or evidence, he or she agrees with the objection and gives it effect.

Syllabus
A headnote; a short note preceding the text of a reported case that briefly summarizes the rulings of the court on the points decided in the case.

Symbolic delivery
The constructive conveyance of the subject matter of a gift or sale, when it is either inaccessible or cumbersome, through the offering of some substitute article that indicates the donative intent of the donor or seller and is accepted as the representative of the original item.

Symbolic speech
Nonverbal gestures and actions that are meant to communicate a message.

Syndicate
An association of individuals formed for the purpose of conducting a particular business; a joint venture.

Synopsis
A summary; a brief statement, less than the whole.

Table of cases
An alphabetized list of the judicial decisions that are cited, referred to, or explained in a book with references to the sections, pages, or paragraphs where they are cited.

Tacit   Implied, inferred, understood without being expressly stated.

Tacking   The process whereby an individual who is in adverse possession of real property adds his or her period of possession to that of a prior adverse possessor.

Taft-Hartley Act   The amendments to the National Labor Relations Act, also known as the Wagner Act of 1935 (29 U.S.C.A. § 151 et seq.), which were enacted to counteract the advantage labor unions had gained under the original legislation by imposing corresponding duties on unions.

Tail   Limited, abridged, reduced, or curtailed.

Takeover   To assume control or management of a corporation without necessarily obtaining actual title to it.

Talesman   An individual called to act as a juror from among the bystanders in a court.

Tamper   To meddle, alter, or improperly interfere with something; to make changes or corrupt, as in tampering with the evidence.

Tangible   Possessing a physical form that can be touched or felt.

Tariff   The list of items upon which a duty is imposed when they are imported into the United States, together with the rates at which such articles are taxed.

Taxable income   Under the federal tax law, gross income reduced by adjustments and allowable deductions. It is the income against which tax rates are applied to compute an individual or entity's tax liability. The essence of taxable income is the accrual of some gain, profit, or benefit to a taxpayer.

Taxable situs   The location where charges may be levied upon personal property by a government, pursuant to provisions of its tax laws.

Taxation   The process whereby charges are imposed on individuals or property by the legislative branch of the federal government and by many state governments to raise funds for public purposes.

Tax avoidance   The process whereby an individual plans his or her finances so as to apply all exemptions and deductions provided by tax laws to reduce taxable income.

Tax court   A specialized federal or state court that decides cases involving tax-related controversies.

Tax deed   A written instrument that provides proof of ownership of real property purchased from the government at a tax sale, conducted after the property has been taken from its owner by the government and sold for delinquent taxes.

Tax evasion   The process whereby a person, through commission of fraud, unlawfully pays less tax than the law mandates.

Taxing costs The designation given to the process of determining and charging to the losing party in a legal action the expenses involved in initiating or defending the action, to which the successful side is lawfully entitled.

Taxpayer bill of rights A federal or state law that gives taxpayers procedural and substantive protection when dealing with a revenue department concerning a tax collection dispute.

Taxpayer's suit An action brought by an individual whose income is subjected to charges imposed by the state or federal government, for the benefit of that individual and others in order to prevent the unlawful diversion of public funds.

Tax rate The amount of charges imposed by the government upon personal or corporate income, capital gains, gifts, estates, and sales that are within its statutory authority to regulate.

Tax return The form that the government requires a taxpayer to file with the appropriate official by a designated date to disclose and detail income subject to taxation and eligibility for deductions and exemptions, along with a remittance of the tax due or a claim for a refund of taxes that were overpaid.

Tax sale A transfer of real property in exchange for money to satisfy charges imposed thereupon by the government that have remained unpaid after the legal period for their payment has expired.

Telecommuni-cations The transmission of words, sounds, images, or data in the form of electronic or electromagnetic signals or impulses.

Temperance movement A movement in the United States to moderate or eliminate the consumption of alcoholic beverages.

Temporary restraining order A court order that lasts only until the court can hear further evidence.

Tenancy A situation that arises when one individual conveys real property to another individual by way of a lease. The relation of an individual to the land he or she holds that designates the extent of that person's estate in real property.

Tenancy by the entirety A type of concurrent estate in real property held by a husband and wife whereby each owns the undivided whole of the property, coupled with the right of survivorship, so that upon the death of one, the survivor is entitled to the decedent's share.

Tenancy in common A form of concurrent ownership of real property in which two or more persons possess the property simultaneously; it can be created by deed, will, or operation of law.

Tenancy in coparcenary A type of concurrent estate in real property by which property rights were acquired only through intestacy by the female heirs when there were no surviving male heirs.

Tenant An individual who occupies or possesses land or premises by way of a grant of an estate of some type, such as in fee, for life, for years, or at will. A person who has the right to temporary use and possession of particular real property, which has been conveyed to that person by a landlord.

Tender An offer of money; the act by which one individual offers someone who is holding a claim or demand against him or her the amount of money that the offeror regards and admits is due, in order to satisfy the claim or demand, in the absence of any contingency or stipulation attached to the offer.

Tender offer A proposal to buy shares of stock from the stockholders of a corporation, made by a group or company that desires to obtain control of the corporation.

Tender years doctrine A doctrine rarely employed in child custody disputes that provides that, when all other factors are equal, custody of a child of tender years—generally under the age of thirteen years—should be awarded to the mother.

Tenement A comprehensive legal term for any type of property of a permanent nature—including land, houses, and other buildings as well as rights attaching thereto, such as the right to collect rent.

Tennessee Valley Authority Act Legislation passed by Congress in 1933 that established the Tennessee Valley Authority (TVA), an autonomous federal corporate agency responsible for the integrated development of the Tennessee River basin.

Tenor An exact replica of a legal document in words and figures.

Tenure A right, term, or mode of holding or occupying something of value for a period of time.

In feudal law, the principal mode or system by which a person held land from a superior in exchange for the rendition of service and loyalty to the grantor. See also feudalism.

The status given to an educator who has satisfactorily completed teaching for a trial period and is, therefore, protected against summary dismissal by the employer.

A length of time during which an individual has a right to occupy a public or private office.

Term An expression, word, or phrase that has a fixed and known meaning in a particular art, science, or profession. A specified period of time.

Termination Cessation; conclusion; end in time or existence.

Term of art A word or phrase that has special meaning in a particular context.

Territorial courts Federal tribunals that serve as both federal and state courts in possessions of the United States—such as Guam and the Virgin Islands—that are not within the limits of any state but are organized with separate legislatures and executive and judicial officers appointed by the president.

Territoriality A term that signifies a connection or limitation with reference to a particular geographic area or country.

Territorial waters The part of the ocean adjacent to the coast of a state that is considered to be part of the territory of that state and subject to its sovereignty.

Territories of the United States Portions of the United States that are not within the limits of any state and have not been admitted as states.

Territory A part of a country separated from the rest and subject to a particular jurisdiction.

Terrorism The unlawful use of force or violence against persons or property in order to coerce or intimidate a government or the civilian population in furtherance of political or social objectives.

Testacy The condition or state of leaving a valid will at one's death to direct the distribution of one's estate.

Testament Another name for a will.

Testamentary Relating to wills.

Testate One who dies leaving a valid will, or the description of this status.

Testator One who makes or has made a will; one who dies leaving a will.

Test case A suit brought specifically for the establishment of an important legal right or principle.

Testify To provide evidence as a witness, subject to an oath or affirmation, in order to establish a particular fact or set of facts.

Testimony Oral evidence offered by a competent witness under oath, which is used to establish some fact or set of facts.

Theaters and shows Comprehensive terms for places where all types of entertainment events can be viewed, including films, plays, and exhibitions.

Theft A criminal act in which property belonging to another is taken without that person's consent.

Theodosian code The legal code of the Roman Empire promulgated in a.d. 438 by the emperor Theodosius II of the East and accepted by the emperor Valentinian III of the West.

Third degree A colloquial term used to describe unlawful methods of coercing an individual to confess to a criminal offense by overcoming his or her free will through the use of psychological or physical violence.

The least serious grade of a specific crime—the grades being classified by the law according to the circumstances under which the crime is committed—for which the least punishment specified by statute will be imposed.

Third party A generic legal term for any individual who does not have a direct connection with a legal transaction but who might be affected by it.

Threats Spoken or written words tending to intimidate or menace others.

Time draft A written order to pay a certain sum in money that is payable at a particular future date.

Time is of the essence A phrase in a contract that means that performance by one party at or within the period specified in the contract is necessary to enable that party to require performance by the other party.

Timely Existing or taking place within the designated period; seasonable.

Time, place, and manner restrictions Limits that government can impose on the occasion, location, and type of individual expression in some circumstances.

Time-price differential A method whereby a seller charges one amount for the immediate cash payment of merchandise and another amount for the same item or items when payment is rendered at a future date or in installments.

Timeshare A form of shared property ownership, commonly in vacation or recreation condominium property, in which rights vest in several owners to use property for a specified period each year.

Tithing In Western ecclesiastical law, the act of paying a percentage of one's income to further religious purposes. One of the political subdivisions of England that was composed of ten families who held freehold estates.

Title In property law, a comprehensive term referring to the legal basis of the ownership of property, encompassing real and personal property and intangible and tangible interests therein; also a document serving as evidence of ownership of property, such as the certificate of title to a motor vehicle.

In regard to legislation, the heading or preliminary part of a particular statute that designates the name by which that act is known.

In the law of trademarks, the name of an item that may be used exclusively by an individual for identification purposes to indicate the quality and origin of the item.

Title insurance A contractual arrangement entered into to indemnify loss or damage resulting from defects or problems relating to the ownership of real property, or from the enforcement of liens that exist against it.

Title search The process of examining official county records to determine whether an owner's rights in real property are good.

Toll A sum of money paid for the right to use a road, highway, or bridge. To postpone or suspend. For example, to toll a statute of limitations means to postpone the running of the time period it specifies.

Tontine An organization of individuals who enter into an agreement to pool sums of money or something of value other than money, permitting the last survivor of the group to take everything.

Torrens title system A system for recording land titles under which a court may direct the issuance of a certificate of title upon application by the landowner.

Tortfeasor A wrongdoer; an individual who commits a wrongful act that injures another and for which the law provides a legal right to seek relief; a defendant in a civil tort action.

Tortious Wrongful; conduct of such character as to subject the actor to civil liability under tort law.

Tort law A body of rights, obligations, and remedies that is applied by courts in civil proceedings to provide relief for persons who have suffered harm from the wrongful acts of others. The person who sustains injury or suffers pecuniary damage as the result of tortious conduct is known as the plaintiff, and the person who is responsible for inflicting the injury and incurs liability for the damage is known as the defendant or tortfeasor.

Totten trust An arrangement created by a person depositing his or her own money in his or her own name in a bank account for the benefit of another.

Towage service An act by which one vessel, known as the tug, supplies power in order to draw another vessel, called the tow.

To wit That is to say; namely.

Town A civil and political subdivision of a state, which varies in size and significance according to location but is ordinarily a division of a county.

Township In a government survey, a square tract of land six miles on each side, constituting thirty-six square miles. In some states, the name given to the political subdivision of a county.

Trade dress A product's physical appearance, including its size, shape, color, design, and texture.

Trademarks Distinctive symbols of authenticity through which the products of particular manufacturers or the salable commodities of particular merchants can be distinguished from those of others.

Trade name Names or designations used by companies to identify themselves and distinguish their businesses from others in the same field.

Trade secret Any valuable commercial information that provides a business with an advantage over competitors who do not have that information.

Trade union An organization of workers in the same skilled occupation or related skilled occupations who act together to secure for all members favorable wages, hours, and other working conditions.

Trade usage Any system, custom, or practice of doing business used so commonly in a vocation, field, or place that an expectation arises that it will be observed in a particular transaction.

Trading stamps and coupons A comprehensive term for any type of tickets, certificates, or order blanks that can be offered in exchange for money or something of value, or for a reduction in price when a particular item is purchased.

Transcript A generic term for any kind of copy, particularly an official or certified representation of the record of what took place in a court during a trial or other legal proceeding.

Transfer To remove or convey from one place or person to another. The removal of a case from one court to another court within the same system where it might have been instituted. An act of the parties, or of the law, by which the title to property is conveyed from one person to another.

Transfer of assets The conveyance of something of value from one person, place, or situation to another.

Transfer tax The charge levied by the government on the sale of shares of stock. A charge imposed by the federal and state governments upon the passing of title to real property or a valuable interest in such property, or on the transfer of a decedent's estate by inheritance, devise, or bequest.

Transitory action A lawsuit that can be commenced in any place where personal service of process can be made on the defendant.

Transnational corporation Any corporation that is registered and operates in more than one country at a time; also called a multinational corporation.

Transnational law All the law—national, international, or mixed—that applies to all persons, businesses, and governments that perform or have influence across state lines.

Traverse In common-law pleading, a denial of the plaintiff's assertions.

Treason The betrayal of one's own country by waging war against it or by consciously or purposely acting to aid its enemies.

Treasury stock Corporate stock that is issued, completely paid for, and reacquired by the corporation at a later point in time.

Treaties in force A publication compiled by the Treaty Affairs Staff, Office of the Legal Adviser, Department of State, which lists treaties and other international agreements of the United States that are on record with the Department of State.

Treatise A scholarly legal publication containing all the law relating to a particular area, such as criminal law or land-use control.

Treaty A compact made between two or more independent nations with a view to the public welfare.

Treble damages	A recovery of three times the amount of actual financial losses suffered which is provided by statute for certain kinds of cases.
Trespass	An unlawful intrusion that interferes with one's person or property.
Trespass to try title	Another name for an ejectment action to recover possession of land wrongfully occupied by a defendant.
Trial	A judicial examination and determination of facts and legal issues arising between parties to a civil or criminal action.
Tribunal	A general term for a court, or the seat of a judge.
Trover	One of the old common-law forms of action; a legal remedy for conversion, or the wrongful appropriation of the plaintiff's personal property.
True bill	A term endorsed on an indictment to indicate that a majority of grand jury members found that the evidence presented to them was adequate to justify a prosecution.
Trust	A relationship created at the direction of an individual, in which one or more persons hold the individual's property subject to certain duties to use and protect it for the benefit of others.
Trust company	A corporation formed for the purpose of managing property set aside to be used for the benefit of individuals or organizations.
Trust deed	A legal document that evidences an agreement of a borrower to transfer legal title to real property to an impartial third party, a trustee, for the benefit of a lender, as security for the borrower's debt.
Trustee	An individual or corporation named by an individual, who sets aside property to be used for the benefit of another person, to manage the property as provided by the terms of the document that created the arrangement.
Trusties	Prison inmates who through their good conduct earn a certain measure of freedom in and around the prison in exchange for assuming certain responsibilities.
Trust receipt	A document by which one individual lends money to purchase something and the borrower promises to hold the item for the benefit of the lender until such time as the debt is paid.
Truth-in-lending act	Legislation contained in Title I of the Consumer Credit Protection Act (15 U.S.C.A. § 1601 et seq.), which is designed to assure that every customer who needs consumer credit is given meaningful information concerning the cost of such credit.
Try	To litigate a legal controversy; to argue a lawsuit in court as an attorney; to sit in the role of a judge or jury to investigate and decide upon questions of law and fact presented in such an action.

Tucker act   Legislation enacted by Congress in 1887 to remedy inadequacies in the original statutory measures that created the former Court of Claims in 1855.

Turpitude   Conduct that is unjust, depraved, or shameful; that which is contrary to justice, modesty, or good morals.

Tying arrangement   An agreement in which a vendor conditions the sale of a particular product on a vendee's promise to purchase an additional, unrelated product.

UCC   An abbreviation for the Uniform Commercial Code.

UCCC   An abbreviation for the Uniform Consumer Credit Code.

UCMJ   An abbreviation for the Uniform Code of Military Justice (10 U.S.C.A. § 801 et seq.).

Ultimate facts   Information essential to a plaintiff's right of action or a defendant's assertion of a defense.

Ultra vires   [*Latin, Beyond the powers.*] The doctrine in the law of corporations that holds that if a corporation enters into a contract that is beyond the scope of its corporate powers, the contract is illegal.

Umpire   A person chosen to decide a question in a controversy that has been submitted to arbitration but has not been resolved because the arbitrators cannot reach agreement, or one who has been chosen to be a permanent arbitrator for the duration of a collective bargaining agreement.

Unauthorized practice   The performance of professional services, such as the rendering of medical treatment or legal assistance, by a person who is not licensed by the state to do so.

Unconscionable   Unusually harsh and shocking to the conscience; that which is so grossly unfair that a court will proscribe it.

Underinclusiveness   A characteristic of a statute or administrative rule dealing with First Amendment rights and other fundamental liberty interests, whereby the statute prohibits some conduct but fails to prohibit other, similar conduct.

Understanding   A general term referring to an agreement, either express or implied, written or oral.

Undertaking A written promise offered as security for the performance of a particular act required in a legal action.

Underwrite To insure; to sell an issue of stocks and bonds or to guarantee the purchase of unsold stocks and bonds after a public issue.

Undue influence A judicially created defense to transactions that have been imposed upon weak and vulnerable persons that allows the transactions to be set aside.

Unemployment compensation Insurance benefits paid by the state or federal government to individuals who are involuntarily out of work in order to provide them with necessities, such as food, clothing, and shelter.

Unenumerated rights Rights that are not expressly mentioned in the written text of a constitution but instead are inferred from the language, history, and structure of the constitution, or cases interpreting it.

Unethical conduct Behavior that falls below or violates the professional standards in a particular field, such as law or medicine.

Unfair competition Any fraudulent, deceptive, or dishonest trade practice that is prohibited by statute, regulation, or the common law.

Unfair labor practice Conduct prohibited by federal law regulating relations between employers, employees, and labor organizations.

Uniform acts Laws that are designed to be adopted generally by all the states so that the law in one jurisdiction is the same as in another jurisdiction.

Uniform commercial code A general and inclusive group of laws adopted, at least partially, by all the states to further uniformity and fair dealing in business and commercial transactions.

Unilateral contract A contract in which only one party makes an express promise, or undertakes a performance without first securing a reciprocal agreement from the other party.

Union shop A type of business in which an employer is allowed to hire a nonunion worker, who, however, must subsequently join the union in order to be permitted to continue work.

United States Government Manual A comprehensive directory, published annually, that contains general information about the federal government with emphasis on the executive branch and regulatory agencies, and also information about Congress and the judicial branch of government.

Unities In real property law, the four characteristics that are peculiar to property owned by several individuals as joint tenants.

Unitrust A right of property, real or personal, held by one person, the trustee, for the benefit of another, the beneficiary, from which a fixed percentage of the net fair market value of the assets, valued annually, is paid each year to the beneficiary.

Unjust enrichment	A general equitable principle that no person should be allowed to profit at another's expense without making restitution for the reasonable value of any property, services, or other benefits that have been unfairly received and retained.
Unlawful	Contrary to or unauthorized by law; illegal.
Unlawful assembly	A meeting of three or more individuals to commit a crime or carry out a lawful or unlawful purpose in a manner likely to imperil the peace and tranquillity of the neighborhood.
Unlawful communications	Spoken or written words tending to intimidate, menace, or harm others.
Unlawful detainer	The act of retaining possession of property without legal right.
Unliquidated	Unassessed or settled; not ascertained in amount.
Unwritten law	Unwritten rules, principles, and norms that have the effect and force of law though they have not been formally enacted by the government.
Upset price	The dollar amount below which property, either real or personal, that is scheduled for sale at an auction is not to be sold.
Usage	A reasonable and legal practice in a particular location, or among persons in a specific business or trade, that is either known to the individuals involved or is well established, general, and uniform to such an extent that a presumption may properly be made that the parties acted with reference to it in their transactions.
USC	An abbreviation for U.S. Code.
USCA®	An abbreviation for U.S. Code Annotated.
USCCAN®	An abbreviation for *United States Code Congressional and Administrative News*, a source of new federal public laws that is published by West Group every two weeks when Congress is in session and once a month when Congress is not in session.
U.S. Code	A multivolume publication of the text of statutes enacted by Congress.
U.S. Code Annotated®	A multivolume work published by West Group that contains the complete text of federal laws enacted by Congress that are included in the U.S. Code, together with case notes (known as annotations) of state and federal decisions that interpret and apply specific sections of federal statutes, plus the text of presidential proclamations and executive orders.
U.S. commissioners	The former designation for U.S. magistrates.
USDC	An abbreviation for U.S. District Court.

Use — The fact of being habitually employed in a certain manner. In real property law, a right held by an individual (called a *cestui que use*) to take the profits arising from a particular parcel of land that was owned and possessed by another individual.

Use and occupation — A kind of action brought by a landlord against an individual who had occupancy of the landlord's land or premises under an express or implied agreement requiring payment, but not under a leasehold contract that would allow the landlord to initiate an action for rent.

Use tax — A charge imposed on the use or possession of personal property.

U.S. Taxpayers Party — A political party with offices and candidates throughout the United States that takes an ultraconservative stance on fiscal and moral issues.

Usufruct — A civil law term referring to the right of one individual to use and enjoy the property of another, provided its substance is neither impaired nor altered.

Usurious — Characterized by an unconscionable or exorbitant rate of interest.

Usurpation — The illegal encroachment or assumption of the use of authority, power, or property properly belonging to another; the interruption or disturbance of an individual in his or her right or possession.

Usury — The crime of charging higher interest on a loan than the law permits.

Uti possidetis — A term used in international law to indicate that the parties to a particular treaty are to retain possession of that which they forcibly seized during a war.

Utter — To publish or offer; to send into circulation.

Uxor — [*Latin, Wife.*] A woman who is legally married.

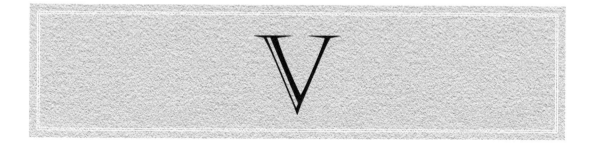

Vacate — To annul, set aside, or render void; to surrender possession or occupancy.

Vagrancy — The condition of an individual who is idle, has no visible means of support, and travels from place to place without working.

Vague — Imprecise; uncertain; indefinite.

Valid — Binding; possessing legal force or strength; legally sufficient.

Valuable consideration In the formation of a valid and binding contract, something of worth or value that is either a detriment incurred by the person making the promise or a benefit received by the other person.

Value The estimated or appraised worth of any object or property, calculated in money.

Vandalism The intentional and malicious destruction of or damage to the property of another.

Variance The discrepancy between what a party to a lawsuit alleges will be proved in pleadings and what the party actually proves at trial.

In zoning law, an official permit to use property in a manner that departs from the way in which other property in the same locality can be used.

Vel non [*Latin, Or not.*] A term used by the courts in reference to the existence or nonexistence of an issue for determination; for example: "We come to the merits vel non of this appeal," means "we come to the merits, or not, of this appeal," and refers to the possibility that the appeal backs merit.

Vendee Buyer or purchaser; an individual to whom anything is transferred by a sale.

Vendor Seller; an individual who transfers property for sale; merchant; retail dealer; supplier.

Vendor and purchaser The legal relationship between the buyer and the seller of land during the interim period between the execution of the contract and the date of its consummation.

Venire facias [*Latin, Cause to come.*] A judicial order or writ addressed to the sheriff of a county where a legal action is to take place, commanding the sheriff to assemble a jury.

Venireman A member of a jury which has been summoned by a writ of venire facias.

Venue A place, such as the territory from which residents are selected to serve as jurors.

A proper place, such as the correct court to hear a case because it has authority over events that have occurred within a certain geographical area.

Verba [*Latin, Words.*] A term used in many legal maxims, including *verba sunt indices animi*, which means "words are the indicators of the mind or thought"; and *verba accipienda ut sortiantur effectum*, or "words are to be taken so that they may have some effect."

Verdict The formal decision or finding made by a jury concerning the questions submitted to it during a trial. The jury reports the verdict to the court, which generally accepts it.

Verify	To make certain, to substantiate, or to confirm by formal oath, affirmation, or affidavit.
Versus	[*Latin, Against.*] A designation used in the caption of a lawsuit to indicate the opposite positions taken by the parties.
Vertical merger	A merger between two business firms that have a buyer-seller relationship.
Vest	To give an immediate, fixed right of present or future enjoyment.
Veto	The refusal of an executive officer to assent to a bill that has been created and approved by the legislature, thereby depriving the bill of any legally binding effect.
Vexatious litigation	A legal action or proceeding initiated maliciously and without probable cause by an individual who is not acting in good faith for the purpose of annoying or embarrassing an opponent.
Vicarious liability	The tort doctrine that imposes responsibility upon one person for the failure of another, with whom the person has a special relationship (such as parent and child, employer and employee, or owner of vehicle and driver), to exercise such care as a reasonably prudent person would use under similar circumstances.
Vice	A fault, flaw, defect, or imperfection. Immoral conduct, practice, or habit.
Vice crimes	A generic legal term for offenses involving immorality, including prostitution, lewdness, lasciviousness, and obscenity.
Vill	In old English law, a division of a hundred or wapentake; a town or a city.
Virginia and Kentucky resolves	Resolutions passed by the Virginia and Kentucky legislatures in 1798 and 1799 protesting the federal Alien and Sedition Acts of 1798.
Virginia Declaration of Rights	Statement of rights adopted by the colony of Virginia in 1776, which served as the model for the U.S. Constitution's Bill of Rights.
Vis	[*Latin, Force or violence.*] A term employed in many legal phrases and maxims, such as *vis injuriosa*, "wrongful force."
Visa	An official endorsement on a passport or other document required to secure an alien's admission to a country.
Visible means of support	A term employed in vagrancy statutes to test whether an individual has any apparent ability to provide for himself or herself financially.
Vitiate	To impair or make void; to destroy or annul, either completely or partially, the force and effect of an act or instrument.

Viva voce [*Latin, With the living voice; by word of mouth.*] Verbally; orally.

Viz. [*Latin, A contraction of the term* videlicet, *to wit, namely, or that is to say.*] A term used to highlight or make more specific something previously indicated only in general terms.

Void That which is null and completely without legal force or binding effect.

Voidable That which is not absolutely void, but may be avoided.

Void for vagueness doctrine A doctrine derived from the Due Process Clauses of the Fifth and Fourteenth Amendments to the U.S. Constitution that requires criminal laws to be drafted in language that is clear enough for the average person to comprehend.

Voir dire [*Old French, To speak the truth.*] The preliminary examination of prospective jurors to determine their qualifications and suitability to serve on a jury, in order to ensure the selection of fair and impartial jury.

Volenti non fit injuria [*Latin, To the consenting, no injury is done.*] In the law of negligence, the precept that denotes that a person who knows and comprehends the peril and voluntarily exposes himself or herself to it, although not negligent in doing so, is regarded as engaging in an assumption of the risk and is precluded from a recovery for an injury ensuing therefrom.

Volstead Act A popular name for the National Prohibition Act (41 Stat. 305), a comprehensive statute that was enacted to enforce the Eighteenth Amendment to the U.S. Constitution and to prohibit the manufacture and sale of intoxicating liquors.

Voluntary act A crime that is the product of conscious choice and independent will.

Voting Rights Act of 1965 An enactment by Congress in 1965 (42 U.S.C.A. § 1973 et seq.) that prohibits the states and their political subdivisions from imposing voting qualifications or prerequisites to voting, or standards, practices, or procedures that deny or curtail the right of a U.S. citizen to vote because of race, color, or membership in a language minority group.

Voting trust A type of agreement by which two or more individuals who own corporate stock that carries voting rights transfer their shares to another party for voting purposes, so as to control corporate affairs.

Vouchee Under a procedure in common law, a person from whom a defendant will seek indemnity if a plaintiff is successful in his or her action against the defendant.

Voucher A receipt or release which provides evidence of payment or other discharge of a debt, often for purposes of reimbursement, or attests to the accuracy of the accounts.

Vouching-in A procedural device used in common law by which a defendant notifies another, not presently a party to a lawsuit, that if a plaintiff is successful, the defendant will seek indemnity from that individual.

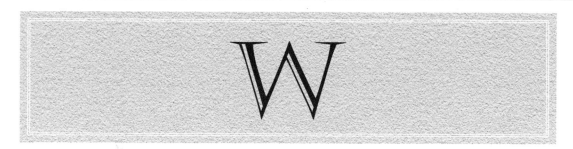

Wadset	In Scotland, the ancient term for a mortgage.
Wage assignment	The voluntary transfer in advance of a debtor's pay, generally in connection with a particular debt or judgment.
Wage earner's plan	A form of bankruptcy under a former federal law whereby an individual retained her property and paid off a debt over a period of time, as determined by a court and subject to supervision by the court.
Wager of battel	A type of trial by combat between accuser and accused that was introduced into England by William the Conqueror (King William I) and his Norman followers after the Norman Conquest of 1066.
Wager of law	A procedure for defending oneself that could be used in a trial before one of the ancient courts of England.
Wait-and-see doctrine	A rule that permits consideration of events occurring subsequent to the inception of an instrument that pertains to the vesting of a future interest. If the specified contingency on which the creation of the interest depends actually occurs within the period of the Rule Against Perpetuities, the interest is legally enforceable.
Waive	To intentionally or voluntarily relinquish a known right or engage in conduct warranting an inference that a right has been surrendered.
Waiver	The voluntary surrender of a known right; conduct supporting an inference that a particular right has been relinquished.
Waiving time	The process whereby an individual permits a court to take longer than usual in trying him or her on a criminal charge.
Want	The absence or deficiency of what is needed or desired.
Want of consideration	A comprehensive term for all transactions or situations where no inducement to a contract was intended to pass between the parties thereto and, therefore, no legally enforceable contract is created.
Wanton	Grossly careless or negligent; reckless; malicious.
Wapentake	A local division of a shire or county in old English law; the term used north of the Trent River for the territory called a hundred in other parts of England.

War   Conflicts arising between the armed forces of two or more nations and the methods employed to guard and protect such nations, under the authority of their respective governments.

War crimes   Those acts that violate the international laws, treaties, customs, and practices governing military conflict between belligerent states or parties.

Ward   A person, especially an infant or incompetent, placed by the court in the care of a guardian.

Warehouseman   An individual who is regularly engaged in the business of receiving and storing goods of others in exchange for compensation or profit.

Warehouse receipt   A written document given by a warehouseman for items received for storage in his or her warehouse, which serves as evidence of title to the stored goods.

Warrant   A written order issued by a judicial officer or other authorized person commanding a law enforcement officer to perform some act incident to the administration of justice.

Warrant of attorney   A written authorization that allows an attorney named in it to appear in court and admit the liability of the person giving the warrant in an action to collect a debt.

Warranty   An assurance, promise, or guaranty by one party that a particular statement of fact is true and may be relied upon by the other party.

Warranty deed   An instrument that transfers real property from one person to another and in which the grantor promises that title is good and clear of any claims.

Wash sale   The buying and selling of the same or a similar asset within a short period of time.

    A fictitious type of arrangement whereby a broker, upon receiving an order from one individual to purchase and an order from another individual to sell a certain amount of a particular stock or commodity, transfers it from one principal to the other and retains the difference in value.

Waste   Harmful or destructive use of real property by one in rightful possession of the property.

Water rights   A group of rights designed to protect the use and enjoyment of water that travels in streams, rivers, lakes, and ponds, gathers on the surface of the earth, or collects underground.

Weapons   A comprehensive term for all instruments of offensive or defensive combat, including items used in injuring a person.

Weight of evidence   Measure of credible proof on one side of a dispute as compared with the credible proof on the other, particularly the probative evidence considered by a judge or jury during a trial.

Weights and measures	A comprehensive legal term for uniform standards ascribed to the quantity, capacity, volume, or dimensions of anything.
Welfare	Government benefits distributed to impoverished persons to enable them to maintain a minimum standard of well-being.
Westminster, First Statute of	A law enacted in 1275 to enforce some of the provisions of Magna Charta and to liberalize the law of England.
Westminster, Second Statute of	An English law enacted in 1285 that converted estates in fee simple conditional into estates in fee entail and rendered them inalienable, thereby strengthening the power of the nobility.
Westminster Hall	A building connected to the houses of Parliament in London, England, that formerly housed the superior courts.
West Saxon lage	The laws of the West Saxons, who lived in the southern and western counties of England, from Kent to Devonshire, during the Anglo-Saxon period.
Whaling	The hunting of whales for food, oil, or both.
Wharves	Structures erected on the margin of navigable waters where vessels can stop to load and unload cargo.
Whereas	On the contrary, although, when in fact. An introductory statement of a formal document.
Whereby	By or through which; by the help of which; in accordance with which.
Wherefore	For which reason.
Whistleblowing	The disclosure by a person, usually an employee, in a government agency or private enterprise; to the public or to those in authority, of mismanagement, corruption, illegality, or some other wrongdoing.
Whiteacre	A fictitious designation used by legal writers to describe a parcel of land.
White primary	A legal device once employed by some Southern states to prevent African Americans from exercising their right to vote in a meaningful way.
White supremacy groups	Organizations that believe the Caucasian race is superior to all races and therefore seek to either separate the races in the United States or to remove all non-Caucasians from the nation.
Wildcat strike	An employee work stoppage that is not authorized by the labor union to which the employees belong.
Will	A document in which a person specifies the method to be applied in the management and distribution of his estate after his death.
Willful	Intentional; not accidental; voluntary; designed.

Williams Act   A 1968 federal law that amended the Securities and Exchange Act of 1934 (15 U.S.C.A. § 78a et seq.) to require mandatory disclosure of information regarding cash tender offers.

Wilmot Proviso   An unsuccessful 1846 congressional amendment that sought to ban slavery in territories newly acquired from Mexico.

Wind up   The last phase in the dissolution of a partnership or corporation, in which accounts are settled and assets are liquidated so that they may be distributed and the business may be terminated.

Wiretapping   A form of electronic eavesdropping accomplished by seizing or overhearing communications by means of a concealed recording or listening device connected to the transmission line.

Witan   An Anglo-Saxon term that meant wise men, persons learned in the law; in particular, the king's advisers or members of his council.

Withholding tax   The amount legally deducted from an employee's wages or salary by the employer, who uses it to prepay the charges imposed by the government on the employee's yearly earnings.

Within the statute   Encompassed by, or included under, the provisions and scope of a particular law.

Without day   A term used to describe a final ending or adjournment of a session of a legislature or a court; the English translation of the Latin phrase *sine die*.

Without prejudice   Without any loss or waiver of rights or privileges.

Without recourse   A phrase used by an endorser (a signer other than the original maker) of a negotiable instrument (for example, a check or promissory note) to mean that if payment of the instrument is refused, the endorser will not be responsible.

Witnesses   Individuals who provide evidence in legal proceedings before a tribunal. Persons who have sufficient knowledge of a fact or occurrence to testify about it and who give testimony under oath in court, concerning what they have seen, heard, or otherwise observed.

Women's rights   The effort to secure equal rights for women and to remove gender discrimination from laws, institutions, and behavioral patterns.

Woods and forests   A comprehensive term for a large collection of trees in their natural setting and the property on which they stand.

Words and Phrases®   A multivolume set of law books published by West Group containing thousands of judicial definitions of words and phrases, arranged alphabetically, from 1658 to the present.

Words of art	The vocabulary or terminology of a particular art, science, or profession, particularly those expressions that are peculiar to it.
Words of limitation	The words in a deed or will that indicate what type of estate or rights the person being given land receives.
Words of purchase	Language used in connection with a transfer of real property that identifies the grantees or designees who take the interest being conveyed by deed or will.
Workers' compensation	A system whereby an employer must pay, or provide insurance to pay, the lost wages and medical expenses of an employee who is injured on the job.
Work product rule	A legal doctrine that provides that certain materials prepared by an attorney who is acting on behalf of his or her client during preparation for litigation are privileged from discovery by the attorney for the opposition party.
Worthier title doctrine	A common law rule that provides that a conveyance of real property by a grantor to another person for life with a limitation to the grantor's heirs creates a reversion in the grantor by which his or her heirs acquire the property only upon the death of the grantor, not upon the death of the person who has been granted the property for life.
Writ	An order issued by a court requiring that something be done or giving authority to do a specified act.
Wrong	A violation, by one individual, of another individual's legal rights.
Wrongful birth	A medical malpractice claim brought by the parents of a child born with birth defects, alleging that negligent treatment or advice deprived them of the opportunity to avoid conception or terminate the pregnancy.
Wrongful death	The taking of the life of an individual resulting from the willful or negligent act of another person or persons.
Wrongful discharge	An at-will employee's cause of action against his former employer, alleging that his discharge was in violation of state or federal antidiscrimination statutes, public policy, an implied contract, or an implied covenant of good faith and fair dealing.
Wrongful life	A type of medical malpractice claim brought on behalf of a child born with birth defects, alleging that the child would not have been born but for negligent advice to, or treatment of, the parents.
Wrongful pregnancy	A claim by parents for damages arising from the negligent performance of a sterilization procedure or abortion, and the subsequent birth of a child.

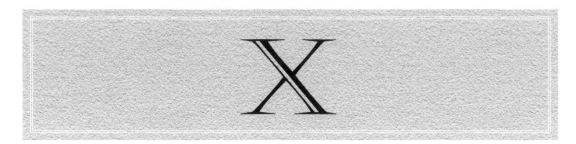

X rating A classification devised by the Motion Picture Association of America (MPAA) and the National Association of Theater Owners (NATO) in 1968 to designate certain films containing excessive violence or explicit sexuality. It was replaced in 1990 by the NC-17 rating (no one 17 and under admitted).

XYY chromosomal abnormality defense A legal theory that holds that a defendant's XYY chromosomal abnormality is a condition that should relieve him or her of legal responsibility for his or her criminal act.

XYZ Affair A diplomatic scandal involving France and the United States in 1797–1798.

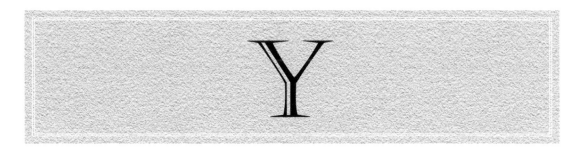

Yalta Agreement A World War II accord made in 1945 between Great Britain, the United States, and the Soviet Union.

Year books Books of legal cases, or reporters, published annually in England from the thirteenth to the sixteenth century.

Yellow dog contract An employment agreement whereby a worker promises not to join a labor union or promises to resign from a union if he or she is already a member.

Yield Current return from an investment or expenditure as a percentage of the price of investment or expenditure.

York-Antwerp rules A group of directives relating to uniform bills of lading and governing the settlement of maritime losses among the several interests, including ship and cargo owners.

Zero bracket amount A lump-sum allowance of income that a taxpayer could receive without imposition of any federal income tax because it was considered equivalent to the standard amount of deductions usually taken by an average taxpayer. It was replaced by the standard deduction in the Tax Reform Act of 1986. 100 Stat. 2085, 26 U.S.C.A. §§ 47, 1042.

Zoning The separation or division of a municipality into districts, the regulation of buildings and structures in such districts in accordance with their construction and the nature and extent of their use, and the dedication of such districts to particular uses designed to serve the general welfare.

TABLE OF CASES CITED

Cases that are main entries
printed in **bold** type.

INDEX

BY NAME

References that include photos or exhibits are printed in *italic* type. Names that are main entries are printed in **bold** type.

INDEX

BY SUBJECT

References that include photos or exhibits are printed in *italic* type.